Ways of Knowing

WAYS OF KNOWING
Kierkegaard's Pluralist Epistemology

M. G. Piety

BAYLOR UNIVERSITY PRESS

Cover Design by Nita Ybarra Design
Cover Image: Søren Kierkegaard (1820–82) (color litho), Klaestrup, Peter (1820–82) / Private Collection / Archives Charmet / The Bridgeman Art Library International

Søren Kierkegaard, *Three Discourses on Imagined Occasions.* ©1993 Howard V. Hong. Reprinted by permission of Princeton University Press.

Søren Kierkegaard, *Works of Love.* ©1995 Postcript, Inc. Published by Princeton University Press, 1998 paperback edition. Reprinted by permission of Princeton University Press.

Søren Kierkegaard, *Concluding Unscientific Postscript,* edited by Alastair Hannay, ©2009. Reprinted with the permission of Cambridge University Press.

Søren Kierkegaard, *"Repetition" and "Philosophical Crumbs,"* translated by M. G. Piety, ©2009. Reprinted by permission of Oxford University Press.

Søren Kierkegaard, *Journals and Papers,* edited and translated by Howard V. Hong and Edna H. Hong, ©1976–1978. Reprinted by permission of Indiana University Press.

Library of Congress Cataloging-in-Publication Data

Piety, M. G. (Marilyn Gaye), 1960-
Ways of knowing : Kierkegaard's pluralist epistemology / M.G. Piety.
p. cm.
Includes bibliographical references (p.   ) and index.
ISBN 978-1-60258-262-0 (hardback : alk. paper)
1. Kierkegaard, Søren, 1813-1855. 2. Knowledge, Theory of. I. Title.
B4378.K56P54 2010
121.092--dc22
                                    2010000801

Printed in the United States of America on acid-free paper with a minimum of 30% pcw recycled content.

CONTENTS

Acknowledgments

Many people have contributed either directly or indirectly to the project this volume represents. I first began working on Kierkegaard's epistemology when I was a graduate student at McGill University. Merold Westphal very kindly agreed to help direct my work even though he was at Fordham and not McGill. I received a great deal of helpful advice and criticism from him, and for that I will always be in his debt. Many other people were helpful as well. C. Stephen Evans, Robert L. Perkins, Sylvia Walsh Perkins, and Anthony Rudd have been tireless supporters and fonts of information. Julia Watkin and Paul Müller helped me to navigate my way through Danish sources during the early stages of my learning Danish. George Kline, who directed my M.A. thesis on Kierkegaard, was almost single-handedly responsible for turning me into a scholar.

Special thanks must go to my dear friend Ebba Mørkeberg, who not only patiently endured my early struggles with Danish but also agreed to tutor me in German over a period of what must have been five years, and to my friends Ole and Jette Püschl, who graciously hosted a philosophy discussion group, of which I was a member. The group, which also included Ebba, began just after my first year in Denmark and continued unabated until I left seven years later. I miss those meetings still.

My parents, Patricia Piety and Harold Piety, deserve thanks for being supportive of my interest in philosophy in general and Kierkegaard in particular, and my father deserves special thanks for being nearly as important an intellectual resource as Google.

Thanks must also go to the chair of my department, Abioseh Porter, and the dean of my college, Donna Murasko, for being consistently understanding and supportive when I was repeatedly overwhelmed by this project.

I would like as well to thank the entire membership of the Søren Kierkegaard Society, or at least the members who show up for the dinner every year at the annual conference of the American Academy of Religion. Where would I be, I wonder, without their warm support? They feel almost like family now.

Two people, however, deserve more thanks than all the rest. My undergraduate professor Robert L. Horn was the single most important influence on my intellectual development. He not only introduced me to Kierkegaard but also generously allowed me to monopolize his office hours for most of my senior year and encouraged me to go on to do graduate work in philosophy. And then there is my husband, Brian J. Foley, who patiently read every single page of the manuscript and whose excellent editing skills have improved it immeasurably. Thank you.

Thank you all.

Preface

I moved to Denmark in the fall of 1990. I had been awarded a Fulbright fellowship to spend a year in Copenhagen working on my dissertation on Kierkegaard. I had no idea that fall that I would spend the next eight years of my life in Denmark. To the best of my knowledge, that is more consecutive years than any other English-speaking Kierkegaard scholar. I did know though, that I would spend the rest of my life working on Kierkegaard's epistemology. I have always been interested in epistemology. It is not an abstract, intellectual interest, but a very practical one. I have always been interested in knowledge because I realized very early that people are inclined to justify their behavior on the basis of what they think they know. My interest in epistemology is thus very much like Kierkegaard's interest in epistemology: it grows out of a more fundamental interest in ethics. This affinity, I believe, has been a great help to me in navigating my way through the sometimes—at least partly—murky waters of Kierkegaard's views on knowledge.

It is not merely my natural sympathy with Kierkegaard's intellectual and ethical interests that have helped to shape the present work in very positive ways. I have benefited enormously from having spent so much time in Denmark. Most scholars cannot manage more than a year in Denmark. Grants do not normally cover more than a year, and scholars who are already gainfully employed as teachers usually have great difficulty securing more than a year of release time to spend on research. This has been a problem for Kierkegaard scholarship. My hope is that this will soon be recognized by grant-giving institutions, and that multiple-year fellowships for study in Denmark will eventually be available.

In the meantime, however, we must muddle through with a collection of seriously flawed translations of Kierkegaard and a community of scholars who, through no fault of their own, are unable to recognize many of the flaws or to correct them. I was taught that scholarly conventions dictate that when a text is referred to in translation, it is incumbent upon a scholar, no matter how good may be his command of the language of the original, to use the wording of the translation that is generally accepted as definitive. I have, with two notable exceptions, endeavored to use the translations in the Kierkegaard's Writings series of Princeton University Press. The two exceptions are that I have used the wording from my own translations of Kierkegaard's *"Repetition" and "Philosophical Crumbs"* (Oxford, 2009) and Alastair Hannay's translation of *Concluding Unscientific Postscript to the "Philosophical Crumbs"* (Cambridge, 2009). The choice to use Hannay's translation was motivated not merely by a desire for consistency (Hannay also translates the Danish *Smuler* as "crumbs") but also because Hannay's translations of Kierkegaard's works are generally superior to the work of the Hongs, who did most of the translations in the Kierkegaard's Writings series. I have occasionally modified the wording of the Hongs' translations when it was particularly unidiomatic or even erroneous. I have also very occasionally used an older translation when it was markedly superior to a newer one. This is always explained, however, in the notes, and references to both translations are included.

I have frequently included the relevant Danish expression either in brackets (if in the middle of a quotation) or in parentheses, if in the text proper. The reader may be slightly confused, however, to find that the same word is not always spelled in the same way. Danish spelling was not regularized until after Kierkegaard's death, so he sometimes spells words such as *Erkjendelsen* (knowledge) with a "j" and sometimes with an "i" and sometimes without either. I have followed his spelling as well as the nineteenth-century convention of capitalizing nouns. All emphasis in quotations is original to the text unless otherwise noted.

I encourage readers with some background in Danish to avail themselves of the online versions of the new *Søren Kierkegaards Skrifter* (Søren Kierkegaard's writings, http://www.sks.dk/forside/indhold.asp). They have been an enormous help to me and will be a help to many other scholars as well.

I have also followed the sigla developed by Robert Perkins for the International Kierkegaard Commentary Series (Mercer University Press). Kierkegaard's works are cited by giving an abbreviation for the work in question followed by a page number in parentheses in the main text rather than in a note. Footnotes are used only for references to works that are not being directly cited.

Sigla

BA   *The Book on Adler*. Translated by Howard V. Hong and Edna H. Hong. Princeton: Princeton University Press, 1998.

C   *Philosophical Crumbs* in *"Repetition" and "Philosophical Crumbs."* Translated by M. G. Piety. Oxford: Oxford University Press, 2009.

CA   *The Concept of Anxiety*. Translated by Reidar Thomte, in collaboration with Albert B. Anderson. Princeton: Princeton University Press, 1980.

CD   *Christian Discourses*. Translated by Howard V. Hong and Edna H. Hong. Princeton: Princeton University Press, 1997.

CI   *The Concept of Irony*. Translated by Howard V. Hong and Edna H. Hong. Princeton: Princeton University Press, 1989.

CS   *Thought on Crucial Situations in Human Life: Three Discourses on Imagined Occasions*. Translated by David F. Swenson. Edited by Lillian Marvin Swenson. Minneapolis: Ausburg, 1941.

CUP

Concluding Unscientific Postscript to the "Philosophical Crumbs." This abbreviation will be used for both the Hannay translation (Cambridge: Cambridge University Press, 2009) and the two-volume translation by Howard V. Hong and Edna H. Hong (Princeton: Princeton University Press, 1992).

EO I and EO II

Either/Or. Translated by Howard V. Hong and Edna H. Hong. 2 vols. Princeton: Princeton University Press, 1987.

EUD

Eighteen Upbuilding Discourses. Translated by Howard V. Hong and Edna H. Hong. Princeton: Princeton University Press, 1990.

FSE and JFY

"For Self-Examination" and "Judge for Yourself." Translated by Howard V. Hong and Edna H. Hong. Princeton: Princeton University Press, 1990.

FT

"Fear and Trembling" and "Repetition." Translated by Howard V. Hong and Edna H. Hong. Princeton: Princeton University Press, 1983.

JC

Johannes Climacus or De Omnibus Dubitandum Est. See *Philosophical Fragments.*

JFY

Judge for Yourself! See *"For Self-Examination"* (FSE).

JP

Søren Kierkegaard's Journals and Papers. Edited and translated by Howard V. Hong and Edna H. Hong, assisted by Gregor Malantschuk. Bloomington: Indiana University Press, vol. 1, 1967; vol. 2, 1970; vols. 3–4, 1975; vols. 5–7, 1978.

KAUC

Kierkegaard's Attack upon Christendom. Translated by Walter Lowrie. Princeton: Princeton University Press, 1944.

LD

Letters and Documents. Translated by Henrik Rosenmeier. Princeton: Princeton University Press, 1978.

NRF

Nutidens Religieuse Forvirring: Bogen om Adler [Contemporary religious confusion: The book on Adler]. *Udgivet med indledning og noter af Julia Watkin* [Edited with an introduction and notes by Julia Watkin]. Copenhagen: C. A. Reitzels Forlag, 1984.

P	*"Prefaces" and "Writing Sampler."* Edited and translated by Todd W. Nichol. Princeton: Princeton University Press, 1998.
Pap.	*Søren Kierkegaards Papirer* [Søren Kierkegaard's papers]. 2nd enlarged edition by Niels Thulstrup, with index vols. 14–16 by Niels Jørgen Cappelørn. 16 vols. Copenhagen: Gyldendal, 1968–1978.
PC	*Practice in Christianity.* Translated by Howard V. Hong and Edna H. Hong. Princeton: Princeton University Press, 1991.
POH	This abbreviation will be used for both the Hong's translation (see UDVS) and for *Purity of Heart Is to Will One Thing: Spiritual Preparation for the Office of Confession.* Translated by Douglas V. Steere. New York: Harper Torchbooks, 1964.
PV	*The Point of View for My Work as an Author.* Translated by Howard V. Hong and Edna H. Hong. Princeton: Princeton Univesity Press, 1998.
R	*Repetition.* See *Philosophical Crumbs* (C).
SLW	*The Stages on Life's Way.* Translated by Howard V. Hong and Edna H. Hong. Princeton: Princeton University Press, 1988.
SUD	*The Sickness Unto Death.* Translated by Howard V. Hong and Edna H. Hong. Princeton: Princeton University Press, 1980.
SV	*Søren Kierkegaards Samlede Værker* [Søren Kierkegaard's collected works]. Edited by A. B. Drachman, J. L. Heiberg, and H. O. Lange. 2nd ed. 15 vols. Copenhagen: Gyldendal, 1920–1936.
TA	*Two Ages: The Age of Revolution and the Present Age: A Literary Review.* Translated by Howard V. Hong and Edna H. Hong. Princeton: Princeton University Press, 1978.
TDIO	*Three Discourses on Imagined Occasions.* Translated by Howard V. Hong and Edna H. Hong. Princeton: Princeton University Press, 1993.

TM   *"The Moment" and Late Writings.* Translated by Howard
              V. Hong and Edna H. Hong. Princeton: Princeton Uni-
              versity Press, 1998.

UDVS   *Upbuilding Discourses in Various Spirits.* Translated by
              Howard V. Hong and Edna H. Hong. Princeton: Prince-
              ton University Press, 1993.

WA   *Without Authority.* Translated by Howard V. Hong and
              Edna H. Hong. Princeton: Princeton University Press,
              1997.

WOL   *Works of Love.* Translated by Howard V. Hong and Edna
              H. Hong. Princeton: Princeton University Press, 1995.

CHAPTER ONE

Introduction
Kierkegaard as Epistemologist

The Project

Kierkegaard is considered one of the most important thinkers of the nine-teenth century, yet very little scholarly work has been done on his epistemol-ogy.[1] This is a serious problem because Kierkegaard's views on knowledge are, and must be, intimately related to his views on religious faith and its role

---

[1] Among the thousands of articles on Kierkegaard, only a half a dozen concern his epis-temology. Steven N. Emmanuel, "Kierkegaard on Faith and Knowledge," *Kierkegaardiana* 15 (1991): 136–46; Robert L. Perkins, "Kierkegaard, a Kind of Epistemologist," *History of European Ideas* 12, no. 1 (1990): 7–18; M. G. Piety, "Kierkegaard on Religious Knowledge," *History of European Ideas* 22 (1996): 105–12; Louis P. Pojman, "Kierkegaard's Epistemology," *Kierkegaardiana* 15 (1991): 147–52; Johannes Sløk, "*En Studie I Kierkegaards Erkendelses-teori*" [A study of Kierkegaard's epistemology], *Dansk Teologisk Tidsskrift* 1 Hefte (1941); and David Wisdo, "Kierkegaard on the Limits of Christian Epistemology," *International Jour-nal for Philosophy of Religion* 29, no. 2 (1991): 97–112. Among the hundreds of books on Kierkegaard, there are only two on his epistemology: Anton Hügli's *Die Erkenntnis der Sub-jektivität und die Objektivität des Erkennens bei Søren Kierkegaard* [Knowledge of subjectivity and the objectivity of knowing in Søren Kierkegaard] (Basel, Switzerland: Editio Academica, 1973) and Martin Slotty's 1915 dissertation, "Die Erkenntnislehre S. A. Kierkegaards" [The epistemology of S. A. Kierkegaard] (Friedrich-Alexanders-Universität, 1915). No use, that I have been able to determine in any case, has been made of these last two important sources in English-language Kierkegaard scholarship.

in human experience. So little is understood about Kierkegaard's epistemology that prominent scholars still debate such fundamental issues as whether
it is possible, according to Kierkegaard, to have propositional knowledge
that God became human in the person of Christ.[2]

Several works have appeared recently that touch on Kierkegaard's epistemology,[3] but there is still no work in English devoted exclusively to the
subject. My objective is to delineate, as clearly as possible, Kierkegaard's
views on knowledge. The project is at once grand and modest. It is grand in
the sense that it is setting out on what is, in English in any case, uncharted
territory. It is modest in that while it will include references both to the
history of epistemological thinking as well as to contemporary work in
this field, it will make no direct attempt to situate Kierkegaard's views
in the history of epistemological thinking, nor any direct attempt to relate
Kierkegaard's views to contemporary epistemological debates. Either project
would be premature. What is needed at this early stage of the understanding
of Kierkegaard's epistemology is a general outline of his views on knowledge.
The objective here is to provide what might serve as part of the foundation
for future scholarship that could be devoted to such specific issues as, for
example, the relation between Kierkegaard's epistemology and Enlighten-
ment epistemologies, or Kierkegaard's potential contribution to contemporary epistemological debates such as those relating to virtue epistemologies
and communitarian epistemologies.

It is also important to acknowledge that no claim is made to the effect
that Kierkegaard consciously thought through his epistemology with the
thoroughness and detail displayed in the present study. Kierkegaard's main
interest is not epistemology but ethics and religion. He does occasionally
look specifically at the nature of knowledge, most notably in the *Concluding
Unscientific Postscript* and in *Works of Love*. More often than not, however,
his attention is focused elsewhere. He never produced anything like an epistemological treatise. It is therefore possible that many of the views attributed
to him here were held more intuitively than as the result of conscious analysis. The argument of the present work is that the views it presents may be

---

[2] See the debate on this issue between Steven N. Emmanuel and Louis P. Pojman
in *Kierkegaardiana* 15 (1991): 136–46 and 147–52, respectively, as well as my response,
"Kierkegaard on Religious Knowledge," 105–12.

[3] See C. Stephen Evans, *Kierkegaard on Faith and the Self* (Waco, Tex.: Baylor University
Press, 2006); Peter Mehl, *Thinking through Kierkegaard: Existential Identity in a Pluralistic
World* (Urbana: University of Illinois Press, 2005); Steven Shakespeare, *Kierkegaard, Language
and the Reality of God* (Aldershot, UK: Ashgate, 2001); and David Willows, *Divine Knowledge:
A Kierkegaardian Perspective on Christian Education* (Aldershot, UK: Ashgate, 2001).

inferred and extracted from various parts of Kierkegaard's corpus and that if the views are sometimes confusing in their complexity, they nevertheless form a largely coherent whole.

Most epistemologies are reductionist in that they take the various senses in which we use the expression "knowledge" and try to reduce them to a single essence that either forces recondite cases onto the model in question in a manner that strains credulity or dismisses them as legitimate instances of knowing. I am going to argue that Kierkegaard, on the other hand, is an epistemological pluralist. That is, I am going to argue that there are several kinds of knowledge according to Kierkegaard and that they can be divided into two basic sorts: "objective knowledge [*den objective Viden*]" and "subjective knowledge [*den subjective Viden*]" (CUP, 169). Knowledge is objective if it is not essentially related to the existence of the individual knower as is the case, for example, with knowledge in the natural sciences, or with any sort of knowledge that is purely descriptive. Knowledge is subjective if it is essentially related to the existence of the individual knower as is the case, for example, with ethical and religious knowledge, or with any sort of knowledge that has a prescriptive dimension. These two basic categories may be further subdivided. Objective knowledge may be subdivided into what I will call knowledge in the strict sense, which is associated with formal certainty, and knowledge in a looser sense, which is associated with probability rather than certainty.[4] This latter sort of knowledge is what Kierkegaard's pseudonym, Johannes Climacus, refers to in the *Concluding Unscientific Postscript* as "approximate knowledge [*Approximations-Viden*]" (CUP, 68).

Subjective knowledge may also be subdivided into two sorts. First there is subjective knowledge proper, and then there is what I will call pseudo-knowledge. Subjective knowledge proper, I will argue, is associated with certitude, or psychological certainty. Pseudo-knowledge refers to a subject's intellectual grasp of propositions that are essentially prescriptive but whose substance is not reflected in the existence of the "knower." This "knowledge" has neither formal nor psychological certainty but amounts to a kind of hypocrisy where the knower professes to have grasped in its essence something that his existence betrays he has not yet grasped.

I will argue that Kierkegaard's epistemology is both foundationalist and nonfoundationalist, both substantive and procedural, and that it includes both internalist and externalist theories of belief justification.[5] Both

---

[4] See Evans, 38–39.

[5] For more information on substantive versus procedural views of knowledge, see Richard Rorty, *Philosophy and the Mirror of Nature* (Princeton: Princeton University Press, 1979). Rorty actually contrasts substantive views of knowledge, or what he identifies specifically as

objective knowledge in the strict sense and subjective knowledge proper are a result of the substantive contact of the knower with the object of knowledge. This contact provides a foundation for knowledge that makes possible an internalist justification of the beliefs in question in the sense that this contact can be discerned through introspection. In contrast, both objective knowledge in the loose sense and pseudo-knowledge are the result, according to Kierkegaard, of the application of a procedure for determining knowledge as such. Despite the necessity, however, of the procedure, the justification of these beliefs will turn out to be essentially externalist in the sense that the procedure must be combined with a relationship on the part of the knower to the conditions in the world that determine the truth of the belief in question. Since these conditions are constantly changing, they can neither be established with certainty by the knower nor provide a traditional foundationalist justification for his beliefs. Kierkegaard's epistemology, as Evans has observed, is both in a sense "premodern" and "postmodern" (Evans, 42). That is, it is premodern, in terms of Kierkegaard's understanding of truth, but postmodern in its nonreductionist account of the complexities of human knowing.

Part of the difficulty involved in understanding Kierkegaard's epistemology stems from the fact that he makes no rigorous terminological distinctions either among the various Danish expressions for knowledge or among the four distinct types of knowledge it appears can be found in his works. I will argue, however, that the variety of uses he makes of the expression "knowledge" does not represent an equivocation on his part as to its meaning. "Knowledge" appears to have a multiplicity of meanings that serve an important purpose within his authorship. Each of these meanings represents what I will argue is a distinct sense in which the expression is used in everyday contexts. Kierkegaard's objective, I will argue, in detailing the various senses in which the expression "knowledge" is used, is to show that there is no sense in which knowledge of the truth of Christianity may legitimately be said to be superior to *faith* in this truth.[6]

---

the "Platonic" view (see "Knowledge as Needing 'Foundations,'" 155–60), to what he calls "representational" views (this term is used throughout the book) rather than procedural ones. That is, the knower, on these latter views, is considered to know something about reality to the extent that he has succeeded in constructing an accurate mental representation of reality. The construction of this representation is the product, however, of the application of a particular procedure for determining the character of reality, hence "procedural" and "representational" may be used interchangeably with respect to epistemological theories.

[6] See Slotty, 43.

Background

It may strike one as peculiar to attribute such significance to the episte-mology of a thinker who has traditionally been considered something of a skeptic.[7] The prominence of epistemological concerns in Kierkegaard's authorship was noticed, however, as early as 1849 by both the Danish theo-logian Hans Lassen Martensen in his *Den Christelige Dogmatik* (Christian Dogmatics)[8] and by the Danish philosopher Rasmus Nielsen in his com-parison of the views expressed in works Kierkegaard published under the pseudonym Johannes Climacus to those of Martensen in his *Dogmatik*.[9] Nielsen argued that the issue around which both theology and philosophy revolved at the time was whether the truth of Christianity could be known objectively.[10] He chose to contrast what was purportedly Kierkegaard's posi-tion to Martensen's not merely because the views expressed by Kierkegaard's pseudonym Johannes Climacus were in direct opposition to Martensen's views but because the issue in question was one with which both thinkers were equally preoccupied.

As I explained in the section above, this study makes no attempt to place Kierkegaard precisely within a historical context. It is important, how-ever, that something be said concerning Kierkegaard's relation to Hegel and, in particular, to the Danish Hegelians. His relation to Hegel has been the subject of heated philosophical debate.[11] The fact that much of Kierkegaard's

---

[7] See Richard Popkin, "Kierkegaard and Skepticism," in *Kierkegaard: A Collection of Critical Essays*, ed. Josiah Thompson (Garden City, N.Y.: Doubleday, 1972), 342–72; Terence Penelhum, "Skepticism and Fideism," in *The Skeptical Tradition*, ed. Myles F. Burn-yeat (Berkeley: University of California Press, 1983), 287–318; and Slotty, 19.

[8] Dr. H. Martensen, *Den Christelige Dogmatik* [Christian dogmatics] (Copenhagen: C. A. Reitzels Forlag, 1849). See also Robert L. Horn, "Positivity and Dialectic: A Study of the Theological Method of Hans Lassen Martensen" (Ph.D. diss., Union Theological Semi-nary, 1969), 262; and Niels Thulstrup, "Inledning Til Philosophiske Smuler" [Introduction to philosophical crumbs], in Søren Kierkegaard, *Philosophiske Smuler, Udgivet med Inledning og Kommentar af Niels Thulstrup* [Philosophical crumbs, edited with an introduction and commentary by Niels Thulstrup] (Copenhagen: C. A. Reitzel, 1977), xli.

[9] R. Nielsen, *Mag. S. Kierkegaards "Johannes Climacus" og Dr. H. Martensens "Christelige Dogmatik": En undersøgende Anmeldelse af R. Nielsen, Professor i Philosophien* [Master S. Kierkegaard's "Johannes Climacus" and Dr. H. Martensen's "Christian Dogmatics": A criti-cal review by R. Nielsen, professor of philosophy] (Copenhagen: C. A. Reitzels Forlag, 1849).

[10] See Nielsen, 4.

[11] Almost every German language work on Kierkegaard addresses this issue at some point, with Heinrich M. Schmidinger's *Das Problem des Interesses und die Philosophie Sören Kierkegaards* [The problem of interest and the philosophy of Søren Kierkegaard], Sympo-sion, *Philosophische Schriftenreihe*, (Freiburg: Verlag Karl Alber, 1983) offering one of the best treatments.

terminology comes from Hegel complicates the issue and makes the task of understanding his views, as contrasted to Hegel's, on almost any issue problematic. It is thus important that one approach Kierkegaard with some appreciation of how his concerns differ from Hegel's.

One of the most prominent Danish Kierkegaard scholars, Johannes Sløk, maintains that despite the fact that their terminology is similar, Kierkegaard and Hegel were very different sorts of thinkers. "Their thoughts," Sløk asserts,

> have nothing to do with each other. Their intentions are completely different; their interests, their methods, their focus, everything is completely different. They are not two philosophers who had opposite thoughts on the same problem. They are two individuals who had completely different thoughts on completely different problems. . . . The difference between them is categorical. Hegel's categories are the world and the idea and Kierkegaard's categories are Man and God.[12]

Sløk argues that when Kierkegaard uses what appear to be Hegelian terms, these terms "as Kierkegaard employs them, have another meaning" (Sløk, 50). This point is reiterated by Kierkegaard scholars Birgit Bertung and J. Heywood Thomas. Bertung argues that "Kierkegaard consciously uses the expressions 'abstract' [*abstract*] and 'concrete' [*conkret*] differently from Hegel, and something similar holds true," Bertung continues, "for almost all the central existential concepts, even though Hegelian terminology is at the same time Kierkegaard's philosophical starting point."[13] Thomas is less radical than Sløk. He does not deny that there is a relation between Hegel and Kierkegaard. He argues, however, that Kierkegaard "took characteristically Hegelian terminology and used it to make his great accusation against Hegel."[14] If Thomas' charge is correct, the question becomes, what *is* Kierkegaard's "great accusation against Hegel"?

Among the works in English that examine Kierkegaard's relation to Hegel or to the tradition of German idealism are Jon Stewart, ed., *Kierkegaard's Relations to Hegel Reconsidered*. Modern European Philosophy, gen. ed. Robert B. Pippin (Cambridge: Cambridge University Press, 2003); Niels Thulstrup, *Kierkegaard's Relation to Hegel*, trans. George L. Stengren (Princeton: Princeton University Press, 1980); Mark C. Taylor, *Journeys to Selfhood: Hegel and Kierkegaard* (Berkeley: University of California Press, 1980); Stephen N. Dunning, *Kierkegaard's Dialectic of Inwardness: A Structural Analysis of the Theory of Stages* (Princeton: Princeton University Press, 1985).

[12] Sløk, 50. See also Schmidinger, 200. Translations of secondary works, unless otherwise noted, are my own.

[13] Birgit Bertung, *Om Kierkegaard, Kvinder og Kærlighed—en studie i Søren Kierkegaards Kvindesyn* [On Kierkegaard, women and love—A study of Kierkegaard's views on women] (Copenhagen: Reitzel, 1987), 29.

[14] J. Heywood Thomas, "Logic and Existence in Kierkegaard," *Journal of the British Society for Phenomenology* 2, no. 3 (1971): 10.

"A convenient starting point," argues Thomas, "is the crucial doctrine of Hegel's *Logic* that there is an identity between thought and being."[15] That is, the Hegelian doctrine of mediation ultimately resolves (or purports to resolve) the opposition between appearance and reality, or between subject and object, by bringing them together in a higher unity which is accessible as such for what Hegel refers to as "pure thought" (Hegel, *Science of Logic*, 46).

Kierkegaard's pseudonym Johannes Climacus argues, however, that while

> [t]he systematic idea is the subject-object, the unity of thinking and being [*Væren*]; existence [*Existents*] is, on the contrary, precisely their separation. . . . Objectively understood, thinking is pure thinking, which corresponds in just such an abstractly objective way to its object, which object is therefore itself, and the truth the correspondence of thought with itself. (CUP, 105)[16]

According to Climacus, what is missing in Hegel's identification of reality with thought is an appreciation of what he refers to as the "distinction between factual being [*faktisk Væren*] and ideal being [*ideel Væren*]" (C, 114–15n3). The being that, according to Climacus, may be identified with thought is ideal being rather than factual, or concrete, being,[17] thus the "systematic" unity of thinking and being, or of subject and object, is, he argues, "a chimera of abstraction" (CUP, 165).[18]

Absolute knowledge is possible for Hegel as the product of pure thought,[19] but what, one may wonder, is pure thought, and how is the individual knower related to it? Thomas argues that, according to Hegel,

> the absolute is because I think it and in order to make his position more secure he [Hegel] turns the statement round and says that my thinking of the absolute is the self-thinking of the absolute in me. But pure thought is then described not only as absolute but also in terms of some subject which is absolute so that unless we are to go on talking of two subjects we are bound to assert the coincidence of

---

[15] Thomas, 4. See also G. W. F. Hegel, *Hegel's Science of Logic*, trans. A. V. Miller (London: Allen & Unwin, 1969), "Introduction," 43–64.

[16] See also Hermann Deuser, "*Kierkegaards Verteidigung der Kontingenz: «Daß etwas Inkommensurables in einem Menschenleben ist»*" [Kierkegaard's defense of contingency: "That there is something incommensurable in a human life"], *Kierkegaardiana* 15 (1991): 104–5; and Hügli, 144.

[17] See CUP, 275–76. See also Hügli's claim that, according to Kierkegaard, concrete, or actual, existence "is another type of being than the being that is thought" (Hügli, 99); and Deuser, 104.

[18] See also CUP, 95.

[19] See G. W. F. Hegel, *Science of Logic*, "Introduction"; and *The Phenomenology of Spirit*, trans. A. V. Miller (Oxford: Clarendon, 1977), chapter 7, "Absolute Knowledge."

the empirical [i.e., the particular, or concrete, individual] and the absolute subject. (Thomas, 7)

Climacus argues, however, that such a coincidence of the individual thinking subject and the absolute subject is "fantastic" (CUP, 165). "[N]o human being," he asserts, "is ever more than a particular individual" (CUP, 165). "Thus to one existing," he continues, "who asks how pure thought relates to one existing, and what he should do to enter into it, pure thought provides no answer" (CUP, 262).[20]

No individual, according to Kierkegaard, can be admitted into the realm of pure thought. So long as a person exists, his thought will always be in some sense relative rather than absolute, even if it is relative only to his existence as a member of the species of human beings. This means that, for Kierkegaard, all knowledge is in some sense relative rather than absolute, or, as Gregor Malantschuk observes, "A human being is tied, in his quest for knowledge, to specific epistemological assumptions."[21] To argue, however, that all knowledge is relative does not in itself imply that it is arbitrary. "Kierkegaard did not dispute the possibility of a logical system, or a system of universally valid thought-determinations," observes Slotty. "What he disputed was the practicable nature of Hegel's absolute method as well as the manner in which this method was actually employed by Hegel" (Slotty, 16). Or, as Hügli explains, "Kierkegaard did not reject the idea of objective knowledge, but only its claim to absoluteness" (Hügli, 33).[22]

What is perhaps most problematic for Kierkegaard about Hegel's philosophy is that it does not, on his view, leave any room for ethics.[23] "Am I the Good," asks Johannes Climacus, "because I think it, or am I good because I think the Good?" (CUP, 276). "With this question," observes

[20] See also Deuser's claim that "Kierkegaard's concept of subjectivity is a response to idealistic philosophy in that the latter, to the extent it centers on *res cogitans*, transcendental apperception and the unity of subject and object, not only misses living, human or, in an existential sense, concrete subjectivity, it positively ignores it" (Deuser, 104).

[21] Gregor Malantschuk, "*Das Verhältnis zwischen Wahrheit und Wirklichkeit in Sören Kierkegaards existentiellen Denken*" [The relation between truth and actuality in Søren Kierkegaard's existential thought], in *Frihed og Eksistens: Studier I Søren Kierkegaards' Tænkning* [Freedom and existence: Studies in the thought of Søren Kierkegaard], ed. Niels Jørgen Cappelørn and Paul Müller. (Copenhagen: C. A. Reitzels Forlag, 1980), 50. See also Hügli, 49; Slotty, 23; and JP, 1:50.

[22] See also Robert L. Perkins, "Kierkegaard's Epistemological Preferences," *International Journal for Philosophy of Religion* 4, no. 4 (1973): 216; Thulstrup, *Kommentar*, 187; Malantschuk, "*Das Verhältnis*," 52; and Slotty, 20.

[23] See CUP, 101, 248–49n; and Hügli, 113.

Hügli, "Climacus identifies the genuine starting-point for ethical skepticism concerning the identity of thought and being" (Hügli, 203).[24] Hegel's philosophy, "in that it tries to prove the idea [*die Idee*] is actual and the actual ideal" (Hügli, 105), eliminates the contradiction between *is* and *ought*.

Part of the difficulty in establishing Kierkegaard's relation to Hegel concerns the fact that there is evidence that much of what had traditionally been interpreted as his criticism of Hegel was directed not against Hegel but against the speculative theology of the Danish Hegelian H. L. Martensen.[25] It has even been suggested that "until Kierkegaard's relation to Martensen is understood in detail we will have little chance to understand Kierkegaard at all" (Horn, 268). A detailed treatment of Kierkegaard's relation to Martensen is beyond the scope of this book. We will look briefly, however, at this relationship as it pertains to the subject of the present study.

Paul Holmer's claim that "Kierkegaard was not primarily an epistemologist" is undoubtedly correct if by "epistemologist" one understands a thinker who is entirely absorbed in the investigation of the nature of knowledge for its own sake.[26] "[T]he religious framework," Hannay observes, "is axiomatic for Kierkegaard" (Hannay, 331). Kierkegaard's interest in the nature of knowledge is inexorably intertwined with theological concerns.[27] He was convinced the speculative theology that was becoming increasingly popular in the Copenhagen of his day was hopelessly confused.[28] Martensen was the leading proponent of this theology, which is presented in detail in both his *Den menneskelige Selvbevidstheds Autonomie i vor Tids dogmatiske Teologie* (The autonomy of human self-consciousness in contemporary dogmatic theology) (Copenhagen, 1841) and his *Den Christelige Dogmatik* (Christian dogmatics) (Copenhagen, 1849).

"[A]ll religion," argues Martensen,

> is a consciousness of God, a relation to God which includes both a consciousness of an opposition between God and the world and a reconciliation [*Løsning, Ophævelse*] of this opposition in unity. Religion may thus be more precisely defined as man's consciousness of his community with God, his union with God. (*Dogmatik*, 8)

---

[24] See also CUP, 275ff.

[25] See JP, 1:707. See also Stewart; Frederik Barfod, *Fortællinger af Fæderlandets Historie* [A narrative history of the fatherland] (Copenhagen: Gyldendal, 1874), 419; and Slotty, 41.

[26] Paul Holmer, "On Understanding Kierkegaard," in *A Kierkegaard Critique: An International Selection of Essays Interpreting Kierkegaard*, ed. Howard A. Johnson and Niels Thulstrup (New York: Harper, 1962), 45.

[27] See Hügli, 223.

[28] See Hügli, 240.

Martensen makes reference to the Hegelian doctrine of the mediation of opposites to resolve the apparent opposition between God and man. According to Martensen, man's consciousness of his community with God means that

> God himself is actively present in our consciousness, in systematic thought and in the rational and conceptual development of this idea; he who is thought by us thinks also in us. This is the true content of the [Hegelian] teaching of the unity of subject and object in speculative thought. . . . The same law that is the foundation of the unity of God and man in religious *love* also applies with respect to religious knowledge. (*Autonomie*, 13)

Hegel's absolute thinking itself thus becomes God thinking himself, and the coincidence of the empirical and the absolute subject to which Kierkegaard objected so strongly in Hegel becomes the coincidence of the human and the divine subject, to which Kierkegaard has even stronger objections.[29] Christianity, argues Kierkegaard, does not teach the essential unity of God and man, but their separation.[30] An attempted resolution of the opposition between God and man, as Hannay points out, "obviates the need for redemption" (Hannay, 172).

Kierkegaard has a number of problems with Martensen's speculative theology. Absolute certainty is, for Martensen, the starting point of speculative theology. But what Martensen "treats as a presupposition," argues the German Kierkegaard scholar Martin Slotty, "is, according to Kierkegaard, the entire essence and purpose of Christianity" (Slotty, 42). Martensen viewed the systematic explication of the content of Christian faith as a more profound development of, or expression of, that faith,[31] whereas for Kierkegaard, the fact that the content of faith admits of explication, at least to a certain extent, does not in any sense imply that such explication may be thought of as higher than faith itself. Faith, as we will see, was considered by Kierkegaard to be the highest achievement of an individual's existence.

There are many more specific points of disagreement between Martensen and Kierkegaard. What is important for the purposes of the present discussion is that Martensen fails to make a rigorous, systematic distinction between knowledge and belief.[32] Christianity, according to Martensen,

---

[29] See Thulstrup, *Kommentar*, xxix.

[30] This view pervades all Kierkegaard's works but is perhaps most clearly present in *Philosophical Crumbs* and in *Practice in Christianity*, trans. Howard V. Hong and Edna H. Hong (Princeton: Princeton University Press, 1991).

[31] See *Autonomie*, 13; and *Dogmatik*, 5–6.

[32] See Horn, 265.

represents a rebirth of the individual through belief in Christ.[33] "Dogmatics," he argues, "takes as its point of departure the fullness of faith [*Troens
Fylde*] and develops from this fullness a wealth of knowledge" (*Dogmatik*, 6).
Martensen also claims, however, that the foundation of dogmatics is immediate (*umiddelbare*) religious knowledge (*Erkendelsen* or *Viden*),[34] which
characterizes every individual as such.[35] It thus appears that he uses "faith"
and "knowledge" interchangeably.

Martensen had been Kierkegaard's tutor, and Kierkegaard attended his
lectures on "Speculative Dogmatics" during the academic year 1838–1839.
The views expressed in Martensen's *Den menneskelige Selvbevidstheds Autonomie* and *Den Christelige Dogmatik* were thus well known to Kierkegaard long
before the publication of the latter work in 1849.[36] It appears that much of
Kierkegaard's authorship up to the publication of Martensen's *Dogmatik* was
directed specifically at clearing up what he felt was a category confusion—
that is, the confusion of faith and knowledge—in Martensen's thought.[37]

Though Kierkegaard, as we will see in chapter 4, has affinities with
ancient skepticism, I will argue that he appears to believe in the possibility of at least a kind of knowledge of reality external to the knower. His
objection is directed toward the Hegelian-Martensenian thesis concerning
the possibility of *absolute* knowledge. Knowledge, for Kierkegaard, is always
based on some presuppositions the truth of which cannot be proved and is
thus relative to those presuppositions.[38] This does not mean, however, that
Kierkegaard rejects as unfounded all claims to knowledge of the external
world. He simply rejects the claim, observes Slotty, "that our thought can
attain a complete grasp of actuality" (Slotty, 18), and in this sense his views
are remarkably contemporary.

Belief in the power of reason to attain knowledge of objective reality
is, for Kierkegaard, more fundamental to human beings than is skepticism
concerning the possibility of such knowledge. That is, "[t]he individual,"

[33] See *Dogmatik*, 20.
[34] See *Dogmatik*, 12–13.
[35] See *Dogmatik*, 13.
[36] See Pap. II C 20. See also Gregor Malantschuk, *Fra Individ til den Enkelte* [From an individual to the single one] (Copenhagen: C. A. Reitzel, 1978), 14; and Thulstrup, *Kommen-tar*, 185. It is important to note at this point that there is material from Kierkegaard's *Papirer* (i.e., papers) that has not yet been translated into English. If only the Danish reference is given, the reader can assume that there is no English translation of the material in question.
[37] See Horn, 261–68. Horn further argues that "the whole Kierkegaardian approach to the relation of faith and knowledge is ridiculed by Martensen in the preface" to the *Dogmatik* (262).
[38] See Slotty, 18.

asserts Kierkegaard in *Works of Love*, "first begins his life with an '*ergo*,' with belief. But most people live so negligently they do not at all notice that in one way or another, every minute they live, they live by virtue of an '*ergo*,' of a belief" (WOL, 230).

All knowledge, for Kierkegaard, ultimately rests on faith, either implicitly or explicitly, in the truth of the presuppositions on which it is based. Thus it is possible to speak of Kierkegaard, as Slotty does, as an "epistemologist of belief" (Slotty, 12). To argue that Kierkegaard is an epistemologist of belief might make it appear that he falls victim to the same conflation of faith and knowledge that characterizes Martensen's thought. There is an important difference, however, between the claim that knowledge rests on a foundation of faith, or belief, and the straightforward identification of the two. An appreciation of the contingency, or relativity, of all human knowledge was precisely what Kierkegaard believed was lacking among his philosophical and theological contemporaries and, in particular, in the thought of Hans Lassen Martensen. It is the "peculiar epistemology" of Martensen which appears, in fact, to be the primary target of much of Kierkegaard's work.[39]

The Problem of Translation

Before turning to the issue of Kierkegaard's terminology, a couple of points need to be made concerning general differences between Danish and English as these differences affect the present project. It is difficult to draw a clear picture of Kierkegaard's epistemology in English because Danish, like German and unlike English, has several expressions for knowledge. They are *Erkendelse*, or *Erkjendelsen*,[40] *Kjendskab*, *Kundskab*, and *Viden*. *Erkjendelsen* is a cognate of the German *Erkenntniss*, hence "epistemology" is *Erkjendelsesteori* in Danish, just as it is *Erkenntnisstheori* in German. The Danish *Viden* corresponds to the German *Wissen*. Both *Erkjendelsen* and *Viden* are normally used to refer to knowledge in the propositional sense, thus it is with Kierkegaard's use of these two expressions that we will be primarily concerned.

---

[39] Arild Christensen, "*Efterskriftens Opgør med Martensen*" [The confrontation with Martensen in the *Postscript*], *Kierkegaardiana* 4 (1962): 45–62.

[40] The definite article in Danish is enclitic. "*Erkjendelsen*" is just "*Erkjendelse*" with the addition of the definite article "*en*." The definite article is often used in Danish to create abstract nouns. It is probably also important to note here that nouns are no longer capitalized in Danish and that there have been certain changes in spelling. Kierkegaard's "*Erkjendelsen*" is thus now written "*erkendelsen*." For a key to these changes, see Julia Watkin, *A Key to Kierkegaard's Abbreviations and Spelling/Nøgle til Kierkegaards Forkortelser og Stavemåde* (Copenhagen: C. A. Reitzels Boghandel, 1981).

English translators of Kierkegaard have chosen to translate each of the Danish expressions for knowledge with a variety of English expressions, depending on the context in which they occur (e.g., *Erkjendelsen*, following the convention associated with *Erkenntniss*, is sometimes translated as "cognition" rather than "knowledge," although no English translator has been consistent in this respect). This is not necessarily a bad practice; its appropriateness depends, however, on the context and the purpose of the discussion at hand. Since the aim of this project is the elucidation of Kierkegaard's epistemology, I translate the relevant Danish expressions as "knowledge" wherever possible and include the original expression in brackets immediately following the translation.

The translation of both *Kjendskab* and *Kundskab* is more problematic than that of *Erkjendelsen* and *Viden*. Both *Kjendskab* and *Kundskab* are translated into contemporary German as *Kenntniss*. Such a translation is slightly misleading, however, in that these expressions do not mean precisely the same thing in Danish. Although there was a German cognate, *Kundschaft*, of the Danish *Kundskab* (knowledge in the sense of "familiarity with"), in the first half of the nineteenth century, the meaning of this term has since altered somewhat.[41] *Kundskab* is related to the verb *kunne*, which means to be able. *Kundskab* may thus be translated as "knowledge" in either the acquaintance, or the skill sense.[42] That is, to have *Kundskab* is to be familiar with something (e.g., a language) in the sense that one is able to make practical use of this familiarity (e.g., to communicate in that language). Kierkegaard occasionally uses *Kundskab* in a manner similar to that in which one would use the German *Wissenschaft*.[43] That is, he occasionally uses it to refer to propositional knowledge that forms a systematic whole that is intimately related to some practice.[44]

Apart from "knowledge," there is no other expression by which *Kundskab* is generally translated. It is not actually a term Kierkegaard uses very much. It occurs most often in specifically religious discussions, perhaps

[41] See, e.g., Friederich Bresemann, *Hand-Wörterbuch der deutschen und dänischen Sprache* [Concise dictionary of the German and Danish languages] (Copenhagen: C. Steen & Sohn 1855) and W. Scholze-Stubenrecht and J. B. Sykes, *The Oxford Duden German Dictionary* (Oxford: Clarendon, 1990).

[42] See, e.g., J. S. Ferrall and Thorl. Gudm. Repp., *A Danish-English Dictionary* (Copenhagen: Gyldendal, 1845).

[43] "*Kundskab*" was often given as a possible translation of "*Wissenschaft*" in the first half of the nineteenth century (see, e.g., Bresemann; and G. H. Müller, *Deutsch-Dänisches Wörterbuch, Revidirt von Profess. Fr. Høeg Guldberg* [German-Danish dictionary, revised by Prof. Fr. Høeg Guldberg] [Kiel, Germany: Akademischen Buchhandlung, 1807–1810]).

[44] See, e.g., TM, 59; CD, 250; and CUP, 454.

because *"Kundskabens Træ"* is the Danish expression for "the tree of knowledge" as it appears in Genesis. Apart from such contexts, references are few
and translation problematic. It is sometimes translated as "attention"[45] and
other times as "information."[46]

The differences between Danish and English with respect to the various expressions for knowledge are not the only obstacles to understanding
Kierkegaard's epistemology. There is no terminological distinction in Danish between "certainty" in the formal sense and "certitude," or certainty, in
the psychological sense. The Danish term that most closely resembles "certitude" is *Overbevisning*, which means literally "above proof" and which is
translated into English as "conviction."[47]

The second point relating to the general differences between Danish
and English concerns the Danish expressions *Videnskab* and *Videnskabelig*.
These expressions often appear as "science" and "scientific," respectively. Such
translations are misleading, however, in that like their German cognates,
Wissenschaft and *Wissenschaftlich*, they are much more general in their meaning than the English "science" and "scientific." They refer to any systematic
discipline including, for example, literary criticism. I have thus occasionally
revised the translations of Kierkegaard's works, replacing, where necessary,
"science" and "scientific" with more general terms such as "scholarship" and
"scholarly." When Kierkegaard refers to science in the sense of the natural
sciences, the Danish term he uses is *Naturevidenskab*, which literally translates as "natural science." "Natural science" quickly becomes cumbersome,
however, so when the discussion turns to that topic, I will generally refer to
it simply as "science."

Kierkegaard's Terminology

It is the various forms of *Erkjendelsen* and *Viden* that are our primary concern. Kierkegaard appears to use these terms interchangeably, as is exemplified by two references to Plato's theory of knowledge as recollection, one
in a journal entry from 1840, where *"Viden"* appears (Pap. II A 5),[48] and

---

[45] See, e.g., KAUC, 50; PV, 123; and CD, 249–50.

[46] See, e.g., SLW, 245; KAUC, 47; and CD, 25.

[47] See, e.g., Ferrall and Repp.; and Herman Vinterberg and C. A. Bodelsen, *Dansk-
Engelsk Ordbog* [Danish-English dictionary], 2 vols., 2nd rev. and expanded ed. (Copenhagen: Gyldendal, 1966).

[48] This reference is to the Danish edition of Kierkegaard's journals and papers, *Søren
Kierkegaards Papirer* [Søren Kierkegaard's papers], 2nd ed., ed. P. A. Heiberg, V. Kuhr,
and E. Torsting, 16 vols. (Copenhagen: Gyldendal, 1968–1978). Work has begun on a

the other in the *Postscript*, where the term is *"Erkjenden"* (CUP, 173). This should not be alarming, however. *Viden* is simply a more general, or colloquial, term for knowledge than *Erkjenden*.[49] Kierkegaard was concerned not "to get out of touch with everyday speech and usage . . . as sometimes happens with a scholar with the result that he constantly collides with the everyday and . . . offends against the genius of the language and the legitimate shareholders in the common property of the language" (P, 41).[50]

Kierkegaard appears, however, occasionally to distinguish between knowledge in the sense of *Erkjendelsen* and knowledge in the sense of *Viden*. We will see, for example, in the chapter on objective knowledge, that he sometimes associates knowledge with skeptical *isostheneia*, or the determination that the reasons for and against the truth of a particular proposition are equally balanced. This association is particularly prominent in *Works of Love*. Knowledge, in these contexts, is always *Viden*, rather than *Erkjendelsen*. Distinctions of this sort appear, however, to be dependent on the context of the references. They cannot be extended to the authorship as a whole and may thus simply reflect an attempt to adapt the discussion to the vernacular of a particular audience rather than an attempt to develop a substantive distinction.

Kierkegaard, I will argue, appears consistent in terms of the substance of his thought. He displays a general disdain, however, for terminological consistency for its own sake. "It is characteristic of Kierkegaard," explains Bertung, "that he often uses commonly employed expressions idiosyncratically, at the same time he uses these expressions in their parallel ordinary sense" (Bertung, 24).[51] Part of the difficulty with trying to understand Kierkegaard's epistemology thus concerns the fact that he makes no rigorous terminological distinctions among the various Danish expressions for knowledge.

---

comprehensive English translation of Kierkegaard's journals and papers. It will be many years, however, before this project is finished. I have thus chosen to use the Hongs' translation, *Søren Kierkegaard's Journals and Papers* (Bloomington: Indiana University Press, 1967–1978). Unfortunately, this edition, though it comprises seven volumes, is still only a selection. I will cite the Danish edition of Kierkegaard's journals and papers if the passage in question is not included in the Hongs' translation.

[49] See, e.g., Poul Lübcke, *Politikens Polikkens Filosofi Leksikon* [Politiken's philosophical lexicon] (Copenhagen: Politikens Forlag, 1983).

[50] This remark would make Kierkegaard appear to be the first "ordinary language philosopher."

[51] See also Schmidinger's reference to the consistency that underlies Kierkegaard's apparently arbitrary use of the term "interest" (Schmidinger, 221); and Adi Schmüeli, *Kierkegaard and Consciousness*, trans. Naomi Handelman (Princeton: Princeton University Press, 1971), 5.

Such play with words was possible for Kierkegaard, at least in part, because he was not an academic philosopher and hence was not subject to the same constraints on terminological consistency to which academics are routinely subject and because, as Hügli points out, Kierkegaard "views the concept, which is independent of particular linguistic indicators, as the meaning constant" (Hügli, 276n4). That is, language, for Kierkegaard, is composed of two elements: the word and what is meant by it.[52] "When I am speaking," explains Kierkegaard in *The Concept of Irony*, "the thought, the meaning, is the essence, and the word is the phenomenon" (CI, 247).

Perhaps the clearest statement of Kierkegaard's philosophy of language is in Lars Bejerholm's "*Meddelelsens Dialektik*" ("The dialectic of communication"), where he explains that

> [t]he relation between a linguistic term and a concept, according to Kierkegaard, is usually such that the linguistic term denotes a concept. This concept may, however, be denoted by a variety of linguistic terms. It is, therefore, a matter of indifference which terms are used to denote a given concept. The most important thing, according to Kierkegaard, is that one "knows what one is talking about"; the particular terms used are, in contrast, inessential. Linguistic confusion arises first when terms are used in such a way that uncertainty arises concerning which concept they denote. "[L]inguistic confusion" is, therefore, a consequence of conceptual confusion or a blending of unlike "categories."[53]

Even if the underlying thought is consistent, terminological inconsistency can understandably create confusion in the reader. One of the tasks of this book is thus to distinguish the different senses in which Kierkegaard uses various philosophical expressions. Kierkegaard observes that occasional linguistic ambiguity can have a positive function to the extent that it reflects a more substantial, ontological, or epistemological ambiguity.[54] He appears, however, to have the equivalent of technical expressions that he uses fairly consistently in their technical senses.

The task of distinguishing these expressions and their associated meaning is complicated, however, by the fact that the first English translations

---

[52] The wording here is important. Language, for Kierkegaard, is *not* made up of words and meanings that are bound to them independently of any reference to a particular speaker.

[53] Lars Bejerholm, "*Meddelelsens Dialektik*": *Studier i Søren Kierkegaards teorier om språk, kommunikation och pseudonymitet* ["The dialectic of communication": Studies of Kierkegaard's theories of language, communication and pseudonymity], Publications of the Søren Kierkegaard Society II (Copenhagen: Munksgaard, 1962), 60. The second of the quotations within this quotation comes from CUP, 215. Bejerholm, unfortunately, did not include references for these quotations. I have been unable to locate the first.

[54] See CA, 9.

of Kierkegaard's works, while stylistic masterpieces, were too free to give a clear picture of Kierkegaard's philosophical terminology. The more recent translations that Princeton University Press began to publish in the 1980s, though more literal than the earlier translations, are sometimes marred by technical errors.[55] Finally, there are numerous instances in which, although the translations are not incorrect, some modification is necessary in order to make the desired point sufficiently clear. I have thus made a number of revisions to the translations in the passages cited in the present work. In many instances I have included a justification for the revision in a note. In those instances, however, where the reasons for the modification would be clear from the context, I have not included a note.

The Issue of the Pseudonymity

My objective here is to show that there is a coherent epistemology that underlies Kierkegaard's authorship as a whole. I have thus included references from as many of Kierkegaard's works, both published and unpublished, as possible. Like Hannay, I believe that "[o]f the forty or so volumes of the collected works and papers none can truthfully be said to be irrelevant to a presentation of his thought" (Hannay, 21). The subject of knowledge figures more prominently, however, in some works than in others. Certain works will thus be more heavily represented in the references than others. There are, for example, significantly more references to the *Postscript* than to any other single work. The reason for this is not only that it is particularly rich with references to knowledge, nor that as one of the "dialectical works" (Hannay, 93) it is particularly well suited for systematic presentation, but also because, as Hannay observes, "the *Postscript* alone offers a synoptic view of the whole range of Kierkegaard's thought" (Hannay, 21).

Most of Kierkegaard's works that are interesting to philosophers because they tackle traditional philosophical problems such as free will and determinism, the reality of time, and the difference between belief and knowledge were published pseudonymously. Some of the pseudonyms make claims that appear inconsistent with the views of other pseudonyms as well as with views expressed by Kierkegaard in his nonpseudonymous writings. The significance of Kierkegaard's use of pseudonyms is far too complicated to be adequately treated in the context of the present discussion. What needs

---

[55] See M. G. Piety, "The Dangers of Clarity," *Times Literary Supplement*, April 18, 1997. See also the notes throughout the present work where I explain corrections I have occasionally had to make to the translations.

to be addressed is the fact that Kierkegaard cautioned his readers against assuming the views expressed in his pseudonymous works were his own.[56] Some Kierkegaard scholars have taken this declaration so seriously that they restrict the attribution of views expressed in Kierkegaard's pseudonymous works to the relevant pseudonyms. Such a practice is unfortunate, however, because it is an impediment to understanding Kierkegaard's thought as a whole. Most Kierkegaard scholars agree that the pseudonymous works contain a wealth of information concerning Kierkegaard's own views.[57] Part of the project of this book is to persuade the reader that Kierkegaard's pseudonymous works are substantially consistent with both his nonpseudonymous works and the views he records in his journals and papers, at least with respect to his epistemology.

It will occasionally be possible to produce references to Kierkegaard's writings that would appear to contradict much of what I will say, or what I attribute to Kierkegaard, in the rest of this book. Kierkegaard is no different in this respect from any other thinker. That is, few of even the most rigorously systematic thinkers are perfectly consistent either terminologically or substantively. My objective, like that of any scholar engaged in an effort to determine the views of a particular thinker, is to develop an interpretation of those views that will be supported by the preponderance of evidence, taken in context.[58] My aim here is to develop what Hannay refers to as a "philosophically amplified" presentation of Kierkegaard's thought, "a version which emphasizes its overall unity and logical structure, as well as the conceptual content of its parts, to a degree and in a way not found in Kierkegaard's own writings" (Hannay, 329).

It has been argued that Kierkegaard is not a philosopher in the usual sense, but a kind of poet.[59] He was certainly a far more accomplished literary stylist than are most philosophers, and understanding the irony and humor that characterize much of his work is essential to understanding the substance of his thought. There is a reason he is studied by philosophers, however, as well as by theologians and scholars from other disciplines. "The 'old' dispute," observes Jochem Henningfeld, "as to whether Kierkegaard ought

---

[56] See CUP I, 527–31.

[57] See, e.g., Alastair Hannay, *Kierkegaard* (London: Routledge & Kegan Paul, 1982), 57.

[58] See Wisdo, 99, for the importance of the contexts in which particular expressions appear in Kierkegaard's works.

[59] See, e.g., Louis Pojman, "Kierkegaard on Faith and Freedom," *International Journal for Philosophy of Religion* 27 (1990): 41; Wisdo, 98; and Louis Mackey, *Kierkegaard: A Kind of Poet* (Philadelphia: University of Pennsylvania Press, 1971). It is interesting to note, however, that there is at least one place in his authorship where he asserts that he is *not* a poet (FT, 90).

to be considered a philosopher . . . has quite properly become obsolete. The diversity of weighty philosophical issues treated in Kierkegaard's works was long ago made famous by scholars."[60] The occasional failure of philosophers to award Kierkegaard the status of a philosophical thinker is based, as Wisdo has observed, "on a rather narrow conception of Philosophy" (Wisdo, 98). Kierkegaard's few assertions that he was not a philosopher were most likely made tongue in cheek. Most of his authorship is concerned with traditional philosophical issues such as the nature of knowledge and its relation to belief.[61] The significance of such issues was clearly not lost on Kierkegaard. He referred to himself as a "philosopher" in a letter to Rasmus Nielsen, who was himself a professor of philosophy at the University of Copenhagen.[62]

I will, for the most part, treat Kierkegaard as a philosopher in the traditional sense not because I believe this method is superior to the method of scholars who study Kierkegaard with the tools of literary criticism but because I believe a more traditional philosophical analysis of the substance of his thought is a vital complement to any other sort of analysis. Moreover, such analysis has long been badly needed with respect to the issue of Kierkegaard's epistemology.

The assumption that Kierkegaard is an important philosophical thinker does not in itself, however, address the issue of how one is to extract Kierkegaard's views from his pseudonymous works without doing violence to his own philosophical and pedagogical intentions. I will thus generally attribute views expressed in Kierkegaard's pseudonymous works to the relevant pseudonyms and endeavor, wherever possible, to accompany references from the pseudonymous works with supporting references from the nonpseudonymous works as well as from Kierkegaard's journals and papers. In this way I will endeavor to show that Kierkegaard's works may be understood as a whole and that his authorship is characterized throughout by consistency in the substance of his views concerning the nature of knowledge.

[60] Jochem Henningfeld, "*Denken der Existenz: Einübung in Kierkegaard*" [The thought of existence: Practice in Kierkegaard], *Philosophische Rundschau* 40 (1993): 310. See also Hügli, 237.

[61] See, e.g., Malantschuk, "*Das Verhältnis*," 49.

[62] See also LD, no. 228; and JP, 6:6256.

CHAPTER TWO

THE KNOWING SUBJECT

Consciousness, Passion, and Actuality

Kierkegaard was a realist in the sense that he believed there was a distinction between what he referred to as "factual being" (*faktisk Væren*) and "ideal being" (*ideel Væren*) (C, 114–15n3). Factual being does not, according to Kierkegaard, refer to tangible existence but to what one could call "objective reality." That is, it refers to the being of everything that has reality in itself and not simply as an idea.[1] Factual being is thus synonymous, for Kierke-gaard, with reality in general, which he variously refers to as "being" (*Væren*), "existence" (*Tilværelsen*), and "reality" (*Realitet*).[2]

---

[1] That this is the sense in which Kierkegaard uses the expression "*faktisk Væren*" is clear from his criticism of Spinoza's proof for the existence of God. That is, he argues that Spinoza tries to deduce the "existence" (*Væren*) of God from an examination of the essence of the idea of God, whereas Kierkegaard argues that it is impossible to deduce from the idea of something that the thing has "factual being" (*faktisk Væren*). That is, Kierkegaard's criticism of Spinoza is that he tries to prove that there is a god—not that God has tangible existence in the sense of, say, the person of Jesus.

[2] See Gregor Malantschuk, *Nøglebegreber I Søren Kierkegaards Tænkning* [Key concepts in the thought of Søren Kierkegaard], ed. Grethe Kjær and Paul Müller (Copenhagen: C. A. Reitzels Forlag, 1993), 210–12.

The best place to start in trying to understand Kierkegaard's views on the nature of the knowing subject is with his views on consciousness. The richest resource in this respect is Kierkegaard's unpublished work, *Johannes Climacus or De Omnibus Dubitandum Est*. Consciousness, asserts Kierkegaard, through the voice of Johannes Climacus, the pseudonym under which he had planned to publish the work, is a relation between "reality" (*Realitet*) and "ideality" (*Idealitet*) (JC, 169). He is careful to distinguish consciousness from "reflection" (*Reflexion*) (Pap. IV B 1 c. 147). The categories of the latter, he explains, "are always *dichotomous*" (e.g., ideality and reality, and soul and body), while those of the former are "*trichotomous*" (JC, 169), as is expressed when I say, "*I* am conscious of *this sensory impression*" (JC, 169). That is, there is a sensory impression, a consciousness of it, and finally an "I" whose consciousness it is. Reflection, argues Climacus, is the *possibility* of a relation between reality and ideality, and as such it is "*disinterested*" (JC, 170). But consciousness as the relation, that is, the actual relation, is *interested*, or "is interest" (JC, 170). Consciousness is an "*interesse*" (JC, 170), or a "being between" reality and ideality.

Climacus' definition of consciousness as trichotomous suggests there is little, if any, distinction in Kierkegaard's writings between "consciousness" and "self-consciousness." Consciousness always involves an object, a consciousness of that object, and an *I* whose consciousness it is. Consciousness of objects, either concrete of abstract, would always appear to involve some degree of self-consciousness according to Kierkegaard.

Kierkegaard does not, however, make consciousness identical to self-consciousness.[3] To the extent that he distinguishes the two, consciousness could be described as characterizing a person in an immediate sense and self-consciousness as relating the individual moments of consciousness, or as an *interesse* of *interesser* (i.e., a being between of being-betweens).[4] Self-consciousness, so defined, is thus interest just as consciousness is interest. The difference is that the interest of self-consciousness is consciousness whereas the interest of consciousness is the object of knowledge, which may happen to be the subject, but only accidentally. That is, the subject of consciousness is not of essential interest to consciousness, but only to self-consciousness.

Kierkegaard is not particularly interested in consciousness as distin- . guished from self-consciousness. His terminology thus sometimes appears

---

[3] See, e.g., Pap. VII 1 A 182.

[4] *Interesse* is Danish for "interest." The plural of *interesse* is formed through the addition of an "r."

to conflate the two. The interest of consciousness, according to Kierkegaard, is not terribly significant with respect to our existence as particular human beings. Only the interest of self-consciousness is crucial to our subjective existence as such.

Interest may be interpreted in two ways. It may be interpreted legalistically as referring to purely formal involvement independent of the presence, or absence, of subjective concern on the part of the "interested" party. The welfare of a ward is, for example, something in which his guardian is "interested," independently of whether the guardian experiences any subjective concern for this welfare. Interest may also be interpreted, however, to refer to subjective concern.

Both these senses of "interest" are involved in Climacus' definition of consciousness as "interest." Consciousness is interest in a purely formal sense in that, as a being between reality and ideality, it is formally involved with both these realms. What is true of either reality or ideality is thus significant for consciousness, independently of whether the conscious subject experiences any concern for these truths. But the fact that this subject is *formally* involved with both ideality and reality is what makes subjective concern relative to these truths possible. Such concern would appear to be a natural consequence of this situation.

If we return to the example of a relation between a ward and his guardian, we can say that the fact that the guardian is legally responsible for the welfare of the ward means we expect her to experience subjective concern for that welfare. We take the absence of such concern to indicate either that the guardian has failed to appreciate the significance of her position or that there is something psychologically amiss with her. Such concern is not, of course, equivalent to affection. The guardian may experience subjective concern for her ward's welfare without feeling any affection for the child. That is, we expect her to be anxious that the child's needs are provided for because she realizes that providing for those needs is her responsibility in both a moral and a legal sense. Her concern for the welfare of her ward stems from the fact that her formal involvement with that welfare has the potential to affect her own circumstances. She may experience feelings of guilt if she fails to look after the child properly. She could experience social repercussions in the form of other people's condemnation, and she could suffer legal repercussions.

But while Climacus' definition of consciousness as interest in a purely abstract sense makes concrete interest possible, even leads us to expect such interest, it is not immediately apparent *how* the transition from the one type of interest to the other is effected. There is no existence code that would correspond to the legal code and thus spell out for a person exactly what sort of practical significance various truths, or aspects of reality, have in relation to his existence.

It appears Kierkegaard believes the transition from abstract to concrete interest is accomplished through suffering. This suffering is not the result of a particular misfortune. That is, it is not accidental but essential to human existence. Human existence is temporally defined. That is, it is constantly in the process of becoming. "All becoming [*Tilblivelse*]," asserts Climacus, who appears again as the pseudonymous author of Kierkegaard's *Philosophical Crumbs*, "is a *suffering* [*Liden*]" (C, 142). "The birth [*Tilblivelse*] of consciousness," asserts Kierkegaard in a draft of *Johannes Climacus*, "is the first pain of existence" (JC, 257). That is, the consciousness of change is itself characterized by change. Thus the suffering Climacus associates with change becomes associated with consciousness itself to the extent that the object of consciousness is change.

"[E]xistence [*Existents*]," continues Climacus in Kierkegaard's *Concluding Unscientific Postscript*, "when one becomes *conscious* of it, yields [*giver*] passion" (CUP, 294; emphasis added). To the extent that one is conscious of existence, he suffers, and to the extent that he suffers (*lider*), he is passionate (*lidenskabelig*). That is, consciousness is associated with suffering, and this suffering generates concrete interest in the sense of subjective, or passionate, concern for one's existence.

"Passion and interest," observes Heinrich M. Schmidinger, "are considered by Kierkegaard to be equivalent concepts."[5] This point can be made more clearly if we return again to the example of the guardian and her ward. The formal interest she has in the child translates naturally into concrete interest because her consciousness of the formal interest generates a kind of suffering. That is, her awareness that her own welfare is connected to the child's creates in her a natural anxiety for the child's welfare.

Consciousness as interest, or as a being-between reality and ideality, represents what one might call the formal involvement of a person in these two realms independently of whether the person experiences any subjective concern in relation to this involvement. To the extent, however, that this involvement gives rise to a kind of suffering, which is to say to the extent that the object of a person's consciousness is existence, the transition from abstract to concrete interest is not merely possible, it is natural. The concern

---

[5] Schmidinger, *Das Problem*. See also Jörg Disse, *Kierkegaards Phänomenologie der Freiheitserfahrung* [Kierkegaard's phenomenology of the experience of freedom], Symposion, *Philosophische Schriftenreihe* (Freiburg: Verlag Karl Alber, 1991).

of an organism to avoid suffering is generally considered to be part of the instinct for self-preservation. It would appear prerequisite to the survival of living organisms and thus a necessary presupposition of any definition of natural or rational behavior.[6]

The suffering (*Liden*) that characterizes the consciousness of existence generates a passionate (*lidenskabelig*) concern for its alleviation. Concrete interest is thus synonymous with passionate interest. The point may also be made, however, by saying that passion is what distinguishes merely abstract interest from concrete, or actual (*virkelig*), interest. Interest in the sense of subjective passionate concern appears to be the vehicle for the transition from ideality, or possibility, to actuality. "For one who exists," asserts Climacus in the *Postscript*, "what interests him most is existing, and his being interested *in* existing [*at existere*] is his actuality [*Virkeligheden*]" (CUP, 263; emphasis added). The fact that a person *has* an interest in existing would not appear to be enough to give him actuality in the technical sense. It would appear that Kierkegaard believes one must actively *take* an interest in one's existence in order to achieve an authentic, or *actual*, existence. Thus Climacus asserts in the *Postscript* that "as a composite of the finite and the infinite, an *actual* human being has his actuality precisely *in keeping these together*" (CUP, 253; emphasis added).[7] That is, a person's actuality is the result of a passionate interest that he takes in his existence.

Self-Consciousness

The consciousness of existence, according to Kierkegaard, is associated with suffering. But to what extent must one be conscious of existence? Can one avoid such consciousness and to that extent avoid suffering? In order to answer this question, we need to know what Kierkegaard means by "existence."

---

[6] This does not compel one to conclude that the avoidance of suffering is always rational or that the choice of suffering can never be rational. It means merely that under normal circumstances the avoidance of suffering is in keeping with the nature of all living organisms. Certain kinds of suffering may rationally be chosen in order, for example, to avoid other and more life-threatening sorts of suffering. One may choose, for example, to endure the suffering of withdrawal in order to avoid the greater suffering that can ultimately be associated with an addiction.

[7] "Kierkegaard," explains Hügli, "considers the Hegelian distinction between 'existence' (i.e., *Dasein*) and actuality to be correct. That is, the outward appearance of a thing is merely '*daseiend*.' It attains actuality only to the extent that it is taken up into the idea [*die Idee*]" (Hügli, 103).

We saw above that Kierkegaard uses at least three distinct terms to refer to being or reality: *Væren*, *Realitet*, and *Tilværelsen*. The terms *Eksistens* and *Tilværelsen* were roughly synonymous in nineteenth-century Danish. *Eksistens* (occasionally spelled *Eksistents*) was merely the Latin equivalent of the Danish *Tilværelsen*.[8] There is a difference, according to Kierkegaard, however, between being (*Væren*) and existence (*Eksistens*).[9] Mathematical objects, for example, have *ideal* being, but they do not have *actual* being. The being of mathematical objects is purely abstract, which is to say that it is timeless, or eternal. According to Climacus, however, everything that "exists" is temporal, or has *come to be* at some point.[10]

Kierkegaard uses two different Danish expressions to refer to change in the sense of becoming: *Vorden*[11] and *Tilblivelse*.[12] *Vorden* appears to denote change in a very general sense—that is, change that may or may not be associated with necessity.[13] *Vorden* is thus the expression Kierkegaard generally uses to refer to the changes that characterize nature. Nature "exists" in the sense that it came to be at some point, but the changes that have subsequently characterized it are not changes in the sense of *Tilblivelse*.[14]

According to Kierkegaard, to say that something "comes to be" is to say that it has gone from a state of nonbeing (*Ikke-Væren*) to a state of being (*Væren*). But this nonbeing cannot be nothing because then the change in question would be equivalent to getting something from nothing. Climacus asserts that "this non-being which the thing that comes to be leaves behind

[8] See Ferrall and Repp.; Christian Molbech, *Dansk Ordbog* [Danish dictionary], 2 vols. (Copenhagen: den Gyldendalske Boghandling, 1859); and Ludvig Meyer, *Fremmedordbog* [Dictionary of foreign words] (Copenhagen: J. H. Schubothes Boghandling, 1863).

[9] See CUP, 276–77; CA, 12; Robert Widenman, "Kierkegaard's Terminology and English," *Kierkegaardiana* 7 (1968): 124–25; Disse, 35–40; and Hügli, 146.

[10] See, e.g., C, 141–43.

[11] See, e.g., CUP, 68, 77; and SUD, 30.

[12] See, e.g., C, 141–43; and CUP I, 490.

[13] *Vorden* is a cognate of the German *Werden*. Hegel uses *Werden* to denote a certain unrest or state of oscillation between being and nonbeing (*Sein und Nichts*). Kierkegaard is not entirely happy with this account of *Werden* (or *Vorden*), which he has Climacus say is "a nevertheless somewhat obscure definition inasmuch as being itself is also the continuity in the alternation" (CUP, 68). Hegel asserts, however, that when the discussion concerns *Werden*, as it pertains to "a particular, actual something [*einem irgend Etwas und Wirklichem*]," the alternation in question is more accurately characterized as one between the positive and the negative (Hegel, *Science of Logic*, 85). It is this latter account of *Werden* that most closely resembles Kierkegaard's *Vorden* (see, e.g., CUP, 68, 77, 485–86).

[14] See, e.g., C, 144; CA, 21 and 89. See also J. Himmelstrup, "Terminologisk Register" [Glossary], in *Søren Kierkegaards Samlede Værker* [Søren Kierkegaard's collected works], ed. A. B. Drachman, J. L. Heiberg, and H. O. Lange (Copenhagen: Gyldendal, 1920–1936), 2nd ed., vol. 15, 746–47 and 765–66.

must also have some sort of being [*være til*]. . . . But the sort of being," he continues, "that is nevertheless non-being is precisely possibility" (C, 141). He thus defines the change of coming to be as the transition from possibility to actuality. Such a transition, Climacus continues, cannot take place with necessity because "[b]ecoming is a change, but the necessary can in no way be changed because it always relates to itself and relates to itself in the same way" (C, 142). The change of coming to be, he concludes, does not come about through necessity but through freedom.

This is the reason the changes that characterize nature do not exemplify genuine becoming (*Tilblivelse*) and that nature does not, properly speaking, have a history according to Climacus.[15] That is, these changes do not come about freely. Deciduous trees, for example, are not free to keep their leaves all year, just as flowers are not free to bloom at any time whatsoever. The changes that characterize nature are determined by the essence of nature itself and are thus changes only in the phenomenal sense. It is clear, however, that phenomenal change is not what Kierkegaard means by "coming to be." But if consciousness of phenomenal change is not equivalent to consciousness of existence, what *does* constitute consciousness of existence?

Humanity, according to Kierkegaard, unlike nature, has a history in what Climacus calls "the stricter sense" (C, 143). It would appear, however, that even the contemplation of human history does not constitute a consciousness of existence for Kierkegaard. Everything that has come to be, asserts Climacus, is historical.[16] The difficulty is that

> [t]he historical cannot be sensed immediately because it has within it becoming's *duplicity*. The immediate impression of a natural phenomenon or of an event is not an impression of the historical, because *becoming* cannot be immediately sensed, but only presence. But the presence of the historical has becoming within it, otherwise it is not the presence of the historical. (C, 147)

To say that the historical cannot be immediately sensed or perceived is to say that actuality cannot be immediately sensed or perceived. "All knowledge [*Viden*] about actuality," asserts Climacus, "is possibility" (CUP, 264). But possibility is opposed to actuality. It would thus appear there is no knowledge of actuality as such. Indeed, Climacus asserts that "[t]he only actuality there is for someone existing [*en Existerende*] is his own ethical actuality" (CUP, 265). All other actuality, according to Climacus, is transformed by thought into possibility, which is to say that it is not actuality for the knowing subject.

[15] See, e.g., C, 144.
[16] See C, 143.

To claim, however, that the only actuality a person has is his own ethical actuality would appear equivalent to saying that this actuality would be an object of immediate apprehension for him. Such a claim is consistent with what has been identified as Kierkegaard's "intuitionism."[17] That is, it appears Kierkegaard believes one can be conscious of his ethical actuality because he is immediately related to it. One would thus be conscious of his own ethical actuality in the same way he was conscious of his own pain. It will turn out, in fact, that this ethical actuality is precisely a kind of pain (i.e., the pain of guilt consciousness).

"Kierkegaard's psychology," observes Alastair Hannay, "flatly acknowledges the reality of ethics and attempts no scientific explanation of it" (Hannay, 160). Everyone, according to Kierkegaard, is presumed to have knowledge of eternally valid ethical norms.[18] Consciousness of one's ethical actuality would appear to be equivalent to the awareness of an abstract, or ideal, ethical standard to which one is responsible for making his existence conform, combined with the conformity, or lack thereof, his existence actually exhibits.[19] According to Kierkegaard, one will always fail to conform fully to the ideal ethical standard,[20] thus consciousness of one's ethical actuality is, to some extent, always equivalent to consciousness of guilt.

A person is always in some sense aware of his ethical actuality according to Kierkegaard. It is possible to try to ignore this awareness, though, in much the same way that one can try to ignore certain physical pains. Guilt consciousness presupposes self-consciousness. Yet Anti-Climacus, the pseudonym under which Kierkegaard published *The Sickness Unto Death*, asserts, "How rare is the person who has continuity with regard to his consciousness of himself! As a rule people are conscious only momentarily, conscious in the midst of big decisions, but they do not take the daily everyday into account at all" (SUD, 105). This point is repeated in Kierkegaard's journal, where he observes, "There are many people, surely the majority, who are able to live without any real consciousness penetrating their lives" (JP, 3:3130). The lives of such people are, he observes, "a simulated posture of a purely sensate existence" (JP, 3:3705). "Consciousness," asserts Anti-Climacus, "is the decisive thing in relation to the self. The more consciousness, the more will, the more will, the more self" (SUD, 29). Consciousness is decisive

[17] See Hügli, 81; and Bejerholm, 30.
[18] See Malantschuk, *Nøglebegreber*, 44–45; and Hügli, 161.
[19] The awareness of this standard, or of what one could call "the moral law," falls under the heading of what Kierkegaard would call immanent metaphysical knowledge. This knowledge will be examined in chapter 4 (see the section titled "Knowledge in the Strict Sense").
[20] See, e.g., Hügli, 218; and Slotty, 70.

because it necessarily involves self-consciousness, or, more particularly, consciousness of the ethical actuality of its subject, which is, in turn, a kind of
suffering. Suffering generates passion, and decisiveness, as we will see below,
inheres in passion.[21]

"Accurate, clear, decisive, impassioned understanding [*Forstaaelse*] is of
great importance," asserts Kierkegaard in his journals, "for it facilitates *action*"
(JP, 3:3705; emphasis added). This view is consistent with the views on the
relation between passion and action expressed by each of his pseudonyms
that touches on this issue. As early as *Either/Or* we find Judge Wilhelm asso-
ciating passion with decisiveness and action when he observes of the young ·
man, A, that "[p]assionate as you are, it was no doubt possible that you with
your passionateness, could decide to forget your great plans, your studies"
(EO II, 13). This position is repeated in another pseudonymous work, *The
Stages on Life's Way*, where we find references to the "passion of action [*Han-
dlings Lidenskab*]" (SLW, 372) and to "pathos-filled passion that wants to act
[*pathetisk Lidenskab at ville handle*]" (SLW, 436) as well as the observation
that "without passion one never arrives at any resolution" (SLW, 163). Lastly,
we find in the *Two Ages* the observation that "[t]he single individual [in
the present age] . . . has not fomented enough passion to tear himself out of
the web of reflection" (TA, 69).

The identification of passion with decisiveness appears unproblematic
at first. It becomes more problematic, however, when one remembers that
passion is generated by suffering. That is, we most often think of suffering as
something one endures, something to which one's relation is passive rather
than active. There are two senses, however, in which Kierkegaard uses the
expression "suffering." Suffering, we saw, is associated by Kierkegaard with
coming to be, which in this context can be understood to refer to a person's
ethical development. This development is not necessarily positive. It is most
likely to be characterized by a combination of ethical failures as well as ethical successes. According to Kierkegaard, ethical failures are not the result of
the positive *choice* of evil. They are rather the result of the failure to choose
good. Anti-Climacus, for example, argues that

> [i]f a person does not do what is right at the very second he knows [*har erkjendt*]
> it—then first of all knowledge [*Erkjendelsen*] simmers down. Next comes the ques-
> tion of how the will appraises what is known [*det Erkjendte*]. The will is dialectical
> and has under it the entire lower nature of human beings. If this does not agree
> with what is known, then it does not necessarily follow that the will goes out and
> does the opposite of what knowledge understood (presumably such strong oppo-
> sites are rare); rather the will allows some time to elapse, an interim called: "We

---

[21] See Hügli, 133.

shall look at it tomorrow." During all this, knowledge becomes more and more obscure, and the lower nature gains the upper hand more and more; alas, for the good must be done immediately, as soon as it is known [*erkjendt*]. (SUD, 94)

A person who fails to act ethically does not positively choose evil. He just fails to choose to do good, which could be construed as his choosing not to do good. There is a sense, however, in which even this "choice" is not really a choice. That is, Johannes Climacus asserts in Kierkegaard's *Concluding Unscientific Postscript* that

there are cases regarding evil where the transition from thought to action goes almost undetected . . . but these call for a special explanation. That has to do with the individual being subject to habit; by frequently making the transition from thought to action, he has, in the end, by becoming a slave to habit, lost control over the transition, which at *his expense* makes it go faster and faster. (CUP, 285)

A person can be in the habit of lashing out in retaliation when provoked. This is probably the most immediately compelling interpretation of the above passage. A person can also be in the habit, however, of procrastinating. He can become so accustomed to putting off decisions, or to extended periods of deliberation before undertaking any action, that he would seem to have lost the ability to act immediately. On either interpretation, ethical failure appears to be a kind of passivity.

"Every person," observes Kierkegaard in his journals,

always understands [*erkjender*] the truth a good deal farther out than he expresses it existentially [*existentielt*]. Why does he not go father out then? Ah there's the rub! I feel too weak (ethically too weak) to go as far out as my knowledge extends [*som jeg erkjender*]. . . . In this way everyone becomes guilty before God and must make this admission. (JP, 2:2301)

One is *guilty* of passivity because it could have been avoided. Much of the consciousness of one's ethical actuality is thus consciousness of such passivity. "[T]he suffering of actuality," asserts Climacus, is "that the possible turns out to be nothing the moment it becomes actual, for possibility is *annihilated* by actuality" (C, 142). The consciousness of existence is thus often a consciousness of the annihilated possibility for ethical action. The moment for acting comes and goes without the required action being taken. It could have been taken, however, thus this annihilated possibility is retained in the actuality of the person who failed to act. What *comes to be* from the annihilation of the possibility for ethical action is guilt.

A person does not actively endeavor to become guilty in the way he actively endeavors to be ethical. To the extent that ethical obligation concerns a person's relations to others, opportunities or demands for ethical action are made on one from without. That is, these demands are made by the people with whom one comes into contact.[22] To fail to respond to these demands is, in a way, to *endure* becoming guilty and is thus to suffer in a passive sense.

It is important to appreciate, however, that the determinations here of "active" and "passive" are relative. That is, there is a sense in which even morally reprehensible actions may be understood to be initiated within the agent. Thus to say that ethical failure is the result of a kind of passivity, or of the surrender of the freedom to determine one's own actions to outside forces, is not equivalent to saying that these forces determine one's actions with *necessity*. The possibility remains for one to take control of his actions.

Strictly speaking, the suffering associated with ethical failure is not in itself the suffering of actuality in an ethical sense. It is rather the individual's acknowledgment of this failure that is associated by Kierkegaard with his ethical actuality. An actual human being, Climacus asserts, "as a composite of the finite and the infinite, . . . has his actuality precisely in keeping these together" (CUP, 253). Guilt represents a relation between the finite and the infinite in the sense that it is equivalent to a particular relation between a finite person and the infinite moral law. It is not equivalent, however, to the ethical actuality of the guilty person in that these factors are not "held together" by the guilt, but only by the consciousness of guilt. That is, the infinite, in the form of the moral law, is brought into relation to the finite in a person's consciousness of his ethical failures. This consciousness amounts to an acceptance of these failures in the sense that it represents the annihilation of the possibility of self-deception concerning one's guilt.

It is not actually possible, according to Kierkegaard, for a person to deceive himself concerning his guilt. "Deep within every human being," he asserts in one of the religious discourses he published under his own

---

[22] Louis Mackey argues in "The Loss of the World in Kierkegaard's Ethics" that one of the difficulties with Kierkegaard's ethics is precisely that the people with whom one comes into contact cannot make such demands. He concludes from Climacus' contention that "[t]he only actuality there is for someone existing is his own ethical actuality" (CUP, 265) that other people are merely possibilities for Kierkegaard and that possibilities cannot "impinge on [one] directly" (CUP, 276) in the sense that is to say they cannot obligate one ethically. It appears, however, that this criticism is based on an identification of reality (*Realitet, Væren,* or *Tilværelsen*) and actuality (*Virkelighed*). The reality of other people is self-evident according to Kierkegaard. Climacus asserts, for example, that it is "nonsense" to demand of a person that he prove he "is there [*er til*]" (CUP, 34; see also PC, 204; and Slotty, 21). It is the reality of other people, not their actuality, that obligates us ethically (see M. G. Piety, "The Place of the World in Kierkegaard's Ethics," in *Kierkegaard: The Self in Society*, ed. George Pattison and Stephen Shakespeare [London: Macmillan, 1998]).

name, "there is a secret sharer who is present just as scrupulously every-where—conscience" (WA, 182).[23] Guilt, Kierkegaard asserts, that could be entirely hidden from the guilty person would no longer be guilt.[24] Guilt will thus always be accompanied by some degree of its acceptance as such. That this acceptance admits of degrees does not change the fact that it is an act and thus distinguished from the relative passivity of the guilt itself. The individual accepts that the reason he suffers is that he is guilty, and, in this sense, the passive suffering of guilt is prerequisite to the active suffering of guilt consciousness.

To the extent that Kierkegaard associates passion with decisiveness, it is positive. Many of the references to passion in Kierkegaard's religious, or nonpseudonymous works, are disparaging. In *The Sickness Unto Death* (a pseudonymous work), *Works of Love, Christian Discourses*, and "Purity of Heart," passion is often presented as a confusing or destructive force.[25] This passion is often qualified, however, as "earthly" or "worldly passion" (*jordisk lidendkab*).[26] It would thus appear that there are two kinds of passion, which may be understood to correspond to the two types of suffering for Kierkegaard. This view is borne out by a reference in his journal from 1844, which reads, "Let no one misinterpret all my talk about pathos [*Pathos*] and passion [*Lidenskab*] to mean that I sanction every uncircumcised immediacy, every unshaven passion" (JP, 3:3127).[27]

There is an essential opposition, for Kierkegaard, between what he identifies in the *Postscript* and *Christian Discourses* as "earthly passion" and in the *Attack upon Christendom* as "immediate passion" and what he considers "higher passion." "All idealizing passion," explains Climacus, "is an anticipation of the eternal in existence in order for one who exists to exist"

[23] See also FT, 75.
[24] See WA, 182.
[25] See, e.g., SUD, 65, 111; WOL, 315, 343; CD, 77; and UDVS, 142.
[26] See, e.g., CD, 77; and UDVS, 142.
[27] One could argue that Kierkegaard considers there are actually more than two types of passion insofar as he refers in various places in both his pseudonymous and nonpseudonymous works to "false passion [*unsand Lidenskab*]" (PC, 185), "primitive passion [*primitiv Lidenskab*]" (SLW, 430), the "passions" of "irony" and "humor" as distinguished from the "passion of faith [*Troens Lidenskab*]" (FT, 51), the "passion of freedom [*Frihedens Lidenskab*]" (CUP, 146; and R, 65), the "passion of possibility [*Mulighedens Lidenskab*]" (R, 24), "thought passion [*Tanke-Lidenskab*]" (CUP, 477), "the passion of existential effort [*Existents-Anstræn-gelsens Lidenskab*]" (CUP, 472), and, finally, the "purposeful passion of repentance [*Angerens intenderende Lidenskab*]" (SLW, 426), "Christian passion [*christelig Lidenskab*]" (TM, 208), and "the passion of eternity [*Evighedens Lidenskab*]" (TM, 162). Each of these passions may be placed under one of the two general headings of "earthly and worldly passion" or "higher passion [*høiere Lidenskab*]" (SLW, 406).

(CUP, 262), whereas all "[e]arthly passion tends to prevent existence by transforming into something momentary" (CUP, 262n).[28] This latter claim is expressed again in one of Kierkegaard's nonpseudonymously published works where he contends that if passion is "continued in a person it changes his life into nothing but moments" (UDVS, 23).

While it is probably accurate to say that Kierkegaard is concerned in the works he published under his own name with sustaining specifically religious passion, it is clear that in his pseudonymous works his overall concern is with stimulating passion in general, as is expressed in *Either/Or* when A says, "Let others complain that the times are evil. I complain they are wretched, for they are without passion" (EO I, 28), and again in *Fear and Trembling* when he says that the age "has crossed out passion in order to serve science" (FT, 7). "What our age needs," argues Kierkegaard, in a journal entry from 1847, "is *pathos* (just as scurvy needs green vegetables); . . . [hence] all my dialectical reckoning of the comic, the pathos-filled and the passionate in order to get, if possible a beneficial pathos-filled breeze blowing" (JP, 3:3129).

Kierkegaard, observes Hügli, "sees in passion, not simply one among a number of psychological abilities, but as it were, the ability *instar omnium*, the fundamental force present in all human expressions" (Hügli, 164). It is important to get a "pathos-filled breeze blowing" because decisiveness inheres in passion in general to the extent that earthly passion, or passive suffering, is prerequisite to active suffering and the idealizing passion to which it is related. The actual subject, which is to say the self as an actuality, is the product of the decisions of the individual. No passion, no decision; no decisions, no actuality; no actuality, no self.[29] Thus Kierkegaard remarks in his journals that "passion is the genuine dynamometer for human beings" (JP, 1:896/Pap. IV C 96) and Hügli observes that "only in passion is the individual 'completely himself'" (Hügli, 141).[30]

---

[28] The wording here is actually from the Hongs' translation (CUP I, 312n) which, though less literal than Hannay's translation, captures the sense better than the latter. The contrast expressed above between "idealizing passion" and "earthly passion" is expressed again in one of Kierkegaard's newspaper articles from 1855, where he claims that "[t]o become a Christian in the New Testament sense is accomplished by separating or loosening (in the sense in which a dentist speaks of loosening the tooth from the gums) the individual from the connection by which he clings in immediate passion and which immediate passion clings to him" (KAUC, 221/TM, 248) and a "higher" or "unconditioned passion," which, as he explains in a journal entry from 1854, "is the formal condition for being able to receive the content of Christianity" (JP, 3:3133).

[29] See Evans, 267.

[30] See also UDVS, 248; and FT, 121.

Climacus claims that "[t]he goal of motion [*Bevægelsens Maal*] for someone existing is decision" (CUP, 261). It is the potential for *activity* inherent
in suffering and, in turn, passion, on which Kierkegaard concentrates. That
is, Kierkegaard's overwhelming concern is with ethics and religion, or with
initiating in his reader the *activity* of striving to conform to the demands of
the ethical, or religious, ideal. It is, in fact, this conformity that constitutes the
existence of the individual in the sense that it constitutes his ethical actuality.

I began this section with the question of to what extent consciousness
must include a consciousness of existence according to Kierkegaard. It is
now clear that "existence," in this context, is equivalent to one's ethical actuality. A person may try to deceive himself concerning the substance of this
actuality, but according to Kierkegaard there is an important sense in which
he is always aware of it. Consciousness thus always includes some consciousness of existence.

The Self

"Consciousness," asserts Anti-Climacus, "is the decisive thing in relation to
the self" (SUD, 29). "[C]onsciousness," asserts Climacus, "is spirit" (JC,
169) and "[s]pirit," according to Anti-Climacus, "is the self. . . . The self," he
continues, "is a relation that relates itself to itself or is the relation's relating
itself to itself in the relation" (SUD, 13). We saw above, however, that consciousness, as distinguished from self-consciousness, is not a relation that
relates itself to itself but is merely a relation between reality and ideality.
"[T]he self," asserts Anti-Climacus, "is not the relation, but is the relation's
relating itself to itself" (SUD, 13). That is, the self is the interest of the *interesse* (or between-beings) of consciousness, which is to say that "the self" is
equivalent to self-consciousness rather than consciousness.[31]

Kierkegaard sometimes appears to equate consciousness and self-
consciousness to the extent that he asserts consciousness always involves
some degree of the awareness of its subject. Though this awareness admits of
degrees, its presence in every moment of consciousness is what makes self-
consciousness, or the self, possible. Consciousness is thus equivalent to the
self in the sense that it represents the possibility of the self.

There is an important sense in which the self *is* possibility for Kierkegaard. He has the character Judge William continually refer in *Either/Or* to the
subject's choice of himself.[32] This self one chooses is "concrete," according to

[31] See Hügli, 57.
[32] See, e.g., EO II, 218, 223–26. There are too many references to list them all here.
They can be found in the index to the second volume of *Either-Or*.

Judge William, "in the sense that it is the particular, determinate self of the subject who chooses it,[33] but it becomes actual only with this choice. This is apparent from William's assertion that "[t]his self was not before, because it came to be with the choice, and yet it was because it was himself" (EO II, 215). This nebulous being that the self had before it was chosen was nothing other than possibility for such a being, asserts Climacus. The choice of oneself is thus a transition from possibility to actuality, as is described by Climacus in the "Interlude" section of *Philosophical Crumbs*. That is, the choosing oneself is a process of self-actualization.

The self, asserts Anti-Climacus, is a "synthesis" of "the infinite and the finite, of the temporal and the eternal, of freedom and necessity" (SUD, 13),[34] or, as Vigilius Haufniensis expresses it, of the "soul and body" (CA, 88). The emphasis is not on the two factors but on the synthesis. "The Kierkegaardian self," explains Hannay, "is not to be identified with the relation between soul and body; for then the self would be merely a dependent factor, mirroring the interplay of the other two with each other and with the environment" (Hannay, 191). Such mirroring would be equivalent to consciousness rather than to self-consciousness, or to an animal rather than a specifically human type of existence. Human beings are to synthesize the opposites of consciousness if they are to become authentic selves. The question is thus how such a synthesis is effected.

Climacus refers to consciousness as "a contradiction" (JC, 168). It is difficult to imagine how a synthesis could emerge from a contradiction. "The contradiction," explains Hügli, "can neither resolve itself nor be resolved because I think it; it can be overcome only as the result of my action, and even then not once and for all, but through constantly renewed efforts" (Hügli, 115).[35] The self thus comes to be (*bliver til*) through a person's actions.[36] Just as was the case, however, with respect to suffering and passion, there are two types of what one could call "acts" according to Kierkegaard. There are genuine acts initiated within a person and then there is behavior that has the appearance of an act but that was determined by something outside that person.[37] Earthly passion, or passive suffering, may lead to "decisions" that do not represent a positive involvement of the higher elements of the synthesis that is the self. It is possible, for example, to say that one "decided" to have an extramarital affair because the immediate

[33] That is, he argues that the individual "has not created himself, but has chosen himself" (EO II, 270). See also Hügli, 176, 210.

[34] See also JP, 4:3854.

[35] See also Slotty, 40.

[36] See Hügli, 211.

[37] See NRF, 53; and Hügli, 171, 216.

presence of the person concerned created an overwhelming desire for such a relationship. This kind of "decision" does not, however, represent a reconciliation of the opposing factors of consciousness but is rather a surrendering to one of these factors—immediacy.

It would appear that, according to Kierkegaard, a person who surrendered to the desire to have an extramarital affair could not really be said to have "decided" to have the affair.[38] On the other hand, such a person could be said to have "decided" to let immediate factors determine the nature of his behavior.[39] That is, one has decided to surrender the autonomy to decide.[40] One endures becoming guilty of having an affair because one failed to exercise control over what Anti-Climacus calls one's "lower nature." "The *person of immediacy* [*den Umiddelbare*] . . . is bound up in immediacy with the other in desiring, craving, enjoying, etc., yet *passively* in his craving, this self is dative, like the 'me' of a child" (SUD, 51).

It is surprising that Climacus refers to such a person as having a dative "self." To the extent that his actions are determined by external, real or finite, forces, it would appear they would not synthesize the elements of finitude and infinitude, or of reality and ideality, and so on, in the manner required to achieve a genuine self. That is, it would appear that such a person could not have any self at all, not even a "dative" one. We saw above, however, that if a person did not positively synthesize finitude and infinitude through conforming his actions to an abstract, or ideal, ethical standard, he would negatively synthesize these elements of the self in guilt consciousness. One does not become guilty in the same way one becomes ethical. One becomes ethical by actively striving to conform his behavior to the moral law and thus initiating himself the synthesis of finitude and infinitude that is exemplified in ethical action and that is necessary to become a self. One becomes guilty, on the other hand, by failing to initiate this synthesis oneself. Such a failure means that the synthesis is effected from outside the person. That is, the moral law clings to morally reprehensible actions in the form of a condemnation that is experienced as feelings of guilt.

Guilt is not equivalent to guilt consciousness. To the extent that Kierkegaard assumes people are immediately aware of their own ethical actuality, guilt consciousness is unavoidable. Just as self-consciousness intrudes on every moment of consciousness, so does guilt consciousness intrude on every

---

[38] See Hügli, 171.

[39] This coheres with Hannay's assertion that "in sin a person positively affirms a willingness to be 'determined' by temporal goals" (Hannay, 163). See also Thomas, 34.

[40] The insight that one can decide to surrender the autonomy to decide is not unique to Kierkegaard. It is precisely what is meant by the saying, "Not to decide is also a decision."

moment of the self-consciousness of the guilty person. But guilt consciousness may characterize self-consciousness to varying degrees, not in the sense that a person may be more or less guilty (although this is, of course, possible) but in the sense that he may be more or less willing to acknowledge his guilt. Anti-Climacus speculates that "a great many people . . . work gradually at eclipsing their ethical and ethical-religious comprehension [*Erkjenden*]" (SUD, 94).

There is an important difference between a person who is merely guilty and a person who wills to acknowledge, or to accept, that he is guilty. The existence of the former represents a synthesis of the finite and the infinite in that those elements are brought together from without in the form of a condemnation of his actions. The existence of the latter represents a synthesis that was initiated within the individual through his act of acknowledging his guilt. Such an act constitutes a transition from possibility to actuality in that accepting one's guilt annihilates the possibility for self-deception. It is thus possible for Kierkegaard to speak of a guilty, or "dative," *self* rather than simply a guilty individual. Everyone has a self in this minimal sense to the extent that no one, according to Kierkegaard, can entirely avoid acknowledging his own guilt.

Consciousness, as we saw, is associated by Kierkegaard with suffering. To the extent, however, that consciousness is also associated with the self, it is possible to identify the self with suffering. According to Frater Taciturnus, the pseudonymous author of "A Note to the Reader" at the end of *The Stages on Life's Way*, "only the suffering that is related to the idea is of interest" (SLW, 458).[41] That is, a person, as temporally defined—that is, as constantly engaged in a process of coming to be—is going to suffer. Only to the extent, however, that this suffering is related to the actualization of the idea through his decision to express that idea in his existence is it of interest to Kierkegaard. The passion that is the active expression for this suffering is the "idealizing passion" identified above, which, according to Climacus, is an "anticipation of the eternal in existence" (CUP, 262), which helps "the individual to exist" by facilitating "the true life of the individual" as that life is expressed in the synthesis of "the infinite and the finite" (SUD, 13). This synthesis is characterized by Kierkegaard in his journals as "the divine [or infinite] inhabit[ing] and find[ing] its tasks in the finite" (JP, 2:1578).[42]

---

[41] There are two senses in which this claim may be understood. It is true, according to Taciturnus, from both an esthetic and a religious perspective. The difference is that "it is only an immediate relationship that concerns esthetics . . . suffering must come from without" (SLW, 457). Religiously, however, "I remove the externality and repeat the correct principle: only the suffering that is related to the idea is of interest" (SLW, 458).

[42] See Hügli, 121, 214.

The self, according to Anti-Climacus, "is a relation that relates itself to itself, or is the relation's relating itself to itself in the relation" (SUD, 13). The self is not merely a relation between the opposing elements of consciousness; it is a synthesis of these elements in the individual subject. It is a relation between these elements that relates to itself in the sense that it is aware of the character of this relation as either positive or negative. The self is the activity of a person both in the sense of his efforts to bring the actuality of his existence into conformity with an abstract ethical ideal and in the sense of his efforts to acknowledge the true extent of the conformity of that actuality to this ideal.

To equate the self with activity is to imply that it is never finished. That is, the self proper, according to Kierkegaard

> [i]s the conscious synthesis of infinitude and finitude that relates itself to itself, whose task is to become [*vorde*] itself . . . to become oneself is to become concrete. But to become concrete is neither to become finite nor to become infinite, for that which is to become concrete is indeed a synthesis. Consequently, the development must consist of an infinite moving away from itself in the infinitizing of the self, and in an infinite coming back to itself in the finitizing process. . . . Yet every moment that a self exists [*er til*], it is in the process of becoming [*Vorden*], for the self *kata dynamin* does not actually exist [*er ikke virkelig til*], [but] is simply that which *ought* to come to be [*skal blive til*]. (SUD, 29–30; emphasis added)

Even while a person is engaged in self-actualization, the self proper, according to Anti-Climacus, does not actually exist,[43] because the self proper is the product of complete self-actualization, and this, if it is achieved at all, can be achieved only when a person's life is finished. As long as one lives, he has his self "as a task" (EO II, 262).

Subjectivity, asserts Climacus, is passion.[44] We saw in the preceding sections that Kierkegaard identifies passion with decisiveness. This would appear to be the reason he emphasizes in the *Postscript* that "[o]nly in subjectivity is there decision" (CUP, 171). The decisiveness required to initiate the conformity of one's existence to the ethical ideal and thus to achieve a genuine, or actual, self inheres in passion. To the extent that he associates subjectivity with passion, it is a mistake to become objective. Or as Climacus puts it, "If the dialectical and reflection are not exploited to intensify

---

[43] Thus Anti-Climacus also asserts that "the majority of people do not exist at all in the more profound sense" (PC, 129). That is, Kierkegaard asserts in his journals that "[m]ost men never become spirit. The stages—child, adult, oldster—they pass through these with no credit to themselves; it is none of their doing, for it is a vegetative or vegetative-animal process. But they never experience becoming spirit" (JP, 1:67). See also Schmidinger, 318.

[44] See CUP, 171, 427.

passion, to become objective is to regress; and even the person who loses himself through passion has not lost as much as the person who lost passion, for the former had possibility" (CUP, 513). To lose passion is to lose the possibility for actual existence.

It is interesting that insofar as the task of the individual is construed by Kierkegaard to be that of bringing his existence into conformity with ethical-religious ideality, which is to say the eternal, it would appear that it could also be characterized as that of bringing one's subjective existence into conformity with objective truth.[45] Hence the effort to become more and more subjective through the cultivation of the decisive passion that inheres in subjectivity would appear to be directed ultimately toward the end of becoming objective.[46] So why not just become objective directly instead of indirectly aiming at objectivity through an effort to become subjective?

The answer appears to be that one is precluded from becoming objective directly by the fact that one is a subject—that is, by the fact that one exists. Or, as Climacus explains, "[s]ince a human being is a synthesis of the temporal and the eternal, the happiness to be had by the speculator will be an illusion, since he desires in time to be merely eternal" (CUP, 49). A person cannot become objective by escaping directly into the purely intelligible, or universal, because part of that person will always remain particular and tangible and hence be excluded from this objectivity. The only way one can really become objective, according to Kierkegaard, is through the conscious effort to make the particularity and tangibility of his existence conform to an objective ideal.

Subjectivity is ultimately untruth for Kierkegaard,[47] but a person will never come to know this unless he comes to a complete appreciation of subjectivity as such. Hence Kierkegaard observes in his journals that "[i]t is absolutely true [that] isolated subjectivity as the age understands it is evil, but restoration to health by means of objectivity is not a hair better. Subjectivity is the way of deliverance" (JP, 4:4555). That is, Kierkegaard argues that "precisely in order to put an end to subjectivity in its untruth we must pass all the way through to the single individual" (JP, 4:4555). We "pass

---

[45] It is important to point out, however, that Kierkegaard would not characterize ethical-religious ideality as "objective" truth. Since ethical-religious truth is essentially prescriptive in nature and thus relates directly to individuals as such, Kierkegaard considers it "subjective" truth. More will be said on this topic on the chapter that looks at the nature of subjective truth.

[46] See Hügli's observation that "if phenomenal actuality is designated as objectivity [das Objektive] and thought as subjectivity, then the goal of appropriation is to make the subjective objective" (Hügli, 31).

[47] See CUP, 179; and JP, 4:4555. See also Hügli, 218.

through the single individual" that each of us is by stirring up the interest, or passion, that inheres in our subjectivity and invoking the decisiveness that inheres in that passion.

Anti-Climacus defines the self as a relation. We can see now that this relation is both something we inherit by virtue of the fact that we are conscious beings, for consciousness itself is a relation, and something we create. That is, the self is our beginning in the sense that it inheres as possibility in consciousness, and it is our end, or goal, in the sense that we strive to actualize it through conforming our behavior to the ideality of the moral law.[48]

Much more could be said on Kierkegaard's views of the self.[49] My concern has been simply to detail those aspects of Kierkegaard's views on the self that will be indispensable to understanding his epistemology. His views on the self have obvious significance with respect to the problem of self-knowledge. There are other, less obvious ways, however, in which the material in this chapter will be significant to understanding Kierkegaard's epistemology in a broader sense.

Scholars have long appreciated that it is not appropriate, according to Kierkegaard, to take a dispassionate, or impersonal, interest in issues essentially related to one's personal existence. We are now in a position to make this point even more strongly. It is now clear that, according to Kierkegaard, it is not appropriate even to aspire to adopt such an interest because it is clearly impossible. No one can really be so "absentminded," according to Kierkegaard, that he fails to notice his own ethical actuality, which is to say that no one can be so absentminded that he fails to notice his own suffering. The closest one could come to a perspective of impersonal interest in issues essentially related to one's own existence would, as we saw, be a "simulated posture" of such an interest.

Ethical and religious knowledge will not be examined until much later in this study. We will be concerned in the next few chapters with identifying the various types of objective knowledge according to Kierkegaard. What

---

[48] "We are clearly presented here," explains Schmidinger, "with a circle, the two sides dialectically bound together; on the one side the necessary preexistence [*das Schon-da-sein-Müssen*] of the self, without which there could be no choice and, on the other side, the self as that which first comes to be [*Erst-zustande-Kommen*] in the choice and without which the choice would be meaningly" (Schmidinger, 230). See also EO II, 181.

[49] See C. Stephen Evans' *Kierkegaard on Faith and the Self*; Mark C. Taylor's *Kierkegaard's Pseudonymous Authorship: A Study of Time and the Self* (Princeton: Princeton University Press, 1975) and *Journeys to Selfhood: Kierkegaard and Hegel*. See also Joseph H. Smith, M.D., ed., *Kierkegaard's Truth: The Disclosure of the Self. Psychiatry and the Humanities*, vol. 5 (New Haven: Yale University Press, 1981).

is important at present is that the reader understand that consciousness, according to Kierkegaard, is essentially interest, and that hence all knowledge is, in some sense, interested. Kierkegaard's views on the nature of consciousness will turn out to be important for understanding his views on knowledge of what he considers to be immanent metaphysical reality as well as to his views on knowledge of actuality as it is represented in scholarship and the natural sciences.

CHAPTER THREE

Defining Knowledge

Objective versus Subjective Knowledge

Despite Climacus' famously equating truth with subjectivity (CUP, 159ff.), Kierkegaard is no enemy of objective knowledge.[1] He wanted simply, as Slotty explains, "to expose . . . the impossibility of absolute knowledge" (Slotty, 20).[2] That is, there is no presuppositionless knowledge according to Kierkegaard.[3] Knowledge is always relative to some set of presuppositions, the truth of which has not been proved.

We saw in chapter 2 that Kierkegaard associates human nature with interest. It follows from this that there is no disinterested knowledge. All knowledge, according to Kierkegaard, is interested.[4] There are two types of interest for Kierkegaard, however: objective interest and subjective interest.[5] A scholar or scientist, observes Climacus, "asks about truth, but not about *subjective* truth, the truth of appropriation. . . . [T]he investigating subject is of course *interested*, but not infinitely, *personally*, *passionately* interested

---

[1] See Evans, 59–60; Perkins, "Kierkegaard's Epistemological Preferences"; Thulstrup, *Kommentar*, 187; and Malantschuk, "*Das Verhältnis*," 52.

[2] See also Evans, 37.

[3] See Malantschuk, "*Das Verhältnis*," 50.

[4] See JP, 2:2283.

[5] See Hügli, 106; and Schmidinger, 215.

in his relation to this truth" (CUP, 19; emphasis added).[6] This is, of course, only right and proper for a scholar or scientist. The truths with which they are concerned are not essentially related to their subjective existence. "Let the scholarly investigator," asserts Climacus, "labor with tireless zeal, let him even shorten his life in the enthusiastic service of science; let the speculative thinker spare neither time nor diligence; they are still not infinitely, personally, impassionedly interested. On the contrary, they would even rather not be so" (CUP, 20).

Science and scholarship are concerned with reality as it is independent of any particular individual, while ethics and religion are concerned with each individual in his particularity. There is no question of a person conforming his existence to the truths of mathematics, natural science, or history. To the extent that these truths concern reality as such and to the extent that he is a part of that reality, his existence must be assumed a priori to be in conformity with these truths.

Ethics and religion, on the other hand, are not merely descriptive, they are prescriptive. They tell us more than how things are. The tell us how they ought to be and thus place on us the responsibility of bringing our existence into conformity with them. To the extent that there are ethical or religious truths, or eternally valid norms for human behavior (and this is not something Kierkegaard ever doubted), then each of us has an interest in determining what they are and conforming our existence to them.[7] This is the reason Climacus asserts that ethical knowing and religious knowing are "essential knowing [*væsentlig Erkenden*]" (CUP, 166).

It is this personal, or subjective, interest that constitutes interest proper for Kierkegaard.[8] That is, despite the reference cited above to the interest (albeit "impersonal") of the "scholarly investigator" (CUP, 20) and similar references to the "enthusiasm of the inquiring scholar" (JP, 3:2807) and the "objective passion of the researcher" (CUP, 482), Kierkegaard refers in other places to systematic, or scientific, thought as disinterested.[9] One might be tempted to assume that Kierkegaard's views on this issue simply changed over time. The dates of the references to systematic knowledge fail, however,

---

[6] See also JP, 3:2807.

[7] That is, we are interested in the technical sense of being formally involved with these truths, quite apart from the issue of whether we experience any subjective concern for them. To the extent that there are ethical or religious truths, our responsibility to conform our existence to them is independent of whether we experience any subjective desire for such conformity.

[8] See Hügli, 106.

[9] See CUP, 126, 262; BA, 100; JP, 3:2807; and JP, 5:5621.

to support such an assumption. There are references of both sorts from 1842 to at least 1846, when the *Postscript* appeared.[10]

One might also be tempted to the view that Kierkegaard simply could not make up his mind on the issue of whether all knowledge was interested. If there was anything, however, about which he could not make up his mind, it appears to have been whether the "impersonal interest" or "objective passion" he often describes as characterizing the scholar and scientist really deserved to be called "interest."[11] It is clear though that, like the various types of knowledge we will examine later, the context of the discussion appears to determine whether impersonal interest counts as real interest. The more abstract, metaphysical, or speculative the discussion, the more likely one is to find Kierkegaard acknowledging that even abstract thought is interested; whereas, the more concrete, ethical, or religious the discussion, the more likely one is to find him characterizing abstract thought as disinterested.

It is important for the purposes of the present discussion that we understand both why Kierkegaard would consider all knowledge to be interested and why, despite this, he frequently refers to various types of knowledge as "disinterested." Kierkegaard's views on the nature of consciousness necessitate that he reject the idea that knowledge could ever be purely objective or disinterested. It is thus not surprising to find that he claims human knowledge is anthropomorphic "in the widest sense, not merely as an expression about God, but about all existence" (JP, 2:2269). That is, if the interests of the knower help define what knowledge is, then the nature of this knowledge will reflect, in some way, the nature of the subject whose knowledge it is.

Impersonal interest characterizes human beings as members of a species—that is, characterizes human consciousness in a general sense. Personal interest, on the other hand, characterizes individuals as such. The proper objects of impersonal interest are things essentially unrelated to the individual

---

[10] See "What knowing is without interest? It has interest in a third (for example, beauty, truth, etc.) which is not myself" (JP, 2:2283); "[When reality is brought] into relation to ideality, this is an act of cognition. [I]nsofar as interest is involved, there is at most a third in which I am interested—for example, the truth. . . . [When ideality is brought] into relation with reality this is the ethical [and] that in which I am interested is myself" (JP, 1:891); and "the investigating subject is of course interested, but not infinitely, personally, passionately interested in his relation to this truth" (CUP, 19). Contrast those references with "Doubt lies in interest and all systematic knowledge is disinterested" (Pap. IV B 1 149, n.d. [1842–1843?]); "Abstraction is disinterested" (CUP, 262); and "The objectivity, the disinterestedness with which the physiologist counts the pulse-beats and studies the nervous system has no real relationship to ethical enthusiasm" (JP, 3:2807).

[11] See, e.g., CUP, 19–20, 482; and JP, 3:2807.

knower, as is the case with respect to the objects of scholarly and scientific knowledge. Kierkegaard's overwhelming concern, however, is with ethics and religion; hence, the apparent lack of any essential relation between the objects of scholarship and science and the individual knower often leads him to refer to this knowledge as "disinterested."[12] Climacus refers to such disinterested knowledge as "objective knowledge [*den objective Viden*]" (CUP, 169). This "objective knowledge" is the subject of the next chapter. It will be contrasted later to what Climacus, in the *Postscript*, famously refers to as "subjective knowledge [*den subjective Viden*]" (CUP, 169).

Objective versus Subjective Truth

Knowledge, according to Kierkegaard, is the result of reality (*Realitet*) having been brought into relation to ideality.[13] This means that it is a representation of reality in the abstract, or ideal, categories of thought.[14] I am going to argue that while Kierkegaard never directly defines knowledge, he appears to be operating with something like the traditional definition of knowledge as justified, true belief. The meaning of each of these terms, however, will turn out to be relative to the object of knowledge, which is to say that it will be relative to the type of knowledge in question. Only knowledge in the strict sense is associated by Kierkegaard with certainty. Justification is more often associated with probability than with certainty. Part of Kierkegaard's interest in epistemology clearly stems from his frustration with what would appear to be the perennial human failure to appreciate that most knowledge, even of the traditional objective sort, is not associated with certainty. In order to understand Kierkegaard's views on knowledge, however, we must look first at his views on truth and then see how these views can be plugged into his claims about knowledge.

Truth, according to Kierkegaard, is an agreement between thought and being.[15] This agreement may be established in two ways, either intellectually or existentially. That is, reality may be represented in ideality, or ideality may be represented in reality (i.e., actuality). There are thus two senses in which Kierkegaard uses the expression "truth," as can be seen in Anti-Climacus' assertion that "[t]here is a difference between truth and truths" (PC, 206).

Truths plural are the result of an accurate representation of being in thought. Since "being," according to Kierkegaard, encompasses both ideal,

[12] See, e.g., JP, 5:5621.
[13] See JP, 1:891.
[14] See Hügli, 106.
[15] See CI, 247; and CUP I, 169. See also Slotty, 28; and Hügli, 78.

or abstract, and actual entities, truths can be defined either as an agreement between some abstract object and thought or as an agreement between some actuality and thought.[16] The first case appears tautological in that "thought and being [*Tænken og Væren*]," according to Climacus, "mean one and the same thing" (CUP, 160). That is, the truth that, according to Climacus, is an agreement between ideality and thought is a "duplication" (CUP I, 160), or "self-identity" of ideality in thought, which in this context may be understood to refer to what Kierkegaard's teacher P. M. Møller described as an "*a priori* system of determinations for everything that is."[17] This redoubling is accomplished in language, of which, according to Kierkegaard, all thought consists and which has the dual nature of being both ideal in itself and an expression of ideality.[18] Abstract, or ideal, being is expressed in language, which is itself abstract. Hence truth, in the sense of "truths," is a property of sentences, or propositions.[19] This is also the case when truth is construed as agreement between actuality and thought. Truth is not what is the case about the world, but the agreement between a particular conception of, or proposition about, the world, and what is the case. The fact, for example, of whether Caesar crossed the Rubicon is not a truth about Caesar, or about the past; it is rather the claim that accurately represents this fact that is true.[20]

Kierkegaard occasionally speaks as if the meaning of "truth" were restricted to truth in the sense of "truths" (i.e., as a property of propositions, or of thought) as when Vigilius Haufniensis, the pseudonym under which Kierkegaard published *The Concept of Anxiety*, observes that "the trilogy—the beautiful, the good, the true—has been conceived and represented in the sphere of the true (namely as knowledge)" (CA, 111), or when Climacus claims that the "truth" of the past is "an object of knowledge [*Erkjendelsens Sag*]" (C, 151).[21] One might thus be tempted to conclude that although Kierkegaard's ontology makes two types of truth possible, he was

---

[16] See Hügli, 78.

[17] P. M. Møller, *Efterladte Skrifter* [Posthumously published writings] (Copenhagen: C. A. Reitzels Forlag, 1843), vol. 2, 186. Møller had a strong influence on the development of Kierkegaard's thought (see Malantschuk, "*Søren Kierkegaard og Poul Martin Møller* [Søren Kierkegaard and Poul Martin Møller]," in *Frihed og Eksistens*, 101–13; and Thulstrup, *Kommentar*, 130).

[18] See CI, 247; and JP, 2:1159. It is important to remember that language, according to Kierkegaard, has two elements—words and their meanings (see chapter 1, "Kierkegaard's Terminology"), so language is not reducible to words in any straightforward sense.

[19] The expressions "proposition" and "mental representation" will be used interchangeably throughout the following discussion.

[20] Con. Disse, 41.

[21] See also JP, 5:5620.

not himself aware of this but used "truth" only in the sense of a property of propositions. Kierkegaard was clearly aware, however, that his views supported the view that there were two kinds of truth. Not only are there the aforementioned references to "truth" as contrasted with "truths," but Anti-Climacus observes in *Practice in Christianity* that "now all the expressions are formed according to the view that truth is cognition [*Erkjendelsen*], knowledge [*Viden*] . . . whereas in original Christianity all the expressions were formed according to the view that truth is a [way of] being" (PC, 206). The truth that is "a way of being" is the result of an agreement between ideality and reality that is established in reality, which is to say, in actuality.

The truth that is a property of actuality rather than of thought, or language, is the truth belonging to ethics and religion. Ethical-religious truth, according to Kierkegaard, is the agreement between the ideality of ethical or religious prescriptions and the actuality of a person's existence.[22] This is what Climacus calls "essential truth" (CUP I, 199n). It concerns a person's subjective existence as such, and thus Climacus also refers to "essential truth" as "subjective truth" (CUP I, 21).

The distinction between "truth" and "truths" is the distinction between subjective and objective truth. "The inquiring, speculating, knowing [*ekjendende*] subject," observes Climacus, "asks about truth, but not about the *subjective* truth" (CUP, 19). It is a mistake to interpret Climacus' claim in the *Postscript* that "[t]ruth is [s]ubjectivity" (CUP, 159) to mean that Kierkegaard believes there is no such thing as objective truth. Kierkegaard was actually a great defender of objective truth, or of the objectivity of certain kinds of truth. "In the case of, for example, a mathematical proposition," Climacus asserts, "the objectivity is given" (CUP, 171). Although the truth of such a proposition is indifferent to the existence of any particular individual, this indifference, Climacus claims, is precisely "its objective validity" (CUP, 163). "The path of objective reflection," he explains, "now leads to abstract thinking, to mathematics, to historical knowledge [*Viden*] of various kinds, and always leads away from the subject, whose existence or non-existence becomes, and from the objective point of view quite rightly, infinitely indifferent" (CUP, 163).

---

[22] See Hügli, 31. It is important to note that, in keeping with the rather loose manner in which Kierkegaard employs terms, he does occasionally refer to ethical or religious truths in the sense of their being the property of propositions, as is the case, for example, when he argues that "the proclaimer, too, certainly needs to have the truth said" (JFY, 135).

Objective Truth

The difficulty with understanding Kierkegaard's views on objective truth is that he is not particularly interested in it, so there are relatively few references to it in his works as compared to the numerous references to subjective truth. We must thus try to construct a picture of Kierkegaard's views on objective truth from what few references are available.

"Objectively understood," asserts Climacus,

> truth can mean: (1) the historical truth, (2) the philosophical truth. Looked at historically, truth must be made out through a critical consideration of the various reports, etc., in short, in the way that historical truth is ordinarily brought to light. In the case of philosophical truth, the inquiry turns on the relation of a historically given and ratified doctrine to the eternal truth. (CUP, 19)

That is, objective truth can signify either (1) historical truth in the sense of the agreement between the past as it is represented in thought and the being of the past or (2) philosophical truth in the sense of the agreement between a particular philosophical doctrine (e.g., Platonism), as it is represented in thought, and eternal being.

To say that thought agrees with being would appear to mean that if the reality represented in thought were something determinate or static, then the representation of it in thought should have this same character. Both philosophical reality and historical reality, according to Kierkegaard, have a fixed character, but while an agreement between philosophical reality and a representation of it in thought will turn out to be relatively unproblematic,[23] this is not, as we will see in the next section, the case with respect to historical reality.

Kierkegaard's views on objective truth appear to have been heavily influenced by Leibniz' views on truth. Kierkegaard's journals from 1842 to 1843 show that he was particularly interested in Leibniz' distinction between "truths of reasoning" and "truths of fact."[24] "Truths of reasoning," argued

---

[23] One might argue that, to the extent Kierkegaard associates thought with language and to the extent language may be argued to be a social phenomenon and thus constantly evolving, no representation of abstract, or "philosophical," reality in language could enjoy the same immutable character as the reality in question. Hügli argues, however, that "Kierkegaard decisively rejects such a conception [of language]." According to Kierkegaard, he continues, "language is not a human creation, but is given to human beings from eternity" (Hügli, 51). See also JP, 3:3281; and CA, 47.

[24] See Pap. IV C; Thulstrup, *Kommentar*, 116; and Leibniz, *Philosophical Writings*, ed. G. H. R. Parkinson, trans. Mary Morris and G. H. R. Parkinson (London: J. M. Dent, 1973), §33, 184.

Leibniz, "are necessary, and their opposite is impossible" (Leibniz, 20). Leibniz' truths of "reasoning" would appear to be the same thing as Kierkegaard's "philosophical" truths. The claim, for example, that the validity of an argument is distinguishable from its soundness was first articulated by Aristotle.[25] That is, it was "historically given," but it is not, in itself, a historical truth. That there is a distinction between an argument's validity and its soundness is built into the definition of what makes an argument (i.e., it is part of the essence of an argument). The correspondence of the claim that there is such a distinction to reality is thus formally necessary. This means that this claim has always corresponded with reality and will continue always to correspond with reality. It constitutes an *adaequatio intellectus ad rem*, or agreement between thought and what is.[26]

While truths of reasoning are necessary, according to Leibniz, those of fact are contingent, which means that their opposite is formally possible. Lessing, Kierkegaard discovered, appropriated Leibniz' distinction and applied it to the problem of historical proofs for the truth of Christianity. That is, Lessing asserted that "accidental historical truths can never serve as proofs for necessary truths of reason."[27] Lessing argued that there was a broad gulf between these two kinds of truths and that the transition from the one to the other could be made only by a leap. Hence there could be no historical proof for the truth of Christianity. Historical "proofs" may be given for historical truths (e.g., the preponderance of historical accounts of the person of Jesus may be taken as "proof" that such a person existed), but only arguments of a purely formal sort could function, according to Lessing, as claims about the nature of God.

Lessing did not actually think it was possible to prove truths of fact in the sense that it was possible to prove truths of reason. That is, he argued that "no historical truth can be demonstrated," but he acknowledged that statements about the past could be more or less well confirmed.[28] This appears to be Kierkegaard's position as well. I asserted above that, according to Kierkegaard, when the reality in question was determinate or static, then its representation in thought should have that same character. The

---

[25] Aristotle, *Prior Analytics*, *The Complete Works of Aristotle*, *The Revised Oxford Translation*, 2 vols., Bollingen Series 81, no. 2, ed. Jonathan Barnes (Princeton: Princeton University Press, 1984), 39–113.

[26] See Hügli, 199.

[27] G. E. Lessing, *Über den Beweis des Geistes und der Kraft* [On the proof of spirit and its power], in *Die Erziehung des Menschengeschlechts und andere Schriften* [The education of the human race and other writings], Universal Bibliotek No. 8968 (Stuttgart: Philipp Reclam Jun., 1976), 34.

[28] See Lessing, 34.

determinacy of the past is what Climacus calls "immutability [*Uforander-lighed*]" (C, 144). Historical truth thus ought to involve a representation of the past that has this character of unchangeableness.

The difficulty is that establishing the correspondence of statements about actuality to actuality, whether what is in question is nature or human events, is problematic. No amount of contemplation will reveal that a particular statement must correspond to actuality because nothing actual is what it is through necessity.[29] But if the correspondence of a statement to actuality cannot be definitely established, then the agreement between this statement and reality, which, according to Kierkegaard, constitutes truth, "becomes a *desideratur*[30] and everything then posed in terms of becoming [*Vorden*], since the empirical object is unfinished, and the existing, cognizing spirit is itself in the process of becoming. The truth thus becomes an approximating" (CUP, 159).[31]

Hügli asserts, however, that while "[t]he first argument, that the empirical object is not complete, is undoubtedly correct with respect to present actuality, which is still in the process of becoming [*im Werden*], it is not correct with respect to the past, which as Climacus stresses in *Crumbs* 'has happened the way it happened' and is thus 'immutable' [C, 144]" (Hügli, 87). The second argument, he continues, "is certainly correct: The knower is in the process of becoming; this does not explain, however, why historical knowledge must be an approximation" (Hügli, 88).

It would appear that historical knowledge can never be more than an approximation for Kierkegaard because nothing historical was necessary in a formal sense. That is, no matter how much data one might be able to collect that would support a particular interpretation of the past, there would always remain the formal possibility, which is to say the possibility for thought, that this interpretation was false. The preponderance of historical evidence may support, for example, that Caesar crossed the Rubicon. It remains conceivable, however, that he did not.

The categories of thought are abstract. According to Kierkegaard, this means that they cannot capture concrete facts as such.[32] Thought, for

---

[29] It is important to remember that when Kierkegaard speaks of "necessity," the reference is usually to formal, or logical, necessity, not to causal necessity.

[30] Something needed, desired. Usually *desideratum*.

[31] The wording here is a combination of the Hannay and the Hongs' translations. Hannay has "on the way to being," where the Hongs have "in the process of becoming." The original Danish text of the passage in question is "*er i Vorden.*" That is, the reference at the end of the passage is to "becoming" (*Vorden*), not "being" (*Væren*).

[32] See Slotty, 54.

Kierkegaard, is language, which is to say that it is an expression of reality. The difficulty, as Hügli points out, is that "whenever the individual is expressed, the expression is an assertion that it should not be individual, but general. The general, however, says nothing about the individual as an individual, but only something about the individual in general" (Hügli, 84).[33] Thus where the reality in question is concrete or actual, rather than abstract, no expression of it is going to capture it in its uniqueness, or particularity, and thus preclude the possibility that it is other than it is represented as being.[34]

It is in this respect that the object of historical knowledge is "unfinished." It is finished in itself, as Hügli rightly observes. It is just that it is not finished for thought. Thus Climacus asserts that "[a]lthough the world-historical is something past, nevertheless as material for cognitive consideration [erkjendende Betragtning] it is incomplete; it is constantly coming into being through ever new observation and research" (CUP, 125). That is, it is always possible to collect more information about the past and thus to get a more complete picture of it.

Hügli asserts that Kierkegaard's "approximation thesis," or his claim that both the subject and the object of historical knowledge are in the process of becoming, is defensible "only if one abandons the Aristotelian assumption—that is, if the concept is not once and for all embodied in the object, but is constituted in the course of the historical development of the relation between subject and object" (Hügli, 280). Kierkegaard himself says in The Concept of Anxiety that if "the phenomenon were not understandable . . . only in and with the concept, and if the concept were not understandable . . . only in and with the phenomenon, then all knowledge would be impossible, inasmuch as in the first case the truth, and in the second case the actuality, would be lacking" (CI, 241–42).

It is clear, however, that actuality is precisely lacking when it is expressed in thought or in language.[35] Language, observes Kierkegaard in his journals, is

> an abstraction and always presents the abstract rather than the concrete [i.e., the actual]. Approaching something scientifically [naturvidenskabeligt], aesthetically, etc., how easily one is led into the conceit that he really knows something for which he has heard the word. It is the concrete intuition that is so easily lost here. (JP, 3:2324/Pap. X 2 A 235)

---

[33] See also Slotty, 35.

[34] Thus Hügli argues that according to Kierkegaard, "language does not express actuality, but produces something new" (Hügli, 52–53).

[35] See Hügli, 52–53; and Slotty, 54.

It would appear that for Kierkegaard, actuality is appreciated as such (to the extent that that is possible) through "concrete intuition." We saw in chapter 2, however, that "the only actuality there is for an existing individual," according to Climacus, "is his own" (CUP I, 316).[36] Thus it would appear that Kierkegaard does, in fact, abandon Aristotle's assumption that the concept is embodied in its object, to the extent that the object in question is an actuality other than the individual's own.

Kierkegaard clearly uses the expression "truth" not merely in a strict sense but in a loose sense as well. That is, sometimes it refers to a genuine agreement between thought and being, but it also occasionally refers to an approximate agreement, as is the case, for example, when Climacus asserts that with respect to claims about empirical reality truth "becomes an approximating" (CUP, 159). It seems reasonable to conclude, therefore, that the "truth" of statements about actuality, to the extent that Kierkegaard uses this expression, *is* identified with the "historical development of the relation between subject and object" (Hügli, 280). Such use would be consistent with Kierkegaard's claims about how historical truth is established as well as with his observation in *The Point of View for My Work as an Author* that "in relation to all temporal and worldly matters the crowd may have competency, and even decisive competency, as a court of last resort" (PV, 110). No single scholar or natural scientist can alone determine that a particular historical or scientific theory corresponds to reality. Theories in science and scholarship are always the product of the cooperative efforts of various individuals throughout the history of these disciplines and need, in order to continue to enjoy acceptance, to be continually reverified within the evolving standards of verification agreed on by practitioners in these disciplines.

This does not mean, however, that Kierkegaard is an idealist (or antirealist).[37] Hügli is right to point out that Kierkegaard insists in *Crumbs* that the past "'has happened the way it happened' and is thus 'unchangeable'" (Hügli, 88). What is in the process of becoming is not the empirical object as such but the object as it is for thought (i.e., *erkjendende Betragtning*). This interpretation is supported both by Kierkegaard's views on the nature of the truth in question (i.e., that as a property of propositions, or thought, it is abstract and cannot thus capture actuality as such) and by the fact that the expression Kierkegaard uses for "becoming" in this context is "*Vorden*," not *Tilblivelse*, the expression Climacus uses in *Crumbs* to refer to "coming to

---

[36] Climacus goes on to assert that "Kant's deviation" was that he "brought actuality into relation with thought, instead of referring actuality to the ethical" (CUP, 275).

[37] See Evans, "Realism and Antirealism in Kierkegaard's *Concluding Unscientific Postscript*," in *Faith and the Self*, 29–46.

be." To "become" in the sense of *at blive til* is to undergo a change in being (*Væren*)—for example, to go from having been possible to being actual.[38] Past events, according to Kierkegaard, have already undergone such a transition. The "becoming" that subsequently characterizes them (i.e., characterizes them to the extent that they are objects of knowledge) concerns their essence (*Væsen*) rather than their being (*Væren*).[39] That is, it represents the determination of their essence for thought. As objects of knowledge, past events are no longer what they were—that is, actualities. As objects of knowledge, they are transformed into intellectual constructions whose correspondence to actuality cannot definitely be established. They thus undergo a number of changes as the result of various efforts to establish this correspondence.[40]

The becoming that characterized the knower, in this context, like that which characterizes the object of knowledge, is also a *Vorden* rather than a *Tilblivelse*. That is, this becoming is not the transition from possibility

---

[38] See C, 141–43; and Hügli, 66. The difference, for Kierkegaard, between "*Vorden*" and "*Tilblivelse*" can be seen in the contrast between Climacus' claim in *Crumbs* that nothing can come to be (*blive til*) with necessity (C, 142) and Vigilius Haufniensis' claim in *The Concept of Anxiety* that there can be a becoming, or change, that is characterized by necessity ("*Vorden med Nødvendighed*"), as is the case with respect, for example, to the development of a plant or the physical as opposed to moral development of a human being.

[39] "As soon as someone who comes later," asserts Climacus, "believes the past (not its truth, for that is an object of cognition [*Erkjendelsens Sag*], that concerns essence [*Væsen*] not being [*Væren*], but believes that it was present by having come to be [*ved at være blevet til*]), then the uncertainty of becoming is there" (C, 151). While Kierkegaard equates "*Vorden*" with Hegel's "*Werden*" (see, e.g., CUP, 68), he appears to reject Hegel's contention that the change in question is an alternation between being and nonbeing (*Sein und Nichts*). The change that for Kierkegaard is from nonbeing (*Ikke-Væren*) to being (*Væren*) is precisely "*Tilblivelse*" (see, e.g., C, 141–43).

Hügli's failure to appreciate the difference between "*Vorden*" and "*Tilblivelse*" may stem from the fact that both expressions are translated into German as "*Werden*." The section, for example, of the "Interlude" from *Philosophical Crumbs* that is titled "*Tilblivelsen*" (i.e., coming to be) in Danish appears in the German translations of *Crumbs* as "*Das Werden*" (see Søren Kierkegaard, *Philosophische Bissen*, Über. Mit Einl. U. Kommentar von Hans Rochol [Hamburg: Felix Meiner Verlag, 1989], 72ff.; Søren Kierkegaard, *Philosophische Brocken*, Übers. von Emanuel Hirsch [Dusseldorf: Eugen Diederichs, 1967], 69ff.; and Søren Kierkegaard, *Philosophische Brocken*, Übers. von Chr. Schrempf [Jena, Germany: Eugen Diederichs, 1910], 67ff.).

[40] These changes are not necessarily progressive in the sense that they represent an increasingly adequate representation of the actualities to which they refer. They may be progressive, but they may also be regressive. We may, for example, be mistaken in our views that some of the works originally attributed to certain artists and writers (e.g., Rembrandt and Shakespeare) were not actually by these individuals. That is, the original attributions may have been correct.

to actuality in any kind of substantial sense. It is rather the process of the determination of the essence of past actualities.

The difficulty with establishing the correspondence of statements of fact to actuality is a result of the inability of thought, with its abstract character, to capture concrete reality as such. There will always be a gap between the expression of an actuality in thought and that actuality as it is in itself because there is a logical gap between individuals and statements made about them. Or as Hügli explains, "In all judgments about individuals, the predicate always encompasses more than the subject" (Hügli, 84). Thus the process, or activity, of the determination of the essence of past actualities for thought goes on interminably.[41] It is for this reason that the "truths" of science and scholarship are "an approximating" (CUP, 159).

Objective Justification

Hannay argues that "Kierkegaard associates the word 'proof' with psychological rather than factual or logical certainty, i.e., with conviction, or certitude, without in any way confusing the former with the latter" (Hannay, 138–39). Slotty concurs in his observation that Kierkegaard "considered a conviction to be higher than any reasons one might have for holding it. He believed that the essence of human beings was expressed in the activity of willing rather than thinking. It was thus irrelevant, on his view, how one came to have certainty concerning reality, as long as one did come to have such certainty" (Slotty, 22).

Truth, as defined by Kierkegaard, may be understood to be independent of any particular individual. Kierkegaard appears, however, to have an internalist view of justification. That is, he appears to associate knowledge with an appreciation of the knower of the correspondence, or at least the probable correspondence, of a particular idea to reality. When the idea is of something abstract, then its justification will be equivalent to an insight on the part of the knower concerning the formal necessity of the correspondence of this idea to reality. This insight, for lack of a better term, may be referred to as an "intuition."[42] The term "intuition" can be misleading, however, in that it has been used in various ways throughout the history of philosophy and in that it rarely appears in Kierkegaard's works. There are fewer than a dozen occurrences in the entire Kierkegaard corpus, with none occurring

---

[41] A particular knower may, of course, contingently halt this process. This has no effect, however, on the essence of the project.

[42] There is a strong connection in Kierkegaard's works between "intuition" and "intimation" (*Anelse*) (see Malantschuk, *Nøglebegreber*, 12–13).

later than 1844.[43] It is possible that Kierkegaard abandoned the expression
because he felt it was too laden with connotations from German idealism
and, in particular, from Schelling. Kierkegaard is critical of Schelling's concept of "intellectual intuition."[44] It may also be that it is effectively synonymous, for Kierkegaard, with another expression, "certainty" (*Vished*) in the
psychological sense, and that he prefers the latter expression because it is
more common. In any case, Kierkegaard associates something on the order
of an insight into the essence of the object of knowledge with certainty in
the sense of subjective conviction. It is this insight, it appears, that justifies
the ideas to which it is connected.[45]

"Intuition," according to Kierkegaard, refers to the appreciation of the
essence of an object of knowledge, or of the object as a whole, rather than as
merely the sum of its parts. He argues, for example, that

> [w]hen a person standing on a high point gazes out over a flat region and sees sev-
> eral roads running parallel to one another, he will, if he lacks intuition [*Intuition*],
> see only the roads, and the fields between them will seem to disappear; however,
> he who has an intuitive eye will see them together, will see the whole section as
> striped. (EO I, 122n)

This ability to appreciate the essence of the object of knowledge is central
to what Kierkegaard calls "true knowledge" (JP, 2:2245). Insight into the
essence of an object makes its outward form insignificant, as is illustrated
by Kierkegaard when he observes that "the image which the mind requires
to fix its object—this and the externality conditioned by it—vanishes when
true knowledge [*sande Erkjendelsen*] appears" (JP, 2:2262). Thus it is appropriate, according to Kierkegaard, that "the great geniuses among poets (such
as Ossian and Homer) are represented as blind . . . for this would seem to
indicate that what they saw when they saw the beauty of nature was not seen
with the external eye but was revealed to their inner intuition [*indre Intuition*]" (JP, 1:117). This "inner intuition" represents what Kierkegaard calls
the "Archimedean point," which, when found, facilitates an understanding
of the object that allows one to deduce the details.[46]

---

[43] There are a few references to Schelling's concept of "intellectual intuition" (*intellektu-
ell Anschauung*, or *intellektuelle Anskuelse* in Danish) in the *Postscript* (CUP, 89, 125n, 281)
and in *The Concept of Anxiety* (CA, 11). The rest of the references are to "intuition" and are
found in the following works: EO I, 122; CA, 152; CI, 32; JP, 1:117; and JP, 2:1182, 36.

[44] See CUP, 89; and Himmelstrup, vol. 15, 605–6.

[45] See Hügli's claim that, according to Kierkegaard, "I grasp an object in knowledge: I
have it in the form of ideality and, what is more, I feel certain that I have its reality in ideality,
its being in thought" (Hügli, 124).

[46] See JP, 1:117.

We saw above that Kierkegaard associates intuition with psychological certainty. This intuition amounts to an insight into the essence of an object that generates certainty concerning its correspondence to reality. When the object is a mathematical proposition, then to stand in an intuitive relation to it would mean one grasped its essence in such a way that one would be able to produce a proof of its truth at will. Vigilius Haufniensis argues that a person who can prove the truth of a mathematical proposition when the variables are designated by the letters A, B, and C, but not when they are designated by D, E, and F, is unable to do so because he "lacks certainty [*mangler Visheden*]" (CA, 140). Such a person "becomes anxious" as soon as he hears the proposition described using terms that are unfamiliar. He was able to prove the truth of the proposition not because he had understood its essence but only because he had memorized the steps in a proof he had been shown. Certainty is thus equated with intuition. That is, certainty is identified by Haufniensis with just such a grasping of the essence of an object of knowledge that Kierkegaard refers to elsewhere as an "intuition."

Certainty, in this sense, renders mental representations unalterable because it refers to the appreciation of the objective necessity of their correspondence to reality. In other words, certainty refers to an appreciation of the formal impossibility—that is, the impossibility for thought—that reality could be other than it is presented as being. This is seen clearly in Kierkegaard's remark that "[p]roof is given for a mathematical proposition in such a way that no disproof is conceivable" (JP, 2:2296). If no disproof of a particular proposition were conceivable, then there would be no chance one would cease to believe that this proposition corresponded to reality. It would be inconceivable that it did not so correspond.

Intuition is sometimes characterized as insight that results from contact with the object of the insight, or from an identification of the subject with the object of the insight. This appears to be a fair characterization of how Kierkegaard uses the expression. Kierkegaard asserts, for example, that a person is easily "led into the conceit that he really knows [*kjender*] something for which he has heard the word" (JP, 3:2324) when it is not the word but a "concrete intuition" that is required for such knowledge.[47]

Thought and being are, at least to some extent, two different things. It is therefore difficult to understand how an identification of the knower with the object of knowledge could be possible. Kierkegaard expresses this difficulty himself when he asks, "[H]ow can true intuition enter in despite man's limited position?" (JP, 2:1182). There are portions of reality, however, to which the knower is immediately related and thus with respect to which

---

[47] See JP, 3:2324.

intuition is possible. One is immediately related to abstract reality through thought, since thought, according to Kierkegaard, is abstract.[48] One is also immediately related to one's ethical actuality through emotion or feeling. The former may thus be the object of what one could call an "intellectual intuition"[49] (keeping in mind, of course, how this use is distinguished from that of Schelling's "intellectual intuition"), and the latter of what Kierkegaard refers to as "concrete intuition."

Both types of intuition would appear to provide what contemporary epistemologists have referred to as a "causal justification" of the knowledge claims with which they are connected.[50] The contact of the knower with the object of knowledge is what makes an intuition concerning the essence of the object possible. Reality itself is ultimately the cause of the mental representation in question and thus of the knower's certainty that this representation corresponds to it. It is thus reality itself that, in a sense, causes the knowledge to be justified.[51] It is ultimately the certainty of the knower, however, concerning the correspondence of his mental representations to reality that constitutes the justification of any knowledge claim. Contact with reality makes certainty possible, but it is the latter that constitutes belief justification, so Kierkegaard's views on justification would appear, ultimately, to be internalist.[52]

There is a significant portion of reality, however, to which we are not immediately related and thus with respect to which intuition is impossible. Concrete intuition is restricted, according to Kierkegaard, to the ethical actuality of the subject whose intuition it is; hence, it cannot justify mental representations of actuality in general. Yet there is a sense, according to Kierkegaard, in which mental representations of actuality in general may be said to be true. That is, he appears to employ, as we saw, both a strict and

[48] See Holmer's claim that, according to Kierkegaard, "ideas and thoughts, categories and principles, are immediately possessed. . . . [I]n respect to their relation to the thinker they are in an immediate relation" (Holmer, 45).

[49] This is presumably what Holmer means when he refers to Kierkegaard's "logical intuition" (Holmer, 44).

[50] See Marshall Swain, "Knowledge, Causal Theory Of," in *Routledge Encyclopedia of Philosophy*, ed. E. Craig (London: Routledge, 1998), http://www.rep.routledge.com/article/P004SECT4 (accessed July 11, 2006).

[51] This does not mean, of course, that Kierkegaard believes all mental representations a person has of abstract reality or of his ethical actuality are either correct or appreciated by that person as correct. It means that in at least some instances, as in the case, for example, of Meno's slave boy, a person can both come to have the correct mental representations of these aspects of reality and achieve certainty concerning their correctness.

[52] This is in contrast to contemporary causal theories of belief justification that tend to be externalist.

a loose sense of "truth." But if he understands truth in both a strict and a loose sense, then it would be reasonable to expect that he would understand justification in both a strict and a loose sense and that while justification, in the strict sense, was causal, there would be a looser sense of justification that was perhaps not causal. A careful examination of Kierkegaard's works reveals that Kierkegaard does, in fact, have two conceptions of how mental representations, or beliefs, might be justified and that the manner in which a belief is justified is relative to the type of belief it is.

Actuality, according to Kierkegaard, is equivalent to the realm of what Leibniz calls truths of fact. While truths of reasoning are necessary, those of fact are contingent. This means that mental representations, or beliefs, about actuality are characterized by probability rather than certainty in the formal sense. Historical truth, for example, is established, according to Climacus, by "a critical consideration of the various reports, etc." (CUP, 19) about the past. These reports may make the correspondence of a particular mental representation to the reality of the past appear probable. If, for example, one has thirty-six documents that refer to Caesar's crossing the Rubicon and three that state he did not cross it, or thirty-six documents that are consistent with such an event and three that are not, it would appear more probable that Caesar crossed the Rubicon than that he did not.

There are two difficulties, however, with such probabilities. The first concerns the fact that one can never be certain one has succeeded in collecting a representative portion of such documents. That is, one can never be certain that there does not lie hidden in some library, cellar, or attic evidence that would tip the scales of probability in favor of the opposite conclusion. That is, what appears probable, based on the evidence actually available at any given point, may not be what is really probable based on all the evidence potentially available. The historian must thus constantly be engaged in a search for new evidence in order to ensure that the available evidence can reasonably be construed as a representative sample.

The second difficulty with the justification of beliefs about actuality concerns the fact that even if the probability of the correspondence of a particular mental representation to reality is based on all the evidence that could, in principle, be available, a probability is not a certainty. No matter how probable the correspondence of a particular mental representation to reality appears to be, the possibility always remains that it does not so correspond. No accumulation of evidence could ever provide more than psychological reinforcement of the acceptance of such correspondence. Yet to the extent a person concludes, in a dogmatic sense, that a particular belief corresponds to reality on the basis of its apparent correspondence, he imagines himself, according to Climacus, "to possess a certainty which can only be had in infinitude" (CUP, 68).

We saw above that, according to Kierkegaard, justification appears to be equivalent to an appreciation of the truth of a given mental representation. Truths of fact, however, appear to be only approximate truths. The justification of mental representations about actuality must thus involve an appreciation of this approximate character. The justification of mental representations of actuality would appear to consist in the appreciation of the knower that the preponderance of available evidence relevant to the representation in question is consistent with that representation as well as that it is possible that more evidence could come to light that would be inconsistent with it. That is, the justification of mental representations about actuality leaves their truth formally uncertain.

The difficulty here is that probabilities are objectively meaningless in the sense that they can be reduced to the claim that something either is, or is not, the case, but this is something one could be said to appreciate even without the benefit of the probability statement.[53] Yet it is precisely probabilities that Kierkegaard associates with knowledge in what one could call the loose sense. The question is, on what basis, or by what reasoning, do these probabilities become meaningful?

"A reason," observes A, the purported author of the collection of papers that make up the first volume of Kierkegaard's *Either/Or*, "is a curious thing; if I regard it with all my passion, it develops into an enormous necessity that can set heaven and earth in motion; if I am devoid of passion, I look down on it derisively" (EO I, 32–33). The apparent probability that a particular mental representation corresponds to reality is interpreted by the "knower" as meaningful because he is not completely objective.[54] That is, he is not entirely disinterested, nor could he be. Consciousness, according to Kierkegaard, is interest. Thus the "knower" cannot help but be interested in—that is, passionately engaged with—the object of his inquiry.

Justification in the loose sense is thus equivalent to the appreciation of the knower of the apparent probability of the correspondence of a particular mental representation to reality, combined with the appreciation that more evidence could come to light that would tip the scales of probability in favor of a competing representation. The knower assumes such probability

---

[53] See Michael Polanyi, *Personal Knowledge* (Chicago: University of Chicago Press, 1962), 21. For a detailed treatment of the views of Polanyi and Kierkegaard, see Willows, chapter 6, 90–109.

[54] See my "Kierkegaard on Rationality," in *Kierkegaard After MacIntyre*, ed. John Davenport and Anthony Rudd (Chicago: Open Court, 2001).

is meaningful in the sense that he views it as supporting the representation with which it is associated. It cannot engender certainty in the formal sense and should not engender it in the psychological sense. The conscientious historian, for example, does not assume that a representation about that past whose correspondence to reality is highly probable *must* so correspond. She assumes rather that it is appropriate to construct theories about the past on the foundation of such a representation. That is, she assumes their provisional acceptance is warranted by their probability.[55]

It is for this reason that knowledge of actuality, according to Kierkegaard, is more properly characterized as a justified true mental representation than as a justified true belief. That is, to the extent that a belief is associated with a dogmatic claim about the nature of reality, it is an improper characterization of knowledge of actuality. Knowledge of actuality is only what one might call provisional knowledge. It represents a judgment that the correspondence of a particular mental representation to reality is probable, not that it is certain. This means, of course, that there is a normative dimension to Kierkegaard's views on knowledge, even in the loose sense of the word. Knowledge is possible, according to Kierkegaard, in science and scholarship, but it is actual only when the scholar or scientist appreciates its provisional nature.

I asserted in chapter 1 that the justification of objective knowledge in the loose sense would ultimately be externalist. Insight on the part of the knower as to the provisional nature of any conclusion in science or scholarship is a

---

[55] There is a striking similarity between Kierkegaard's views on knowledge of actuality and the views of the Pyrrhonist skeptics, who also claimed to hold all their views only provisionally. Some contemporary scholars have actually argued that it is not possible to avoid dogmatism in the way the Pyrrhonists purport to (see Burnyeat, ed., *The Skeptical Tradition*). I have been assured, however, by a man of science, my good friend Danish physician Ole Püschl, that this is precisely what physicians do. Dr. Püschl argued that diseases are diagnosed and treatments prescribed on probabilistic rather than dogmatic bases. He explained, for example, that a patient who complained of fatigue and a sore throat could very well have mononucleosis. If the symptoms persisted over time, he continued, the patient would be more likely to have mono. Finally, a patient whose blood test for mono came back positive would be even more likely to have the illness. Such a patient, Dr. Püschl explained, would be treated as if he had mono because the combination of his symptoms would make it probable that he would respond positively to such treatment. That is, such a patient is treated by the physician *as if* he has mono because this is *probably* what he has. A good physician suspends judgment, Dr. Püschl maintained, however, concerning whether the patient actually has mono because there are always those few cases that do not respond to the treatment most commonly associated with their symptoms and that thus may require another kind of treatment. Even if the treatment is successful, the physician, according to Dr. Püschl, concludes not that the patient must have had mono after all but that this was *probably* what he had.

necessary condition for knowledge in these disciplines, and this makes it appear that the justification of such knowledge is internalist. The reason it is not is that such insight, while necessary, is not sufficient to justify knowledge claims. Holocaust deniers, for example, could acknowledge that the truth of their claim that there was no Holocaust was objectively uncertain. It is clear, however, that Kierkegaard would not accept as legitimate any claim to know there had been no Holocaust. We saw above that with respect to "worldly goals," such as those of science and scholarship, the crowd is, in the end, the decisive authority. The overwhelming majority of historians subscribe to the view that there *was* a Holocaust, so even though the truth of the claim is formally uncertain, no claim to the contrary could be said to be knowledge. The situation is the same with respect to the natural sciences. A good scientist must appreciate the provisional nature of scientific theories, but his views must also be more or less in line with the prevailing views in his discipline if they are to count as knowledge. This latter qualification is what makes the justification of knowledge in the loose sense ultimately externalist. The issue is not whether a person is in a position to *establish* that his views are in line with the prevailing views on the matter, but simply whether they are. This may appear to leave the door open for all kinds of disturbing phenomena such as, for example, the rise of Nazism, to enjoy epistemological legitimacy. I believe, however, that there are two strains in Kierkegaard's thought that would prevent this. First, he has enormous respect for genuine science and scholarship. He would predict, I believe, the rejection with which the racial and sociological theories of the Nazis were met by most legitimate anthropologists and sociologists. Second, Kierkegaard emphasizes that in situations of formal uncertainty (which would be the case with respect to any anthropological or sociological theory, or indeed any scientific theory at all), the ethical must take precedence. Kierkegaard could never condone the use of any human being merely as a means to the end of some other human being's purpose, because a theory that purported to prove that the former, though apparently a human being in the same sense as the latter, was not *actually* so would be inherently uncertain.[56]

[56] See WOL, 231.

CHAPTER FOUR

OBJECTIVE KNOWLEDGE

Knowledge in the Strict Sense

Experience alone cannot yield knowledge according to Kierkegaard. The knower must have something like a collection of innate ideas. Kierkegaard's pseudonym Frater Taciturnus asserts, for example in *The Stages on Life's Way*, that "*if* I know that Caesar was great, *then* I know what greatness is, and this is what I see" (SLW, 438).[1] Greatness is an idea and "ideality," he continues, "I know by myself, and if I do not know it myself, then I do not know it at all, and all the historical knowledge does not help" (SLW, 438).

The difficulty with knowledge claims relating to Caesar's greatness is that Caesar is a particular individual and the categories of thought are general and thus cannot capture individuals as such. Knowledge, in the strict sense, that Caesar was a great man requires more than an appreciation of the nature of the abstract quality of greatness; it requires that one be able to establish definitively that Caesar instantiates this quality. Unfortunately, this cannot be established definitively. To do so would require, first, that one could be certain one's mental representation of Caesar corresponded to the

[1] The emphasis here has been added to help the reader appreciate that Kierkegaard is not claiming that knowledge of Caesar's greatness, or lack thereof, is possible, but only describing some of the conditions that must be met for it to be possible.

63

actuality of this individual and, second, that one could be certain this representation corresponded to the abstract qualification of greatness. According
to Kierkegaard, however, all mental representations of actuality are intellectual constructions whose correspondence to reality is uncertain. The inability of language, or thought, to capture actuality as it is in itself means that,
no matter how well defined, or well confirmed, a particular statement about
actuality may be, the possibility always remains that that actuality is other
than it is represented in the statement as being.

Statements of fact, according to Kierkegaard, can never, no matter how
well confirmed, preclude the possibility of their opposites because nothing
actual is what it is necessarily.[2] The truth of such statements can thus never
definitively be determined. This would appear to exclude them from the
realm of knowledge claims. This is consistent with the strict sense in which
Kierkegaard uses the expression "knowledge." It is inconsistent, however,
with the way we ordinarily use language in that we often claim to have
knowledge when we cannot definitively establish the correspondence of the
beliefs in question to the reality to which they refer. Thus in keeping with
his desire not to alienate his reader through the development of a technical
vocabulary at odds with ordinary language,[3] Kierkegaard often relaxes the
certainty criterion of knowledge.[4] This relaxation appears very well thought
out, however, in that it appears relative to the nature and significance of the
object of knowledge as well as to the context of the discussion. We will look
first at an area of inquiry with respect to which certainty is possible and then
move on to an area where it is not possible and where knowledge can be
spoken of in only a loose sense.

"Reality," as we saw, is a very general expression for Kierkegaard. It refers
to everything that is, whether the being in question is abstract, as in the
case of concepts, or actual, as is the case with everything that is temporally
defined. A large part of reality, according to Kierkegaard, is again what one
could call immanent metaphysical reality.[5] This is the reality of ideas and their
relations. Because thought is itself abstract, our relation to immanent metaphysical reality is relatively unproblematic. "With respect to all problems of
immanence," asserts Kierkegaard, "recollection applies; it exists altogether in
everyone" (JP, 3:3606). Kierkegaard clearly does not believe we have any sort

---

[2] Of course, whatever is factually true precludes its opposite in some sense, even if not
logically. It is for this reason Climacus argues that while truths of fact are not necessary (*Nød-
vendige*), they are "immutable" (*Uforanderlige*) (C, 144).

[3] See chapter 1, "Kierkegaard's Terminology."

[4] See Evans, 39.

[5] See JP, 3:3606.

of existence prior to the one in which we find ourselves at present. "Recollection" is simply the expression he uses to refer to the process by which one can come to know something about reality on one's own (i.e., without the help of revelation). Hügli helps to make this clearer. "Ideality," he explains, "is already there, but it is reality that first causes it to become apparent in its own medium, namely language. This means that viewed subjectively, I both have ideality and do not have it and that I must thus appropriate it, or make conscious what [in some sense] I already have" (Hügli, 47).[6]

According to Kierkegaard, there is a substantial portion of reality with which reason is well equipped to deal, even if it is not sufficient in itself for understanding all reality. Each of us, to the extent that each is rational, is capable of attaining knowledge of abstract realities, or of what Leibniz called truths of reason. All that is required is that one care—that is, will—to attain such knowledge. Other people may serve as teachers to the extent that they can assist us in the acquisition of such knowledge, but their role in this regard cannot be more than that of a Socratic midwife.[7]

"The different sciences," asserts Kierkegaard, "ought to be ordered according to the different ways they accentuate being [*Væren*]" (JP, 1:197). He divides these different sciences into two groups. Ontology and mathematics form one group and "[e]xistential [s]cience [*Existentiel-Videnskab*]" forms the other.[8] We will examine what Kierkegaard means by "existential science" later. Part of immanent metaphysical reality is indifferent, however, to what it means to exist. This is the reality that is the object of what he calls the sciences of "ontology" and "mathematics" (JP, 1:197).

"The definition of science which Aristotle gives," writes Kierkegaard in his journals, "is very important. The objects of science are things which can be in only one way. What is scientifically knowable is therefore the necessary, the eternal" (JP, 2:2281). "The certainty," he contends, of the sciences of ontology and mathematics, "is absolute" (JP, 1:197). The certainty of these sciences is absolute, according to Kierkegaard, because "here thought and being are one" (JP, 1:197). These sciences are not concerned with being that transcends thought. They are concerned with the character of thought itself. They represent an investigation, in the abstract medium of thought, of thought objects. Since the medium in which the investigation takes place, agrees, in its essence, with the objects of the investigation, it can capture those objects as they are in themselves and thus preclude any uncertainty as to whether the effort to capture them has been successful.

---

[6] See also JP, 2:2557; and JP, 2:2274.
[7] See C, 88–91.
[8] See JP, 1:197.

It is not yet clear, however, precisely what the objects of ontological knowledge are. Mathematical objects are easy enough to identify, but what Kierkegaard means by "ontology" is far from clear. It will help in this context to turn to the works of Poul Martin Møller, Kierkegaard's teacher and friend. "Ontology," according to Møller, "is the study of the eternal form of thought and being [*Tilværelesen*]" (vol. 3, 342). Gregor Malantschuk persuasively argues that "ontology," according to Møller, "is synonymous with logic" and that Kierkegaard appropriated this view from Møller.[9] Møller observes, however, that "ontology, like mathematics, contains a sum of hypothetical claims which provide an *a priori* development of all the predicates that may be applied to anything that can exist. But knowledge that a thing actually exists," he continues, "must be obtained in another way" (vol. 2, 186ff.).

Kierkegaard expresses this situation with characteristic sarcasm when he has Climacus observe that "[i]t is generally very difficult to prove that something exists [*er til*]. And what is worse for those brave souls who nevertheless dare to undertake such a project, the difficulty is not one that will confer celebrity on those who preoccupy themselves with it" (C, 113). That is, it is impossible, according to Kierkegaard, to demonstrate, in the sense of to provide an objective proof, that anything exists, and anyone who tries to do it comes off looking a fool.[10]

It is important to appreciate that when Kierkegaard argues that it is impossible to demonstrate that anything exists (*er til*), he does not mean merely that it is impossible to demonstrate that anything has temporal or phenomenal existence (i.e., *Exsistens*). His claim is of much broader significance than that. It appears what he means is that it is impossible to demonstrate that anything has reality in itself rather than simply as an idea.[11] The idea of God, for example, has reality as an idea. That is, it is a real idea. The question of interest, however, is whether there *is* a God.

It is impossible, according to Kierkegaard, to demonstrate that something exists because such a proof must proceed in one of two ways: either by assuming that the thing whose existence is to be demonstrated does not exist—in which case the "proof" involves a contradiction—or by assuming it does exist—in which case the proof is a tautology. This problem is expressed by Climacus in the *Postscript* where he addresses the issue of proofs for the existence of God. "When," he asserts, for example,

[9] See Malantschuk, "S. Kierkegaard and P. M. Møller," 105.

[10] See Slotty's claim that "Kierkegaard steadfastly maintains that reality cannot be proved, that it always requires a leap on our part" (Slotty, 20).

[11] See Hügli, 70–71.

it is said that God must possess all perfections, or that the supreme being must possess all perfections, and since being is a perfection, *ergo* God or the supreme highest must be, then the whole train of thought is a deception. For if in the first part of this talk God is really not conceived as being, then the talk cannot even begin. It will go as follows: a supreme being, who (please note) does not have being, must possess all perfections including that of being; *ergo*, a supreme being who does not have being has being [*er til*]. . . . Otherwise the inference must be kept purely hypothetical: if a supreme being is assumed to be, it must be assumed to possess all perfections; to be is a perfection, *ergo*, it must be—assuming that it is. By drawing a conclusion within a hypothesis, one cannot draw a conclusion outside a hypothesis. . . . When the inference is made, God's being [*Væren*] is just as hypothetical as it was in the beginning. (CUP, 280)

"My reasoning is never to the conclusion that something exists," explains Climacus in the *Crumbs*, "but from the assumption that something exists.[12] . . . Thus I do not prove that a stone exists [*er til*], but that something that exists is a stone. A court does not prove that a thief exists but proves that the accused, who certainly exists, is a criminal" (C, 113).

This is the reason ontological knowledge and mathematical knowledge are hypothetical for Kierkegaard. That is, they determine what thought says about how things must be *if* they have a reality that transcends thought reality, but not *that* they are real in that way. It may be, for example, that the idea of God includes perfection. That is, it may be that the idea of God and the idea of perfection are related in such a way that, if there were a God, then he would have to be perfect. But logic alone could never compel one to accept that there was a God.

Ontology and mathematics are concerned with abstract, or ideal, being, and, as Hügli expresses it, "Assertions about ideal being can be reduced to purely hypothetical conclusions of the form: 'If A, then B.' Whether A is the case or not remains uncertain, but if A, then necessarily B. The conclusions are necessary, but the premises are, and remain, hypotheses" (89). It would appear, however, that when Kierkegaard says ontology and mathematics are hypothetical, he is referring to those sciences to the extent they purport to describe reality as it is in itself. If we return to Møller's definition of ontology, we see that ontology describes not merely "*Tilværelsen*" but also thought. Logical principles, such as the principle of non-contradiction, do not necessarily purport to describe reality in itself; they may be interpreted simply as describing rules of thought.

Møller argues that "[i]t is certain that the sum of the angles of a triangle is 180°, but this in no way implies that a triangle is given. One knows

---

[12] The expression that I have here translated as "exists" is actually *Tilværelsen* rather than *Eksistens*, or *Existents*. The former should be understood more broadly than the latter.

something about actual being [*virkelig Tilværelsen*], however, only if one knows that it includes triangles, and this is not something one learns in mathematics" (vol. 2, 181). One might be tempted to interpret Møller's reference to "actual being" as reference to empirical reality. That it is not is clear in his observation that when one moves from mathematical claims to "claims regarding reality that transcends sense experience [*det Oversandselige*], one is no longer concerned merely with relations among ideas . . . rather one makes oneself out to know something about reality itself" (vol. 2, 181). That is, there is a reality that transcends sense experience, and yet while it must clearly include the reality of thought, it must also, according to Møller, include far more than the reality of thought. Thus "actual being" (*virkelige Tilværelsen*) would appear equivalent, according to Møller, to reality that transcends sense experience (*det Oversandselige*).

Ontological and mathematical knowledge is more certain, according to Kierkegaard, than sense knowledge (*Sandsning*), although he observes in his journals that "it is usually stated the other way around," as when it is stated that some thing X is "as certain as it is certain that I hold this cane in my hand." This, he continues, "is a shabby certainty which even Greek skepticism would deprive one of" (JP, 4:4589).

Ontology, according to Møller, concerns the eternal form of thought and being. To the extent, however, that ontology is interpreted merely to refer to the eternal form of thought, ontological knowledge is entirely unproblematic. That is, the agreement between thought and being that constitutes truth, according to Kierkegaard, would be a tautology since here thought and being would "mean one and the same [thing]" (CUP, 160). But if thought and being mean the same thing, then the correspondence of the one to the other is objectively necessary. An appreciation of this necessity would amount to a kind of intuition. The mental representation in question would be immediately identified with its object, and this identification would preclude any uncertainty on the part of the knower concerning whether the representation had captured the object as it is in itself. A mental representation whose correspondence to reality is appreciated as objectively necessary is true. Such a representation thus satisfies the definition of knowledge, set out in the previous chapter, as a justified, true mental representation. Ontological knowledge is thus composed of justified, true mental representations of the relations among ideas.[13] It is hypothetical only to the extent that it purports to extend beyond the relations among ideas to describe relations among things in themselves.

[13] See Hügli, 57, 79.

A person does not begin life, according to Kierkegaard, with comprehensive objective immanent metaphysical knowledge. It is implicitly present
in his consciousness. He must be actively interested in it, however, if it is to
become explicit for him. One usually starts with an unsubstantiated claim of a
logical or mathematical nature for which one must produce a proof. The proof
is a product of one's determination to understand reality. A person sets out to
construct proofs in an effort to understand reality, and a successful proof is
appreciated as such to the extent that it engenders the relevant intuition.[14]

There is a distinction between proofs and the insights they engender.
This does not necessarily mean, however, that the proof becomes superfluous
once it has given rise to the relevant intuition. It may well be that, in the case
of claims that are not obviously tautological, the insight can be sustained
only when attention is directed toward the proof. It is not the proof, however,
that justifies the mental representation in question, but the intuition through
which the proof is understood as such.[15]

No mental representation that has been determined to cohere with the a
priori system of determinations for everything that is for thought could fail
to cohere with this system. That is, no representation whose correspondence
to reality had been demonstrated to be objectively necessary could ever be
found to fail to correspond to reality. The correspondence of such representations is not probabilistic—it is certain. Ontological knowledge is fixed
as such through an intuition that amounts to an intersection of formal, or
objective, certainty and psychological, or subjective, certainty.

While some ontological knowledge is clearly objective, it is important
to appreciate that some will turn out to be subjective. That is, ontology, to
the extent that it goes beyond purely formal logic to include the semantics
of expressions such as "God" and "perfection," is not entirely indifferent to
the situation of the individual knower. Even the idea of God, as we will see
when we examine subjective knowledge, is significant, according to Kierkegaard, with respect to what it means to exist.

Mathematical knowledge is less problematic, according to Kierkegaard,
than ontological knowledge. Mathematics, according to Møller, is never
concerned with being in itself, but only with thought. The objects of mathematics are restricted to the rules governing the relations between ideas.
Whether these rules are valid independently of thought is not, according to

---

[14] See CI, 32.

[15] This distinction is important to the extent that it is necessary to account for the
fact that there is a difference between simply reading a proof and reading it with understanding. For more on this distinction, see George Weaver, "Reading Proofs with Understanding,"
Theoria 54 (1988): 31–47.

Møller, a mathematical question.[16] Thus mathematical knowledge is essentially unproblematic. That is, mathematics, according to Kierkegaard, is not essentially significant with respect to what it means to exist.[17] This does not mean that it could never have any subjective significance, but only that such significance would be only accidental.

Ontology, as we saw, if not restricted to the relations among ideas but interpreted as extending to the way things are in themselves, is problematic in that one has no way, objectively, of knowing the nature of the relations among things in themselves. Mathematics, on the other hand, clearly satisfies the criterion for a science articulated by Aristotle and affirmed by Kierkegaard. That is, the objects of mathematics are things that can be in only one way and with respect to which objective thinking, according to Kierkegaard, may be considered to be within its rights.[18]

We have seen that Kierkegaard appears to define knowledge as something like a justified, true mental representation. Mathematical knowledge can clearly be expressed in such terms. That is, "[p]roof," asserts Kierkegaard in his journals, "is given for a mathematical proposition in such a way that no disproof is conceivable" (JP, 2:2296). To the extent that a proof of a particular proposition renders any disproof of it inconceivable, it establishes the formal necessity of the correspondence of the mental representation in question to reality. An appreciation of this necessity is equivalent to an intuition concerning the essence of this proof. That is, it is equivalent to an appreciation of its coherence with the rest of the fundamental axioms of mathematics, and it is this appreciation that serves to justify it. The conclusions of mathematics, like those of ontology, are hypothetical only to the extent that they purport to refer to a reality that transcends the reality of thought. But this is something they do not essentially do.

Though our epistemological relation to the truths of mathematics is less problematic, according to Kierkegaard, than our relation to any other sort of truth, he seldom writes about mathematical knowledge. This is not because he has any problems with it but because he is not particularly interested in it. Kierkegaard's overwhelming concerns were ethics and religion. "All essential knowing," he has Climacus claim in the *Postscript*, "concerns existence [*Existents*]" and "only such knowing as has an essential relation to existence is essential, is essential knowing" (CUP, 166).

---

[16] See Møller, vol. 2, 181.

[17] See Hügli, 90.

[18] See, e.g., CUP, 64n. Hannay's translation of "*i sin Ret*" may be misleading to speakers of American English. The word Hannay translates as "place," "*Ret*," would normally be translated as "right" (see, e.g., Ferrall and Repp.).

Knowledge in a Loose Sense

While knowledge of immanent metaphysical reality is expressed, according to Kierkegaard, in ontology and mathematics, knowledge of actuality is the goal of the humanities and the natural sciences. It would appear, however, that knowledge in the strict sense is not really possible in these disciplines. That is, according to Kierkegaard, certainty that a particular mental representation of actuality agrees with the actuality that is its object is possible only when that actuality is the subject's own ethical actuality.[19] We commonly speak, however, as if knowledge were possible in both the humanities and the sciences. There is thus a looser sense in which Kierkegaard uses the expression "knowledge," as is suggested in his remark in *The Point of View for My Work as an Author* that "with regard to all temporal, earthly and worldly goals the crowd can have its validity, even its validity as the decisive factor, that is, as the authority" (PV, 106n). Kierkegaard even goes so far as to say that the fact that the crowd may be the authority with respect to worldly matters is "self-evident" and something he has "never denied" (PV, 106n).

Strictly speaking, knowledge, for Kierkegaard, is associated with certainty in the sense of the necessity of the correspondence of a given mental representation to reality. The difficulty with representations of actuality is that, according to Kierkegaard, nothing actual is what it is necessarily. But if everything actual could have been other than it turned out to be, then the correspondence of any particular representation of actuality to reality can never be more than contingent. This means proofs cannot be given for propositions in the humanities or natural sciences in such a way that no disproof is conceivable. Disproofs will always be conceivable. Claims about actuality cannot be justified in the sense that one can be certain of their correspondence to their objects.

There is a sense, however, in which claims about actuality can be justified. If it appears probable that a particular claim about actuality is correct, then one is going to be inclined to accept that it is correct. The foundation of this inclination is the passion, or interest, that Kierkegaard argues is the essence of the knower. The foundation of the inclination is thus subjective. This does not mean, however, that it is arbitrary. One's inclination to accept that a particular interpretation of actuality is correct is going to be generally proportional to the apparent probability of the correspondence of this claim to the facts. The "justification" of a particular claim about actuality is thus the appreciation of the knower, not of the necessity of its agreement with the

---

[19] See Slotty, 35.

facts but of the probability of such agreement based on the amount of data collected that is consistent with it.

Climacus claims in the *Crumbs* that "immediate sensation and immediate cognition [*Erkjenden*] cannot deceive" (C, 147). Later, however, in the *Postscript*, he argues that "[t]he trustworthiness of sense perception is a deception. This has been sufficiently demonstrated," he continues, "by Greek skepticism and likewise by modern idealism" (CUP, 265).[20] This latter claim appears, at first, to be at odds with the former. There is an important difference, however, between these two references. In the first instance, "sensation" is qualified as "immediate," and in the second instance it is not qualified in this way. Immediate sensation cannot deceive because it does not make any claims, in the sense of draw any conclusions, about objective reality, whereas sensation in the second sense does. Immediate sensation cannot deceive because there cannot be any question of the correctness of a sensation, or impression, in the immediate sense.[21] Sensory states simply are what they are. It does not make sense to speak of a false sensory state. "Immediacy," argues Climacus, "is just indeterminateness" (JC, 167).[22] The possibility of deception arises only when immediate sensation and immediate cognition are brought into relation to something else.[23] That is, error becomes possible only when immediate experience is mediated by reflection in thought,[24] which is precisely what takes place when a person makes knowledge claims based on sensation.

There is an important distinction, for Kierkegaard, between sensory states and our interpretations of their significance. Thought, according to Kierkegaard, is language. Our interpretations of the significance of our sensory states may thus be assumed to involve language. An impression of color, for example, simply is what it is before it is mediated by language. As an experience, it has immediate validity. Even if, for example, it is induced by drugs, it is still an experience. At the level of belief, which is to say, at the level where sensory experience is interpreted as presenting a world that transcends such experience, the situation is more problematic. An impression, as such, cannot be mistaken, but a person can be mistaken in his interpretation

[20] I have corrected Hannay's translation. Hannay repeats "skepticism" after "modern," whereas he should have "idealism" (*Idealisme*).

[21] See Pap. IV B 1.

[22] See also CA, 37, where immediacy is referred to as "nothing [*Intet*]."

[23] See Pap. IV B 12.

[24] This is not to deny that a great deal of neurophysiological activity is required before there can be such a thing as immediate experience but merely to distinguish such activity, to the extent that it is not conscious, from "thought."

of its significance. He may, for example, interpret a particular sense experience as an impression of the color pink. It is possible, however, that he
is mistaken in his belief about how the expression "pink" is used by most
speakers of English. He may, for example, mistakenly believe that violet is a
shade of pink and thus mistakenly conclude that an impression of the color
violet is an impression of pink.

"The Greek skeptic," observes Climacus, "does not deny the correctness
of sensation and immediate cognition [*Erkjendelsen*]. Error, he says, has a
completely different source; it comes from the inferences I draw" (C, 149).
He continues in a note that begins on the same page as the above reference that both Plato and Aristotle emphasize that immediate sensation and
immediate cognition (*Erkjendelsen*) cannot deceive and that "later Descartes
says, precisely as the Greek skeptics said, that error comes from the will that
is too eager to draw conclusions" (C, 149n).

Thus when Kierkegaard says that "the trustworthiness of sense perception is a deception," it appears he means that sense experience will support
a variety of conclusions concerning its significance. That is, sense experience
underdetermines any conclusions concerning its objective significance. "If,
for example," explains Climacus,

> my senses present to me an object that appears round at a distance, but which
> appears square when viewed more closely, or shows me a stick that appears bent in
> water despite the fact that it is straight when it is taken out of the water, the senses
> have not in any way deceived me, but I am deceived only when I infer something
> about the stick or the object. (C, 149)

To turn to another example: I may infer, from a visual impression of a bird
of a certain sort, that there is a goldfinch in my garden. I may not be close
enough, however, to distinguish a real goldfinch from a stuffed one, a robotic
one, or a mutant bird of some other sort. If I move closer, I reduce the possibility of error. As in the former instance, however, I may also be mistaken
about the proper application of the relevant expression—that is, "goldfinch."
I may only vaguely understand what type of bird this expression applies to.
If I take care to do a little research on this issue, I reduce the possibility of
error. It is clear, however, that this possibility cannot be entirely eliminated.

Sense experience does not in itself deceive according to Kierkegaard.
It is rather that the information provided by such experience is insufficient
to determine the correspondence of conclusions about its objective significance to reality. It is clear that, for Kierkegaard, what is the case about the
world transcends experience or perception. We attempt to gain knowledge
of empirical reality, according to Kierkegaard, through an expression, or
repetition, of that reality in thought—that is, language. The difficulty is that

the essence of language, according to Kierkegaard, is ideality,[25] and ideality is qualitatively different from actuality, which is to say from empirical reality.

"[A]ll knowledge," argues Climacus in the *Postscript*, "is a cancelation of, a removal from existence" (CUP, 291). "All knowledge about actuality [*Virkelighed*] is possibility" (CUP, 264). That is, "[a]ll cognition of actuality," explains Holmer, "is a transition process, out of actual and factual being into possible and essential being" (Holmer, 44). Knowledge, by taking its objects out of existence—that is, by bringing empirical reality into relation with thought—transforms them from actualities to mental representations that may or may not correspond to actuality. It is in this sense that they become possibilities. That is, they become mental constructs that may *possibly* correspond to the way the world is in itself.[26]

Knowledge, in the strict sense according to Kierkegaard, is associated with certainty in both the formal and psychological senses. Formal certainty appears impossible, however, with respect to sense experiences. Psychological certainty may be possible, but how is one to be certain that one has properly interpreted the significance of a particular sense impression? That is, how is one to be certain that this impression corresponds to reality? Evidence for, and against, various conclusions must be weighed until the correspondence, or lack thereof, of a particular conclusion to reality may be determined. In what sense, however, could one be said to weigh evidence for and against the correctness of various sense impressions?

Kierkegaard was very interested in ancient skepticism.[27] The Pyrrhonists maintained that whenever one attempted to determine the objective truth of a particular claim, careful application of the skeptical modes, or tropes,[28] would reveal that the claims that might be made on behalf of one's subjective impressions would always be equally balanced by, for example, the possibility of conflicting impressions on the part of other subjects, or the possibility of conflicting impressions under other circumstances. This balance was referred to by the skeptics as *isostheneia*.[29]

If, for example, one attempted to determine from one's subjective impression of warmth whether it was actually, or objectively, warm, what

---

[25] See JC, 168; CI, 247; FT, 113; JP, 2:1590; and Hügli, 47.

[26] See Slotty, 22.

[27] See JP, 1:42; JP, 2:2280; JP, 4:4589; Pap. IV B 2:14; Pap. IV B 10:17; Pap. IV B 13:3; and Pap. VI C 52. See also Thulstrup, *Kommentar*, 165.

[28] See Sextus Empiricus, *Outlines of Pyrrhonism*, vol. 1 (Cambridge, Mass.: Loeb Classical Library, Harvard University Press, 1933), 21–107.

[29] This is actually a simplification of the Pyrrhonist position. It will suffice, however, for the purposes of the present discussion.

one could be said to "know" was (1) that one had a subjective impression of warmth and (2) that such impressions varied from subject to subject (e.g., people who are either feverish or who have just come in from a colder environment often feel warm when others around them do not). What one does not know, in such an instance, is whether one ought to privilege one's own impression relative to the impressions of others. One does not even know whether one should privilege one's own impressions relative to those of other creatures.[30] One may assume, for example, that one's subjective impression of ambient temperature would often conflict with the impressions of cold-blooded creatures such as reptiles.

It is tempting to argue that there must be some veridical sense experience for Kierkegaard, or it would be impossible to recognize sense deception as such. Kierkegaard uses the example of the illusion created when a stick is placed in water, that the stick is broken, to demonstrate the thesis that error arises from the conclusions drawn on the basis of sense experience rather than from the experiences themselves. It would appear, however, that one could make this argument only if the impression of the stick when it was drawn out of the water were veridical. That is, it is commonly assumed that the skeptical argument from illusion undermines itself to the extent that it is dependent upon veridical impressions against which illusions are distinguished as such. This is not the sense, however, in which Kierkegaard uses the argument. That is, what appears veridical is not a particular sense experience but the principle of non-contradiction. That is, it would appear that two conflicting impressions of the same object (e.g., a stick) necessitate the conclusion that *at least* one of these impressions must be false. A stick, for example, cannot be both straight and broken, which is to say that it cannot be both straight and not straight. The assumption that two conflicting impressions cannot both be true in no way necessitates the conclusion that they cannot both be false.

All that is needed, according to Kierkegaard, to cast doubt on the idea that sense experience could ever be veridical is a single occurrence of two conflicting experiences. This is apparent in his remark that "it is easy to see that if all sense perception were not a fraud, there would be no illusion at all" (JP, 5:5620). What he means when he says all sense perception is a fraud is that we are inclined to believe we are immediately related to physical reality in sense experience even though we are not. Sense experience, according to Kierkegaard, as distinguished from "immediate experience," is, in a way, an interpretation of the reality we believe lies behind it. It is only because it is an interpretation that it can be mistaken.

[30] See JP, 1:42.

Despite Kierkegaard's claim that all sense perception is a "fraud," it would be a mistake, argues Slotty, "to call Kierkegaard a skeptic."[31] That is, Kierkegaard "recognizes," Slotty continues, "that certain knowledge can develop from the unavoidable presuppositions of a belief . . . , but this knowledge remains within a hypothesis" (Slotty, 27).[32]

But if certainty is the goal, in what sense could one be understood to have "finished" weighing the evidence for and against a particular conclusion about the objective significance of a given sense experience? To the extent that there is such a thing as knowledge, in the strict sense, that relates to actuality, this knowledge would appear to be associated with the skeptical phenomenon of *isostheneia*. That is, "[k]nowledge," Kierkegaard argues, "is simply a placing of opposite possibilities in equilibrium. To be able to do this is to be knowing [*være vidende*]" (WOL, 231). "Knowledge," asserts Kierkegaard, "is infinitely indifferent . . . like an auctioneer who puts existence [*Tilværelsen*] on the block. The auctioneer then says 'ten dollars' (the value of the property)—but it means nothing; only after someone says 'I bid,' only then is the bid ten dollars" (JP, 2:2297).

"Kierkegaard merely means to stress here," explains Slotty, "that there is no necessary transition from knowledge to conviction, that the relation of the knower here is active" (Slotty, 19–20). Left to itself, reflection would simply heap up data and contrast various interpretations of these data indefinitely.[33] Reflection, according to Climacus in the *Postscript*, cannot be halted by itself. To ask reflection to stop itself, he asserts, is like asking a disease to devise its own cure.[34] Only an act of will can stop reflection. The knower says, "enough," and determines the contrasting possibilities to be equal, where reflection, left to itself, would simply heap up data interminably.

The judgment that contrasting interpretations of a particular set of data are equally probable is a result, according to Kierkegaard, of the fact that there is more to thought than reflection. Reflection contrasts opposites, but consciousness brings opposites into relation to each other in such a way that they can be understood. One can determine that contrasting possibilities constitute an equilibrium because the possibility of conflicting sense experience—combined with the principle of non-contradiction—implies that reality itself must be independent of sense experience. The appreciation of this independence generates the intuition, or insight, that even if all actual experience happened to support a particular conclusion about objective

---

[31] See Evans, 38.
[32] See also Evans, 44.
[33] See JP, 2:1902; and CUP, 95.
[34] CUP, 95.

reality, the weight of the experience would be counterbalanced by the recognition of the divide between sense experience and objective reality. To the extent that such a divide is assumed, no amount of convergence of disparate sense data would be sufficient to outweigh the possibility that the reality to which the experiences refer is other than it is represented by them as being.

What does it mean, however, to say that knowledge is the placing of conflicting possibilities in equilibrium or that to be able to do this is to have knowledge? This becomes clearer if we return to the definition of knowledge as a justified, true mental representation. If, for example, we start with the subjective impression of warmth and conclude, from this impression, that it *might* be warm, our conclusion could be understood to be both justified and true. That is, the reality to which such a conclusion refers is not physical reality but thought reality. The mental representation of reality as possibly warm does not make any claim one way or the other about what the temperature actually is. It refers to the formal possibility—that is, the possibility for thought—that it might, or might not, be warm. That the reality in question is thought reality rather than actuality can be deduced from the fact that to the extent that temperature could be attributed to actuality, it would be determinate.[35] It cannot actually be the case that it might be warm. Either it is warm or it is not warm. One can be certain that it *might* be warm because this certainty is nothing other than the recognition, or intuition, that the ontological split between thought and being means thought can come no closer, in such an instance, to objective reality than to an account of what it *might* be like. The representation of reality as possibly warm is thus justified to the extent that its correspondence to the reality in question—that is, thought reality—is appreciated by the knower as necessary, and it is true in that it agrees in its essence with the reality to which it refers.

The conclusion that it might be warm would appear an odd candidate for knowledge to the extent that knowledge is associated with certainty and the conclusion that it *might* be warm expresses an uncertainty as to the actual temperature. There is an important difference, however, between uncertainty and certainty regarding uncertainty, or between the view that it *might* be warm and the view that one could never be in a position to assert more than that it might be warm. The latter is, after all, a kind of certainty. Kierkegaard's position that subjectivity is essentially interest, or passion, means that the knower is not going to be able to rest content with

---

[35] This would be the case even if there were substantial disagreement among various subjective impressions concerning the temperature. That is, to the extent that temperature may be attributed to reality in itself, it is unaffected by what could, at the extreme, be a complete lack of consensus of subjective impressions concerning what the temperature was.

an uncertainty because "the ultimate potentiation of every passion," according to Climacus in the *Crumbs*, "is always to will its own annihilation" (C,
111). A person cannot rest with an uncertainty because uncertainty leaves
him to his own devices. Since the knower is himself passion and passion
wills its own downfall, he must continually seek rest outside himself. That is,
he must continually seek support from a reality outside himself. One cannot
rest with an uncertainty, according to Kierkegaard, but one can rest with the
certainty that something is uncertain. "When a judge is uncertain," asserts
Kierkegaard in his journals,

> he conducts an investigation, pursues every clue, and then pronounces judg-
> ment—that is, he comes to the conclusion: guilty or innocent; but now and then
> he dismisses the charge. Is then nothing accomplished by the judgment? Indeed,
> there is—the uncertainty is determined. He was uncertain as to how he should
> judge; now he is no longer uncertain, now his verdict is ready: he judges that he is
> uncertain. He rests in that for one cannot rest in an uncertainty, but one can rest
> when one has determined it. (JP, 5:5620)

One can determine the indeterminacy (i.e., for thought), or be certain of
the uncertainty, of the correspondence of a mental representation of reality
to reality through the appreciation of the relation, explained earlier, of the
data to the fact. That is, no amount of data can preclude the possibility that
a particular interpretation of the significance of a given sensory experience
corresponds to the real significance of that experience. No matter how much
the margin of error may be reduced, it cannot be entirely eliminated.

Kierkegaard's skepticism concerning the possibility of veridical sense
experience is actually overdetermined by the arguments he gives to support it. One argument would have been sufficient, yet there are at least
three arguments in his works to support it. The first, which concerns what
one might call the essential incompatibility of thought and actuality, was
examined in the "Objective Truth" section of chapter 3. The second is not
directly developed by Kierkegaard but is easily inferred from what he says
about the relation between thought and reality. This argument could be
called the argument from the indeterminacy of language. Here the problem is that language is constantly evolving. Neither the set of speakers of a
particular language nor the manner in which expressions are used is static.
Since thought, for Kierkegaard, is language, for a representation of empirical reality to correspond to the way that reality is in itself would be for the
language of the representation to cohere with the way the relevant expressions were used by most speakers of that language. But such coherence can
be expressed only in statistical terms, which is to say that the correspondence
of the representation in question to reality can be established in only an

approximate sense. The third argument in Kierkegaard's works against the possibility of veridical sense experience is "the argument from illusion." That is, since knowledge of empirical reality is a representation of that reality in thought, this representation must accord with the laws of thought, one of which is the principle of non-contradiction. The recognition of the possibility of conflicting sense experiences thus leads to the conclusion that there can be no veridical sense experiences.

The supposition that there is a distinction between appearance and reality means it is formally impossible to get behind appearances to find out what reality in itself is like. Strictly speaking, the only knowledge possible, according to Kierkegaard, with respect to empirical reality is reducible to the justified, true mental representation that sense experience underdetermines any conclusion made on its basis, or that the correspondence of such conclusions to actuality is uncertain. Knowledge that conclusions about the objective significance of sense experience are inherently uncertain is not, however, actually empirical knowledge. It is rather knowledge of the consequences for thought of the assumption that there is a split between reality itself and reality as it is represented in sense experience. There is thus no empirical knowledge in the strict sense according to Kierkegaard.

It is possible, however, to speak of empirical knowledge in a looser sense. The scientist is not entirely disinterested relative to his investigations of reality. Consciousness, according to Kierkegaard, as we saw in chapter 2, is interest, thus the scientist cannot help but be interested in—that is, passionately engaged with—the object of his inquiry. His passion is again not subjective passion in that it is not directed at himself but is what Climacus calls the "objective passion of the researcher" (CUP, 482). But to say that the inquiry of the scientist is characterized by objective passion is not to say that it is an entirely objective inquiry. To the extent that it is passionate, it is subjective, or interested. That is, according to Kierkegaard, "[u]derstanding," as Hügli explains, "is a subjective activity" (Hügli, 20), even when the object of inquiry is not essentially subjective.

All actual evidence (as opposed to abstract possibilities) relating to the correspondence of a given interpretation of some set of phenomena to reality may point the inquirer in the direction of a particular conclusion. To the extent that the correspondence of a mental representation of empirical reality to that reality appears probable, it may be considered to be true in an approximate sense, and to the extent that this "truth" is appreciated as such, the representation in question may be considered to be justified.[36] Few

---

[36] See Holmer's claim that, according to Kierkegaard, "[e]mpirical knowledge . . . is only probable" (Holmer, 46).

people ever consciously weigh evidence for and against the veridicality of particular sense impressions. We are too interested in our own experiences to be able systematically to adopt the disinterested stance relative to them that would be required to sustain skepticism concerning their veridicality. We take it for granted that sense experience provides us with a generally accurate picture of the reality that lies behind it.[37]

Simple empirical "knowledge" is distinguished, however, from "knowledge" of actuality as it is represented in scholarship and science. That is, while it may make little sense to say we "decide" that, for example, it is cold outside, it does, as we will see, make sense to say we "decide" that a given scholarly or scientific theory provides the best available representation of the reality to which it purports to correspond.

The loose sense in which Kierkegaard uses the expression "knowledge" is crucial to understanding his views concerning scholarly and scientific knowledge because it is only in this loose sense that scholarship, or science, can yield knowledge according to Kierkegaard. This is not, for Kierkegaard, an indictment of scholarship and science;[38] it is simply a defining characteristic of these disciplines that their conclusions lack certainty. Kierkegaard even praises science and scholarship.[39] What he objects to is the failure of scholars and scientists, as well as people more generally, to appreciate that these disciplines lack certainty. That is, "He wants merely to emphasize the impossibility of *absolute* knowledge" (Slotty, 20; emphasis added).[40] Kierkegaard has no objection in principle to scientists and scholars making knowledge claims, so long as they do not lose sight of the fact that what they have in terms of knowledge is at best ultimately uncertain.

The failure of scientists and scholars to appreciate the uncertainty of their conclusions becomes an issue for Kierkegaard only when it begins to have religious ramifications. That is, he objects when this failure begins to obscure what he believes is the relation between faith and knowledge that is expressed in the New Testament. As long as people are aware that science and scholarship are based on the *faith* that reality is more or less transparent to the human understanding, these disciplines, and the "knowledge" to which they give rise, represent no threat to what Kierkegaard believes is the Christian position on the relation between faith and knowledge.

---

[37] It is for this reason, perhaps, that Kierkegaard has Johannes de Silentio observe that "proficiency in doubting is not acquired in days and weeks" (FT, 6–7). See also Evans, 44.

[38] See, e.g., Slotty, 38.

[39] See JP, 1:386; JP, 2:2288; JP, 3:3368; and CUP, 49.

[40] See also Hügli, 148; and Evans, 48–51.

Science and scholarship, while related in the sense that both are attempts to grasp actuality, are not the same thing. Scholarship refers essentially to what is more commonly identified as "the humanities." Science, on the other hand, refers to the natural sciences—chemistry, physics, biology, and the like. We will look first at scientific knowledge since it is arguably more closely related to straightforward empirical knowledge.

Despite the fact that there are relatively few references to the natural sciences in his works, there is evidence that Kierkegaard was actually attracted to them.[41] He appears also to have had a sophisticated understanding of the nature of scientific inquiry and the use to which such inquiry is inclined to be put by people who do not fully understand it.

Hannay argues that Kierkegaard "does not disparage science in itself as the investigation into nature" (Hannay, 140). It is just that, for Kierkegaard, it very often represents a distraction from ethical concerns. "Why," asks Kierkegaard,

> should I need to know about the afferent and efferent nerve impulses, about the circulation of blood, about the human being's microscopic condition in the womb? *The ethical has tasks enough for me*. . . . I wonder if I am not weakening my whole ethical impulse by becoming a natural scientist? I wonder if with all this diverse knowledge of analogies, of abnormalities of this and that, I do not lose more and more the impulse of the ethical. . . . I wonder if it is not a way of providing myself with a lot of sly evasions and excuses. I wonder if my gaze is not turned away from the most important thing by letting myself begin with physiology instead of assuming the whole of physiology and saying: Begin. (JP, 3:2807)

There are even stronger condemnations of the preoccupation with natural science in Kierkegaard's works. "What the race tends toward," he asserts in his journals, "is apparently the establishment of natural science in the place of religion" (JP, 2:2821). Kierkegaard is not merely concerned about what he sees as the supplantation of theology by metaphysics. This is only the beginning of a development that "will end with physics supplanting ethics" (JP, 1:197).

The difficulty is that "natural science" is concerned with appearances, or with phenomena, whereas ethics and religion are concerned with noumena. This is not a condemnation of empirical science. It is simply a fact about the nature of this sort of effort to grasp reality. The problem first arises when the scientist, or the person who does not fully understand the nature of empirical inquiry, confuses human beings with phenomena and thus mistakenly assumes a phenomenal account of human behavior is an exhaustive account.

---

[41] See Kierkegaard's letter to the biologist P. W. Lund, whose brothers were married to two of Kierkegaard's sisters (LD, no. 3, 41–47).

Appearances, as we saw above, are associated with probabilities rather than certainties. But an account of human behavior in terms of probabilities leaves no room, according to Kierkegaard, for decision,[42] wherein, he believes, the ethical resides.[43] Probabilities do no more than tend in particular directions. Any halt to such tendencies, that is, any conclusion about how to react to such tendencies, must, according to Kierkegaard, be established through an act of will. But the empirical sciences give no account of will as such. This is not to say that the will is incompatible with empirical science but merely that it is neither an object of observation nor an entity the existence of which is a necessary inference from observation. The will as the locus of moral activity is something that transcends empirical science. Thus a conflict arises between ethics and science only when science is taken to give an exhaustive account of reality.

Such pretensions are not essential to science though. Kierkegaard argues, in fact, that they are incompatible with all legitimate forms of systematic inquiry. "The quiet scholar [*Videnskabsmand*]," he asserts,

> does not bring confusion into life; he is erotically lost in his glorious occupation. If, however, a noisy scholar wants to force his way into the existence-spheres [*Existents-Sphærerne*] and confuse what is there the life principle of the whole, the ethical, then, as a scholar and scientist, he is no faithful lover, and science hands him over for comic treatment. (CUP, 127)

The assumption that science can give an exhaustive account of reality would appear, at least in part, to be a result of the fact that, as Kierkegaard charges, it has been the object of "a popularization campaign" (JP, 1:386). That is, people with little understanding of the true nature of systematic inquiry have begun to draw mistaken conclusions based on such inquiry. But what is the true nature of systematic inquiry or, more specifically, the true nature of inquiry in the natural sciences?

Nature came to be at some point, according to Kierkegaard,[44] but the changes that subsequently characterize it are understood by him to come about with necessity in the sense that they are determined by the essence of nature itself.[45] Thus the objects of scientific inquiry would appear to fit the criteria cited earlier that the objects of science are things that can be in only one way.

---

[42] See, e.g., SLW, 110; PC, 90, 98–103. See also the references to "approximation" in CUP, 32, 35n, 36.

[43] See, e.g., JP, 5:5804; and CUP, 111–13, 257n, 284–88.

[44] C, 143.

[45] See PC, 246.

Unfortunately, however, the fact that nature is assumed, by Kierkegaard, to have come to be at some point and to have "*oversandselig*," or transcendent, reality means that knowledge, in the strict sense, of nature is impossible. The development of a plant, for example, is determined, according to Kierkegaard, by the essence of the plant itself rather than by the character of thought.[46] That, for example, deciduous trees lose their leaves in the fall may be a necessary consequence of the essence of these trees, but this "necessity" is not a necessity in the same sense that it is necessary that that the sum of the angles of a triangle is 180°. That is, the former "necessity" characterizes the essence of the thing in itself, not as it is for thought. It is conceivable that deciduous trees could keep their leaves year round, or lose them at some other time of year.[47] Truths of nature, although maybe necessary in themselves, cannot be necessary for thought, for nature exists independently of thought. Truths of nature are a species of truths of fact and thus cannot for the reasons given above be transparent to the knower.

Nature, according to Kierkegaard, was created by God. It could thus have taken any number of forms depending on what one could call the whim of God. Nothing constrained God to create nature in a particular way or to give it a specific character. One cannot, therefore, say that it has the specific character that it has by necessity. But if nature is what it is only contingently, then the correspondence of any mental representation to reality must also be contingent. This means, of course, that one can never be certain that a particular mental representation of nature corresponds to the reality of nature.

The scientist assumes, however, that sense impressions may be relied on to supply a more or less accurate representation of a substantial reality that lies behind them. We saw above that there is reason, according to Kierkegaard, to suspend judgment concerning the veridicality of sense impressions. Yet science is constructed substantially on the basis of such impressions; thus if the status of these impressions is itself uncertain, the entire edifice of science is going to be ultimately unstable. That is, "When everything is explained by an X [e.g., the relation of sense impression to objective reality] which is not [itself] explained, then, viewed as a whole, nothing at all is explained" (JP, 3:2820). It is for this reason Kierkegaard argues that "empirical knowledge [*Empirie*] is a perpetually self-repeating

---

[46] See CA, 21; C, 143; and Pap. IV B 111.
[47] There is actually a small number of trees, such as the pin oak, that lose their leaves in the spring with the emergence of the meristems.

false sorites" (JP, 2:2254) and that "modern science and scholarship [*Viden-skab*] . . . [are] dishonest" (JP, 1L:649).[48]

Natural science is less problematic than the humanities to the extent that its objects are not endowed with a freedom that would complicate explaining their nature or development. It is just as problematic, however, to the extent that its objects are independently existing things to which we are related only through sense impressions. One might argue that the real object of scientific inquiry is not concrete reality but laws, principles, or forces, which, as abstract, are not subject to the difficulties associated with knowledge of actuality. The difficulty is that these abstract objects are often assumed by scientists to correspond to the way physical reality is in itself.

Even if the scientist is modest enough to restrict his account of physical reality to the way reality is for us rather than the way it is in itself, he will have problems. Improvements in the instruments of observation will continually facilitate new discoveries concerning how reality appears to beings equipped with the faculties of reason and observation with which we are equipped.[49] Thus even if we assume that there are determinate physical laws, these laws, as objects of knowledge, are incomplete in the same way we saw in the preceding chapter that the objects of historical knowledge are incomplete.

The process of collecting data would thus appear to be something in which the scientist must continuously be engaged. That is, he could never possess a complete set of data, hence any dogmatic conclusions he might draw concerning the significance of his data would, technically speaking, be premature.

"All natural science," argues Kierkegaard,

> like all modern scholarship is sophistical. Do an experiment using Socrates' simple question: "Does natural science know something or does it not?" It can answer neither Yes nor No, for the whole secret of it is that it is almost and as good as and not very far from and almost, just as if it knew something. (JP, 3:2815)

The process of collecting data would go on interminably, however, if the scientist maintained a purely objective, dispassionate, or disinterested, position relative to his data. The scientist does not, however, simply heap up data. To the extent that there really are physical laws, the data will tend in a particular direction. The more probable an interpretation appears, however, the less seriously the scientist will take the possibility that it might be mistaken. Eventually, the collection of data stops, not because there are enough data

---

[48] See also JP, 4:4878; and CUP, 68.
[49] See CUP, 125; and SUD, 91.

to prove that the theory in question corresponds to reality, in the sense of establishing the necessity of this correspondence, but because the scientist decides that the probability has become great enough to support at least the provisional acceptance of the theory.

I argued in the preceding chapter that Hügli was right to point out that Kierkegaard's theory of "approximate knowledge" is sustainable only if one abandons the Aristotelian view that the concept is anchored in the object in favor of the view that it is the product of the continuing historical dialogue between subject and object. Indeed, concepts in natural science cannot be anchored in their objects, according to Kierkegaard, because these objects (to the extent that these objects actually exist) are essentially inaccessible to the scientist. All scientists have are impressions, not the substantial reality of nature itself.

It is for this reason "the crowd" of natural scientists, according to Kierkegaard, is competent to determine what is scientific knowledge. No individual scientist can determine precisely which among the multitude of interpretations of physical reality is "correct." These determinations are made by the community of scientists as a whole. This does not mean that in order for a theory to be accepted by the scientific community, it must be accepted by every scientist. It means rather that it must have most of the community behind it. Even after a theory has been accepted by the majority of scientists, it must be continually reverified as improvements in the instruments of observation mean that more, and potentially conflicting, information comes to light.

Truths in the natural sciences are thus identified with the "historical development of subject and object" (Hügli, 280n). The appreciation of the scientist that the preponderance of available empirical evidence is consistent with a particular theory combined with his appreciation that more evidence could come to light that would be inconsistent with it and which would thus cause him to abandon it in favor of a competing theory amounts to an appreciation of the "truth" of this theory. It is this appreciation that serves to justify the theory with which it is connected. The difficulty is that while truth here is an "approxima*ting*,"[50] any particular knowledge claim is going to be an approxima*tion*. That is, people making knowledge claims, often even scientists, tend to view things as finished when, in an important sense, they are not.

That the objects of science are unfinished is simply a fact, however, about all of what we generally refer to as "empirical knowledge." There is

[50] Emphasis added.

nothing in principle wrong with such knowledge, according to Kierke-gaard.[51] Kierkegaard's main concern, in this context, is with the tendency of the knower to forget that the foundation of his knowledge is, to a certain extent, subjective rather than purely objective as is often believed. That is, a scientist continually strives for objectivity. Yet a scientist

> who is really enthusiastic about grasping and understanding, does not himself dis-cern that he continually posits what he seeks to abrogate. He is enthusiastic about understanding everything else, but the fact that he himself is enthusiastic he does not come to understand, i.e., he does not conceptualize his own enthusiasm at the same time he is enthusiastic about conceptualizing everything else. (JP, 3:2807)

Such enthusiasm on the part of the scientist is, of course, essential if science is going to do more than heap up data interminably. It is merely the failure of the scientist to recognize its significance with which Kierkegaard has a quar-rel. Scientists often pretend to be purely objective or to base their conclusions entirely on observation. Yet no conclusion, according to Kierkegaard, could ever be based entirely on observation. "[T]he inspiration for the scientific investigation," on his view, is always "an internal presupposition, the cer-tainty of which seeks its corroboration in the observation" (SLW, 282).[52]

It is natural, however, that one would be curious as to why the ten-dency of scientists, or lay people, to misinterpret the significance of scientific inquiry so concerned Kierkegaard, given that his overwhelming interests were ethics and religion, which, by his own admission, are essentially discon-tinuous with empirical science and which would thus not appear threatened by any tendency to misinterpret the significance of scientific knowledge. Kierkegaard's concern appears to have been the result of an appreciation that people have difficulty keeping the phenomenal and noumenal realms sharply separated and that thus a mistake that might be relatively harmless in the one realm was likely to creep into the other where it could have dev-astating consequences. Nowhere is this more apparent, of course, than in the tendency to reduce psychology to a natural science, a tendency of which Kierkegaard is aware and about which he is very concerned.[53]

Kierkegaard has no objection to the systematic study of human psy-chology. Indeed, two of his most important works, *The Concept of Anxiety* and *The Sickness Unto Death*, represent such study. What is important for

---

[51] See CUP, 482; Slotty, 20; and Hügli, 148.

[52] This sounds remarkably like much contemporary work in the philosophy of science. Compare this, for example, to Polanyi's account of Einstein's development of the theory of relativity (Polanyi, 9–11).

[53] See JP, 3:2808, 2809, 2813; and JP, 4:4267.

Kierkegaard is that one not reduce human behavior to a natural phenomenon on the order of the development of a plant, that one not, in one's study
of psychology, dispense with the ethical through the confusion of an *ought*
with an *is*. "Along with the growing sensibleness," observes Kierkegaard,

> there is an increase in a certain kind of knowledge about human nature [*Menneske-
> Kundskab*]: familiarity [*Kjendskabet*] with how we human beings *are* now or *are* at
> this time, a natural-scientific [*naturvidenskabelig*] statistical knowledge about the
> human moral state as a natural product, explained by the situation, the air cur-
> rents . . . etc. Whether we human beings may have degenerated from generation to
> generation is of no concern to this kind of knowledge; it merely states accurately
> how we are. (JFY, 157)

The reduction of a human being to a natural phenomenon is, however, for-
tunately not the only way to go about a systematic study of human behavior.
"I am happy," writes Kierkegaard,

> to acknowledge that Carus' book (*Psyche*) is excellent, and if he will give the quali-
> tative its due, then I will gratefully take a few of his good psychological observa-
> tions. At all decisive points he makes unqualified room for the miracle, for the
> creative power of God, for the absolute expression of worship, and says: This no
> one can grasp, no science, neither now nor ever. Then he communicates the inter-
> esting things he knows. But there must never be any proximity between these two
> categories; above all they must never be brought into proximity with each other. If
> that happens, I will not read or buy a single one of his psychological observations;
> it is too costly. (JP, 3:2818)

No discipline, according to Kierkegaard, that involves the study of human
nature or behavior, no matter how rigorous or systematic, can give rise to
knowledge in the strict sense because the "scientifically knowable" is "the
necessary, the eternal" (JP, 2:2281). That is, human beings are assumed by
both Kierkegaard and his readers to possess free will. Sociology, political science, economics, history, and even philosophy are thus problematic in that
each is to some extent or another concerned with human behavior. "[T]he
objects of science," asserts Kierkegaard, "are things which can only be in a
single way" (JP, 2:2281). But to say that human behavior is free is to say
that, in any given instance, there are numerous possibilities for action open
to a person.

The sociologist, political scientist, or economist can try to explain why
people live the way they do, elect particular public officials, or spend their
money in particular ways, but the specific character of individual behavior is
the responsibility of the individual whose behavior it is. Even if these scholars
acknowledge that the correspondence of their theories to actuality is uncertain, they are ultimately deluding themselves, according to Kierkegaard, if

they believe there could be impersonal forces that did more than influence human behavior.

The failure to appreciate the shaky nature of the foundation of what one believes is one's knowledge of empirical reality, is significant with respect to every sort of knowledge that is related to empirical reality. It is particularly important, however, when the reality in question is presumed to have religious significance, as is the case with philosophy, psychology, history, and, of course, theology. Historical scholarship figures prominently in Kierkegaard's authorship precisely because it is so often presumed to have such significance.

"Kierkegaard," explains Slotty, "did not dispute the reality of historical knowledge,[54] and would not have contested the possibility of a philosophy of history, but only of an absolute philosophy of history" (Slotty, 27). There can be no absolute philosophy of history because "the interpretation of facts is a matter of belief" (Slotty, 41).

What is distinctive about the historical, according to Kierkegaard, concerns *how* it is rather than *what* it is. A historical fact is not like a truth of reason. It has not always been what it is. Facts about the past have become what they are by having come to pass, and this is what gives them their distinctively historical character. The difficulty is that the manner in which something exists—that is, whether it has eternal being or has come to be at some point—is not present to sensation.

This problem is more clearly expressed by Kierkegaard in the "Interlude" section of the *Philosophical Crumbs* under the heading of "The Apprehension of the Past" (C, 145–52). "Immediate sensation," explains Climacus,

> and immediate cognition cannot deceive. This in itself shows that the historical cannot be the object of either, because the historical has within it the duplicity that is becoming's. In relation to the immediate, becoming is namely a duplicity through which that which was most certain is made doubtful. Thus when an observer sees a star, the star becomes dubious to him the moment he desires to become certain that it has come to be. It is as if reflection removed the star from his senses. (C, 147–48)

Climacus remarks that "[i]t is assumed, however, that there is knowledge of the past" (C, 147). Hence the text turns to the conditions that must be met in order for such knowledge to be possible. "The genuinely historical," he asserts,

> is always the past (it is over, whether a year ago or only days makes no difference), and has actuality as the past, because it is certain and dependable that it happened.

---

[54] See Hannay, 105.

But that it happened is again precisely its uncertainty, which will constantly prevent apprehension from taking the past as something that had been that way from
eternity. Only in this contradiction between certainty and uncertainty, which is
the *discrimin*[55] of that which has come to be and thus also of the past, is the past
understood. If it is understood in any other way, then apprehension has misunder-
stood itself (that it is apprehension) and its object (that such a thing could become
an object of apprehension). (C, 146)

Since everything historical has come to be, nothing historical can be necessary. That is, coming to be, according to Kierkegaard, is a change and "the
necessary can in no way be changed because it always relates to itself and
relates to itself in the same way" (C, 142). If the necessary cannot come to
be, then everything that comes to be must do so freely. But this freedom,
according to Kierkegaard, cannot be sensed or known immediately. "One
might think," observes Climacus,

> when faith decides: this exists, ergo it has come to be, that this is an inference
> from effect to cause. This is, however, not exactly the case, and even if it were, one
> must remember that the inference of knowledge [*Erkjendelsens Slutning*] is always
> from cause to effect, or more correctly, from ground to consequent. . . . I cannot
> immediately sense, or know, that that which I immediately sense and know is an
> effect. Immediately, it simply is. (C, 150)

Only the presence of an event can be the object of immediate sensation or
cognition, not the manner in which it has come to be present. Thus Climacus concludes that belief must be "the organ [*Organet*]" (C, 148) through
which a genuine grasp of the historical is attained. "There is an uncertainty,"
explains Hügli, "associated with every historical event in that I can never be
certain whether what I immediately see is the result of a causally necessary
process or of a free act. . . . I cannot see that an event is historical in the
genuine sense; I can at most only believe it" (Hügli, 226).[56] This discussion
of "the historical" is important for Kierkegaard because it is precisely the
conclusion that the historical can be grasped as such only by faith that precludes knowledge that God became man, or that the eternal became historical in the person of Christ.

We saw above that nature, according to Kierkegaard, does not have a history. It is thus properly speaking human beings, or human events, to which
Kierkegaard refers when he refers to historical objects. We also saw, however,
that it is impossible, according to Kierkegaard, to prove that anything exists.
One might conclude from this that he is skeptical concerning the reality of
the external world and, in particular, the reality of other people. It is clear,

---

[55] Distinguishing mark.
[56] See also Thulstrup, "Inledning," xxxi.

however, that Kierkegaard is a realist.[57] The impossibility of proving the existence of anything external to the knower is not essentially significant for Kierkegaard because his view is that human beings are naturally inclined to believe in the reality of things external to us and, in particular, in the reality of other people. Indeed, he asserts that "an individual first of all begins his life with an *ergo*, with faith" (WOL, 230). This faith may be expressed as the confidence of the knower that his relation to reality is such that it may be known by him and that thus his subjective inclination to accept sense perception as providing a generally accurate representation of empirical reality, as well as his subjective inclination to extend the validity of the laws of thought to reality in itself, is objectively vindicated.

It is because, as Kierkegaard observes, most people live their entire lives by virtue of an "*ergo*," by faith in the sense that they never seriously question the reality of the external world and, in particular, the reality of other people, that he argues it is "nonsense" to demand of someone that he demonstrate that he exists (*er til*).[58] Climacus contends, however, that "[t]he *only* historicity superior to proof is contemporary existence [*Tilværelse*]" (CUP I, 35; emphasis added).[59] But if it is impossible, according to Kierkegaard, to prove anything exists, what role do proofs have with respect to knowledge of the past?

To claim that faith is the organ for the historical is, of course, not to claim that one is free to believe anything at all about the past. It was Kierkegaard's opinion, argues Slotty, that

> the more developed a thinker was, the more possibilities he would discover that would make his knowledge hypothetical. He was convinced that the interpretation, or explication, of a fact would inevitably reveal that there was no absolute certainty, but only an assumption made on the basis of a choice. There is no evidence, however, that Kierkegaard considered such choices to be arbitrary. (Slotty, 20)

The past, according to Kierkegaard, is composed of a series of determinable events, each of which at some point "happened" (*skete*), or came to be (*blev til*). Through having come to be, each of these events must be understood to have, in one sense, annihilated the possibility through which this transition took place. That is, before Caesar crossed the Rubicon, it must have been possible for him to have decided otherwise—that is, to have decided not to cross it. According to Kierkegaard, however, we must not confuse the impossibility of changing the past with necessity and as a result attribute

---

[57] See Evans, 29–46.

[58] See CUP, 35 (Hannay translates "*er til*" as "is there"); and PC, 204.

[59] I have chosen the wording of the Hongs' translation here because I believe it is clearer. The passage in question is on p. 35 of the Hannay translation.

necessity to historical events. We must, despite the fact that it is not now possible for Caesar not to have crossed the Rubicon, believe that once it was possible for him not to cross it.

It would appear that insofar as the labor of the historian is directed toward a grasp [*Opfattelse*] of the historical as such, it cannot give rise to knowledge, not even in the loose sense. That is, knowledge, according to Kierkegaard, concerns the truth of a thing,[60] and this is related to its essence [*Væsen*], not to its being [*Væren*]—that is, not to the manner in which it exists or has come to be. This is, however, not the only sort of labor in which the historian is engaged. When the historian is concerned with determining the essence of historical events, he is not concerned with how they were but with what they were. The proper task of the historian, in such an instance, is to determine the truth values of statements about the past, and it is with respect to this activity that proofs can be offered by historians.[61]

"The world-historical view [*Betragtning*]," argues Climacus, "as an act of cognition [*Erkjendelses-Akt*], is an approximation" (CUP, 125).

> The material of world history is endless and the limit must accordingly in one way or another be arbitrary. Although the world-historical is something past, as material for cognitive consideration [*erkjendende Betragtning*] it is incomplete, it is constantly coming into being through ever new observation and research, which makes ever more new or corrective discoveries. Just as the number of discoveries in the natural sciences increases through refining the instruments, so too is it with critically refined observation in the world-historical. (CUP, 125)

But if the past, as an object of knowledge, is unfinished—that is, indeterminate—then there can be no historical knowledge in the strict sense. Just as was the case, however, with the empirical scientist, the job of the historian involves more than just heaping up data. These data will often appear to support a particular interpretation of the past. This is explicable in that there are historical facts, according to Kierkegaard, in the form of past actualities; hence the more data a historian collects, the more these data, taken as a whole, will seem to support a particular conclusion about the essence of the fact in question. If Caesar really did cross the Rubicon, for example, the

---

[60] JP, 5:5620.

[61] It is tempting to consider the question of whether Caesar was a great man to be one with which the historian would also be concerned. It is important to appreciate, however, that according to Kierkegaard even if the answer to such a question possessed a determinate truth value, knowledge of this truth value would not be historical knowledge. Historical knowledge, according to Kierkegaard, concerns the "palpably material" (SLW, 438) and is thus distinguished from knowledge of such abstract qualifications as greatness (SLW, 438). A historian may indeed be interested in the question of Caesar's greatness, but he is not interested in this, according to Kierkegaard, in his capacity as an historian.

more data the historian collects relating to this event, the more these data will appear to support this interpretation of the past.

The only certainty the historian has, however, is that the correspondence to reality of a particular interpretation of the past is formally uncertain. We saw above that probability, viewed objectively, is meaningless. All it says, objectively, is that something either is or is not the case. It is precisely on such probabilities, however, that historical knowledge, in the loose sense of knowledge, is constructed. The probable correspondence of a particular interpretation of the past to reality is going to be meaningful to a historian not because this correspondence has more objective support than the correspondence of competing interpretations but because it has more subjective support in terms of the inclination of the historian to attribute positive significance to probabilities. The historian, like the natural scientist, is not merely allowed to subscribe to particular interpretations of reality; he is expected to subscribe to them, albeit on a provisional basis. The question is, what is the mechanism that allows the historian, or any scholar or scientist, to go from being certain that the correspondence of any theory in his discipline to reality is uncertain to the view that a particular theory nevertheless deserves provisional acceptance?

"A reason," observes A, the anonymous author of the first volume of Kierkegaard's *Either/Or*, "is a curious thing; if I regard it with all my passion, it develops into an enormous necessity that can set heaven and earth in motion; if I am devoid of passion, I look down upon it derisively" (EO I, 32–33). The apparent probability that a particular view about the essence of a past event corresponds to the past is interpreted by the historian as meaningful precisely because, like the natural scientist, he is not completely objective in his contemplation of the issue.

The task of the historian, and indeed the task of any thinker, according to Kierkegaard, whether he is a humanist or a natural scientist, is to collect data and develop provisional interpretations of these data while suspending judgment concerning the actual correspondence of these interpretations to reality. Kierkegaard, as should be clear now, has no objection to science and scholarship (except to the extent that they can distract one from ethical concerns).[62] He even praises them in his journals.[63] What he objects to is the failure of scholars and scientists to appreciate the provisional nature of their conclusions.

It is important, asserts Climacus, that the prospective knower avoid "illusory finality, whether in sense certainty, historical knowledge, or

---

[62] See JP, 3:2807, 2824; and Slotty, 38.
[63] See JP, 1:386; and JP, 2:2286.

speculative result" (CUP, 68). The impression made on a scholar or scientist by the nature of his data is often so strong that he is barely aware of having a subjective role in accepting this direction as meaningful. He does have such a role, however, according to Kierkegaard, even if he fails to notice it. This is what Kierkegaard means when he says knowledge "requires an expression of will" (JP, 2:1094).[64] That is, "knowledge," in the sense in which scholars and scientists use the term, is the result of a decision (albeit, often an unconscious one) of the scholar, or scientist, to accept the direction in which his data are tending as significant. This is not the same thing, however, as allowing the scholar, or scientist, to accept approximate knowledge as certain. What the scientist is allowed to assent to, according to Kierkegaard, is that his knowledge is meaningful, not that it is certain. Such provisional knowledge is meaningful because it is part of the way we are constructed as thinking organisms that we are irresistibly inclined to interpret probabilities as making significant statements about objective reality.

Kierkegaard is aware that the impression created in the scholar, or scientist, by the direction in which a particular set of data is tending can be so great that we would seem to have little choice but to accept the data as conclusive, and he is not, for the most part, concerned to preclude such acceptance. Indeed, he recognizes full well, unlike the Pyrrhonist to whom he is so indebted, that a life without beliefs is impossible. His concern is rather to expose the nature of such acceptance, that it is a choice, no matter how well founded or reasonable it may appear relative to alternative choices.

"It is true of all historical learning and knowledge [*al Viden eller al Kundskab*]," asserts Climacus, "that, even at its maximum, it is only an approximation" (CUP, 481–82). Hence in "historical knowledge [the knower] gets to know a great deal about the world," but he is "moving constantly in the sphere of approximation-knowledge while in his supposed positivity imagining himself to possess certainty" (CUP, 68). One might well ask whether it is intrinsic to science and scholarship that they assume this positivity. It would appear the problem lies in the scientist or scholar and not in the disciplines as such. "The historian," observes Climacus, "seeks to arrive at the greatest possible certainty. . . . As a researcher he is part of a major endeavor from generation to generation; it is always objectively and scientifically important to him to come as close to certainty as possible" (CUP, 482). The difficulty is that the historian, according to Kierkegaard, has what one might call a propensity to assume not that he has come as close to certainty as possible but that he has actually arrived at certainty.

---

[64] See also Slotty, 20.

Kierkegaard observes in his journal that

> [f]or a thinker there is no more horrible anguish than to have to live in the tension that while one is heaping up details it continually seems as if thought, the conclusion, is about to appear. . . . This is the most dreadful tantalization of the intellectual! A thinker is literally in hell as long as he has not found certainty. (JP, 3:2820)

"For one feels a constant urge," observes Climacus, "to have something finished" (CUP, 73).

The difficulty is precisely that neither scholarship nor even science is ever finished or complete. Truth, in these disciplines, is identified with the "historical development of the relation between subject and object" (Hügli, 280). Truth, even in historical scholarship, is not immutable, as is the past itself, but is constantly in the process of becoming. Knowledge of this truth, however, is characterized by a kind of inertia that, although it resembles immutability in that it resists change, ultimately allows one theory to give way to another theory whose correspondence to the reality of the past is considered even more probable.

Each of the disciplines traditionally associated with what we call the humanities is problematic according to Kierkegaard. Psychology, sociology, and economics, in short any discipline that is directly concerned with human behavior, is problematic to the extent that Kierkegaard considers human beings have free will and this is going to necessarily limit the extent to which one can achieve certainty relative to any theory that would involve speculation about human decision making. Art, music, and literature are problematic to the extent that their objects are particular works. That is, there is a gap between a particular work of art, and so on, and the general concept of beauty, a logical gap of the same sort that was discussed in chapter 3. The *School of Athens*, for example, is a particular painting that came to be at a particular point. But beauty, as such, is eternal, according to Kierkegaard, and thus cannot be adequately instantiated in any particular historical object. There is, in fact, something paradoxical, according to Kierkegaard, in the effort to attribute eternal unchanging characteristics such as beauty to particular existing (i.e., temporarily defined) objects such as works of art.[65]

This does not mean, however, that there is no sense, according to Kierkegaard, in the systematic study of the disciplines that fall under the heading of the humanities. It means that such disciplines can be considered to produce knowledge only if that expression is understood in the loose sense.

---

[65] See JP, 3:3085.

CHAPTER FIVE

Redefining Knowledge

Subjective Knowledge

I argued in chapter 4 that Kierkegaard's main quarrel with his contemporaries concerned the possibility of absolute knowledge. Kierkegaard "was content," observes Slotty, "to have convinced himself that there was no such thing as presuppositionless knowledge [in philosophy] and proceeded hurriedly to demonstrate the impossibility of such knowledge in other spheres" (Slotty, 22).

Kierkegaard was not particularly interested in objective knowledge. Subjective knowledge or, more specifically, ethical knowledge and religious knowledge, were his main concerns.[1] "Ethical-religious realities," observes Slotty, "presuppose themselves and knowledge of these realities is attained, according to Kierkegaard, by means which conform to laws unique to these realities" (Slotty, 40).[2] We have already seen that all knowledge is interested according to Kierkegaard and that all knowledge thus has a subjective element. We also saw, however, that there are two fundamentally different

---

[1] See Slotty, 40; and Harald Høffding, *Kierkegaard som Filosof* [Kierkegaard as philosopher] (Copenhagen: Gyldendal, 1919), 59.

[2] Compare this to Deuser's claim that "the inner perspective has its own being and demands, therefore, an epistemology of its own" (Deuser, 105–6).

types of interest: the first where the object of interest is some third thing such as beauty or truth and the second where the object of interest is the knower himself.[3] These two types of interest are associated with two different types of knowledge. We examined objective knowledge in chapters 3 and 4. The remainder of the book will look at what Kierkegaard calls subjective knowledge.

I have not so far drawn much attention to the various Danish expressions Kierkegaard uses to refer to knowledge. This is because the distinctions he makes between the two Danish expressions normally translated into English as knowledge of the propositional sort—that is, *Erkjendelse* and *Viden*[4]—appear to be relative to the context in which they occur.[5] That is, Kierkegaard does not appear to make any general, or systematic, distinction between these expressions. Much of the confusion, however, surrounding the efforts of various philosophers to determine the substance of Kierkegaard's epistemology is a direct result of the fact that Kierkegaard's discussion of subjective, or essential, knowledge often involves reference to acquaintance knowledge (*Kendskab*) rather than to propositional knowledge. To avoid confusion, from now on I will indicate the Danish term in question when quoting Kierkegaard if the term in question would not normally be translated as knowledge in the propositional sense.

It is important to appreciate that subjective knowledge is not distinguished from objective knowledge in the way one might think. Some sorts of subjective knowledge will have a relation to the knower such that if the knower were different, so the content of the knowledge would be different. This does not mean, however, that subjective knowledge is subjectivist. There is, for Kierkegaard, a single ethical and religious reality in the sense that there is one set of eternally valid ethical norms for human behavior and one God who requires of every human being that he actualize these norms in his existence. Kierkegaard, as Slotty observes, "was personally convinced of the truth of Christianity" (Slotty, 63).[6] There is, for Kierkegaard, a single ethical-religious reality—that is, Christianity—it is just that the way

---

[3] See chapter 3, "Objective versus Subjective Knowledge."

[4] See Poul Lübcke, *Politikens Filosofi Leksikon* [Politiken's philosophical lexicon] (Copenhagen: Politikens Forlag, 1983), 16 .

[5] See chapter 1, "Kierkegaard's Terminology."

[6] Compare this to the observation of Kierkegaard's pseudonym Johannes de Silentio in *Fear and Trembling*: "If a human being did not have an eternal consciousness, if underlying everything there were only a wild fermenting power that writhing in dark passions produced everything, be it significant or insignificant, . . . what would life then be but despair? . . . But for precisely that reason it is not so" (FT, 15).

to knowledge of this reality is through the individual, through attention to his subjective experience as such, rather than through becoming objective.[7]

Subjective knowledge proper, we will see, is like objective knowledge in the strict sense in that it is characterized by an immediate relation between the knower and the object of knowledge. That is, subjective knowledge proper involves contact with, or participation with, the reality in question. Just as was the case, however, with objective knowledge in both the strict and looser senses, subjective knowledge is restricted to certain sorts of objects. Only these objects can be known in this way, and they are known in this way because they are specifically suited to this type of knowing.

There are, as we saw earlier,[8] two types, or aspects, of reality to which the knower has an immediate relation according to Kierkegaard. The first is thought. That is, the knower is immediately related to his own ideas as such.[9] The second is ethical actuality. That is, the knower is immediately related to his own ethical actuality. As one might expect, subjective knowledge can be divided into two sorts: knowledge of ideality, or thought reality, and knowledge of actuality. The first sort of subjective knowledge, like the first sort of objective knowledge, falls under the heading of what Kierkegaard calls immanent metaphysical knowledge. Now, however, rather than ontological and mathematical knowledge, we have knowledge of God, self-knowledge, and ethical-religious knowledge.

We learned in chapter 3 that knowledge, according to Kierkegaard, is a representation of reality in thought. Even subjective knowledge is such a representation. What distinguishes it from objective knowledge is not its nature as a representation but how it arises and the manner in which it is related to the individual knower. That is, while objective knowledge is essentially descriptive, subjective knowledge is essentially prescriptive. Subjective knowledge proper is not the product of an observation of reality; it is the product of the participation of the knower in that reality. To the extent, however, that the knowledge in question is distinguished from such participation, it is not properly knowledge. There is thus, for Kierkegaard, a distinction between subjective knowledge proper and what one could call pseudo-knowledge. Objective knowledge in the loose sense is really no worse, for Kierkegaard, than objective knowledge in the strict sense. It is simply the only sort of knowledge that is possible with respect to certain sorts of objects; thus it is the proper way to know those objects. It is not

---

[7] See, e.g., JP, 4:4555.
[8] See chapter 4, "Knowledge in the Strict Sense."
[9] See Holmer, 45.

the objects of pseudo-knowledge, however, that give it this determination but the failure of the "knower" to exhibit the proper relation to the mental representation in question.[10]

There is, again, no knowledge, according to Kierkegaard, that is the product of purely objective, disinterested, dispassionate inquiry. "Just to make the celebrated distinction between what one understands and what one does not understand," asserts Kierkegaard's pseudonym Johannes de Silentio in *Fear and Trembling*, "requires passion" (FT, 42n). Passion, for Kierkegaard, is what stimulates, as well as sustains, inquiry of any sort, whether the inquiry is directed toward some truth that is completely independent of the inquirer or whether it is directed toward some truth that is essentially related to the inquirer. Reality, according to Kierkegaard, does not simply imprint itself on the intellect of the observer. Even the most objective inquiry thus has a subjective element. The difference between objective and subjective knowledge is that while both are the product of activity on the part of the knower, the activity in question is of two sorts. The activity of the inquirer after objective knowledge is consciously directed away from himself toward some object that exists independently of himself and that has no essential relation to his subjective existence. The activity associated with subjective knowledge, on the other hand, is directed toward the experience of the individual knower as such.

Subjective knowledge concerns what is true for the knower both in terms of what his experience is like (i.e., what it is like to have experiences of a certain sort) and in terms of what it should be like (i.e., not what it should be like to have experiences of a certain sort, but what sorts of experiences the individual ought to have, or what sorts of things the individual ought to do). Subjective knowledge is thus both descriptive and prescriptive of subjective experience, but it is also still a mental representation of the reality in question. Subjectivity can be treated abstractly, and this, according to Kierkegaard, is precisely what is done when subjective experience becomes the object of a mental representation.[11] But subjectivity treated in this way (i.e., merely as the object of a mental representation) is distinguishable from subjectivity itself, as Kierkegaard's pseudonym Vigilius Haufniensis observes when he says that "[a]bstract subjectivity is just as uncertain and lacks inwardness to the same degree as abstract objectivity" (CA, 141).

[10] See, e.g., Hannay, 140.

[11] See the remark by Kierkegaard's pseudonym Constantin Constantius that "[a]s soon as knowledge comes into play . . . the elasticity of the test is weakened and the category becomes something other than it was" (R, 68).

Objective knowledge, according to Kierkegaard, as we saw in chapter 3, can be understood to be a justified, true mental representation of reality. A mental representation was true in the strict sense, according to Kierkegaard, when it agreed with the reality to which it referred and was justified by a kind of insight, or intuition, concerning this agreement. Even empirical knowledge, which is knowledge only in the loose sense, involves such an intuition to the extent that it must be understood by the knower to be ultimately uncertain. We will see in this chapter, however, that subjective knowledge, viewed independently of the participation of the "knower" in the reality to which it refers (i.e., what I identified above as pseudo-knowledge), is neither justified nor true and that for this reason it is actually a kind of pseudo-knowledge.

But if pseudo-knowledge lacks both justification and truth, in what sense can it be considered knowledge? The answer to this question concerns the manner in which the relevant expressions are used in ordinary communication. We will see that, just as was the case with objective knowledge, there are two senses in which Kierkegaard uses the expression "truth" and thus two senses in which subjective knowledge (or "knowledge") may be said to be justified.

Before we proceed to an examination of subjective knowledge, we must set out a few questions to which we will return at the end of this chapter. We have already seen that subjective knowledge and objective knowledge have different sorts of objects according to Kierkegaard. This does not necessarily mean, however, that objective knowledge of the objects properly belonging to subjective knowledge is impossible; hence the first question we must address concerns whether such knowledge is possible and, if so, whether it is what Kierkegaard would call knowledge in the strict sense or whether it is knowledge in the looser sense. If objective knowledge of the objects of subjective knowledge is possible, we must address the issue of what advantage, if any, is to be had, according to Kierkegaard, in a subjective knowledge of them. Finally, we must decide whether it is appropriate to subsume Kierkegaard's views on subjective knowledge under the general heading of his epistemology.

Subjective Truth

Truth, as we saw in chapter 3, is defined by Kierkegaard as an agreement between thought and being. This agreement may be established in two ways. It may be the result of the accurate representation of being in thought, or of the accurate representation of thought in being. There are thus two senses in which Kierkegaard uses the expression "truth." This is the distinction referred to in chapter 3 as that between truth and truths.

"[O]bjectively," explains Hügli,

> truth is an agreement between thought and being. Ideality is true only to the extent that it has reality in itself. Truth is—in the classical sense—an *adaequatio intellectus ad rem*. Subjectively, the relation is reversed. Ethics is not concerned with expressing reality in ideality. The individual is only in the truth to the extent that he has ideality in himself. Truth in the subjective sense could thus be designated as an *adaequatio rei ad intellectum*. (Hügli, 199–200)

Truths, according to Kierkegaard, are the result of the accurate representation of being in thought, whether the being in question is ideal, as is the case with what we have called immanent metaphysical truths, or whether it is actual, as is the case, for example, with scholarly and scientific truths. Truth, on the other hand, is the accurate representation of thought in being—that is, in actuality.[12] It is the latter sort of truth to which Anti-Climacus refers when he observes that "now all expressions are formed according to the view that truth is cognition [*Erkjendelsen*], knowledge [*Viden*], whereas in original Christianity all the expressions were formed according to the view that truth is a [way of] being" (PC, 206).

Truth that is a property of actuality rather than of mental representations is restricted, according to Kierkegaard, to aspects of reality that are essentially related to the individual knower as such. Ethics and religion are essentially prescriptive, thus ethical and religious truth is an agreement between the ideality of ethical and religious prescriptions and the actuality of the individual's existence. This, again, is what Kierkegaard refers to as "essential truth" (CUP, 168n) because it is related to the essence of an individual's existence as such—that is, as an individual rather than as an example of a human being in general—and is thus also referred to by him as "subjective truth" (CUP, 159ff.).

Subjective truth, according to Kierkegaard, is a way of existing.[13] It is an existence that instantiates the moral law. This is why Anti-Climacus argues that Christianity demands not that one know the truth but that one "be the truth" (PC, 205). To be the truth is to manifest in one's being—that is, existence—the agreement between thought and being that was identi-

---

[12] Thus Hannay argues that "in Kierkegaard we have the idea that the sensible world can itself come to bear the imprint of an ideal, even thought the 'source' of that ideal remains ineradicably transcendent" (Hannay, 257).

[13] See, e.g., Benjamin Daise, "The Will to Truth in Kierkegaard's *Philosophical Fragments*," *Philosophy of Religion* 31 (1992): 1–12; and Jeremy Walker, "Ethical Beliefs: A Theory of Truth without Truth Values," *Thought* 55, no. 218 (1980): 295–305.

fied above as truth. Subjective truth is not the correspondence, in an external sense, of the existence of the knower to his mental representation of ethical-religious ideality. It is the assent of the subject to the substance of ethical-religious prescriptions as such that represents a genuine correspondence of his existence to these prescriptions.[14] That is, subjective truth is the result of a conscious effort of this person to bring his existence into conformity with these prescriptions.[15] "What is actual," asserts Johannes Climacus, "is not the external action, but an internality in which the individual cancels the possibility and identifies himself with what is thought, in order to exist in it" (CUP, 284). Ethical, or religious, prescriptions are thus actualized not in the sense that a person succeeds in conforming his "historical externality" (CUP, 482) to these prescriptions but in the sense the he has truly willed such correspondence.

I argued in chapter 3 that, strictly speaking, truth was equivalent to an agreement between ideality and reality in the sense of the formal necessity of the correspondence of the one to the other. Such formal necessity is what one could call objective necessity. There is another kind of necessity, however, that one could refer to as subjective necessity. That is, it is necessary, as we saw in chapter 2, for a person to bring his existence into conformity with the substance of ethical-religious prescriptions in order for him to attain genuine existence.[16]

Climacus observes, in the context of a discussion of subjective truth, that

[i]t is not for a single moment forgotten here that the subject is existing and that existing is a becoming, and that the notion of truth as the identity of thought and being is a chimera of abstraction, and truly only a longing on the part of creation, not because the truth is not so, but because the knower is one who exists and thus, as long as he exists, truth cannot be so for him. (CUP, 165)[17]

[14] See, e.g., Hügli's observation that what he refers to as "external actuality" is not under the control of the individual and that "it is unethical to be concerned about something which does not depend upon the ethical itself. So what remains in the end [i.e., as a candidate for ethical action] is simply the intention, the will, to want to act" (Hügli, 216).

[15] See, e.g., Daise, 5–7.

[16] See, e.g., Hügli's claim that, according to Kierkegaard, "a human being is only human to the extent that he acts ethically" (Hügli, 204).

[17] See Slotty's observation that, according to Kierkegaard, "truth, for an existing subject, cannot be appropriated once and for all in the eternity of pure being. There is no absolute continuity. Truth, for an existing subject, consists merely in the passionate anticipation of eternity, in an approach [to eternity]" (Slotty, 38).

"No human being," asserts Anti-Climacus, "with the exception of Christ, is the truth. In relation to every other person, the truth is something infinitely higher than his being" (PC, 204).

What Kierkegaard means when he says that no human being is the truth is that no human being is in "absolute possession" (SV XI, 85–86) of the truth. The difficulty is that a person, as a relation between thought and being (i.e., an *interesse*), or as the relation's relating itself to itself, "strives infinitely, is constantly coming to be [*i Vorden*]" (CUP, 77). "Truth," asserts Kierkegaard's pseudonym Vigilius Haufniensis, "is for the particular individual, only as he produces it in action" (CA, 138).[18] This means that a person's every action (at least every action that has any ethical or religious significance) must produce truth if his existence is to be an expression of the truth. To the extent, however, that a person never finishes acting, he can never be said to have fully succeeded in bringing his existence into conformity with the ideal ethical-religious prescriptions or to have produced truth in the sense of having fully conformed the actuality of his being with the ideality of his mental representation of these prescriptions.[19]

Subjective truth is thus like the self in that it is constantly in the process of becoming and to that extent is potentiality rather than actuality. That is, subjective truth, like the self, does not actually exist (*er ikke virkelig til*) but is simply that which ought to exist (*skal blive til*).[20] Thus Kierkegaard can argue that "what is Christian" (i.e., what Christianity is, or what it means to be a Christian) is never concluded but always "has the future open and can still become what it ought to be" (P, 33).[21] As long as a person exists, he has the future open, and although his existence is not a complete expression of the truth, it can still become this—that is, can still become what it ought to be. A person's task is thus to perfect himself, to make his life an expression of ethical-religious truth, which task is never completed so long as he exists.

We saw in chapter 3 that Kierkegaard uses the expression "truth" in both a strict and a loose sense and that he refers to truth in the latter sense as an approximation. It appears, however, that there is a sense in which even subjective truth proper is an approximation. That is, Anti-Climacus asserts that

---

[18] See Slotty, 39; and Hügli, 228.

[19] See Høffding, 60, 63.

[20] See chapter 2. See also SUD, 29–30; CA, 138; and Pap. V B 60.

[21] I have altered the translation slightly. Nichol has "what it is to be" where I have "what it ought to be." The Danish is "*hvad det skal være*," which literally translates as "what it ought to be."

> [t]he being of truth is the redoubling of truth within yourself, within me, within
> him, that your life, my life, his life expresses the truth approximately in the striving
> for it, that your life, my life, his life is approximately the being of the truth in the
> striving for it, just as the truth was in Christ a life, for he was the truth. (PC, 205)

Only Christ, according to Kierkegaard, expresses truth in an absolute sense. Even if a person is successful in bringing his existence into conformity with ethical or religious prescriptions, his existence, as a whole, can do no more than approximate this truth. This sort of approximation differs, however, from the sort that characterizes knowledge in the loose sense. In both cases truth may be described as a *desideratum*. In the latter case, though, a person has no guarantee that the apparent probability of the correspondence of a mental representation to reality is objectively vindicated in the sense that the more probable the correspondence appears, the closer one is to its absolute determination. An increase in the probability of the correspondence brings one no closer to establishing absolute correspondence. Thus an approximation, according to Kierkegaard, "has the remarkable property of being able to continue as long as you please" (CUP, 36). It can keep going indefinitely because it never actually gets closer to what one could call its destination.

To approximate ethical and religious truth, however, is precisely to "approach" it. This can be seen if we look at the Danish expression Kierkegaard uses to refer to this sort of approximation. The expression in question is not *Approximation*, the expression Kierkegaard uses in the context of his discussion of approximate knowledge, but "*Tilnærmelse*."[22] *Tilnærmelse* is a compound composed of two words: *Nærmelse*, which translates literally as "the act or movement, to approach, to come closer to,"[23] and the preposition *til*, which translates as "to." *Tilnærmelse* may thus be translated into English as either "approximation" or "approach." It is clearly the latter, however, that Kierkegaard has in mind. It was customary in theological circles in Copenhagen in the mid-nineteenth century to speak of *Tilnærmelse til Gud* (approaching God). J. P. Mynster, the bishop of Zealand during most of Kierkegaard's adult life, argued, for example, that "*Tilnærmelsen til Gud kan ikke finde sted uden Betragtning af Gud* [one cannot approach God without a contemplation of God]."[24] A person comes nearer to ethical or religious truth, according to Kierkegaard, "in the striving for it,"[25] in a sense in which he cannot come nearer to objective truth through probability.

[22] See, e.g., JFY, 208; and PC, 205.

[23] See Ferrall and Repp., Molbech, and Vinterberg and Bodelsen.

[24] J. P. Mynster, *Blandede Skrifter* [Miscellaneous writings], 3 vols. (Copenhagen: Gyldendalske Boghandlings Forlag, 1852), vol. 1, 49.

[25] See, e.g., EUD, 306; and SUD, 41–42.

Subjective Justification

Subjective knowledge differs from objective knowledge in that even subjective knowledge proper only approaches truth. But if it cannot be said to be true in an absolute sense, can it be said to be justified? We saw above that Kierkegaard associates knowledge in the strict sense with certainty in the sense of the necessity of the correspondence of the mental representation in question to reality. The justification of this knowledge turned out to be a kind of insight into this necessity that was possible as a result of the fact that the knower was immediately related to the reality in question. This insight was, in turn, equivalent to psychological certainty. That is, it was the contact of the knower with reality that caused the representation of it and that thus also caused that representation to be justified. When contact with reality was not possible, as was the case, for example, when the object of a mental representation was some actuality other than the knower's own ethical actuality, reality could be said to cause the mental representation in question, and thus to justify it, in only a loose sense.

Subjective knowledge proper, like objective knowledge in the strict sense, is characterized, according to Kierkegaard, by a causal account of justification, while pseudo-knowledge, as we will see, like knowledge in the loose sense, can be interpreted as having a causal account of justification only if "cause" is understood in a relatively loose sense. There are thus, just as was the case with objective knowledge, two senses in which subjective knowledge may be justified, and these senses correspond to the two senses of subjective truth detailed above. In this case, however, the different senses in which subjective knowledge may be understood to be justified are not relative to the nature of the object of knowledge but to the nature of the individual's relation to the knowledge as such.

Just as was the case with objective knowledge in the strict sense, subjective knowledge proper appears to be justified by an insight on the part of the knower into the essence of the object of knowledge, an insight that is generated by contact with the reality in question.

Objective knowledge was essentially descriptive. Subjective knowledge, on the other hand, to the extent that it concerns ethics and religion, is essentially prescriptive. This means that contact with the reality to which subjective knowledge refers would appear equivalent to living according to the substance of the prescriptions in question. To bring the actuality of one's existence into conformity with these prescriptions is to establish contact with ethical-religious ideality. This contact would, in turn, constitute an agreement between thought and being (or *adaequatio rei ad intellectum*) that, according to Kierkegaard, constitutes truth.

Objective knowledge in the strict sense is associated with both formal and psychological certainty. Subjective knowledge proper is not associated with formal certainty, but it is associated with psychological certainty. That is, insight into the essence of an object of subjective knowledge is made possible through the knower's contact with that object, and this insight produces psychological certainty concerning the correctness of the mental representation, just as it did with objective knowledge in the strict sense. For example, the existence of a person who is honest is an expression of the ethical obligation to be honest that constitutes contact with the reality of that obligation. This contact, in turn, affirms the reality of this obligation such that this person can be said to experience the reality of the obligation in fulfilling it. And, in fact, people do sometimes say things like, though they believed that what they were about to do was the right thing, they became convinced of this in the act itself.

Subjective knowledge is, again, ethical-religious knowledge. That is, subjective knowledge is related to the existence of the knower in the sense that it prescribes the manner in which this person ought to exist. Since the object of subjective knowledge is ethical-religious ideality, an appreciation of the correspondence of a representation of this ideality to reality is, I will argue, equivalent to an appreciation of the necessity of the correspondence of one's existence to the substance of this representation.

In what sense, however, can the correspondence of the knower's existence to the ideality of ethical and religious prescriptions be understood to be necessary? The obvious answer is that it is necessary for him to attain eternal blessedness, which Christianity offers to those who are properly related to it. Even if this is the case, however, and such a claim is extremely problematic to the extent that it would make eternal blessedness appear something the individual would have to earn, such necessity would appear only hypothetical. That is, *if* a person were interested in eternal blessedness, *then* it would be necessary for him to bring his existence into conformity with ethical-religious ideality. If a person were not interested in such blessedness, however, then such conformity would be unnecessary.

It is possible to argue that every person, according to Kierkegaard, is interested in his own eternal blessedness (i.e., everyone has at least a formal interest in it), apart from the issue of whether he experiences any subjective concern for it,[26] just as he claims that everyone is in despair, whether he knows it or not.[27] There is another way, however, to explain the necessity

[26] See, e.g., Slotty, 40; and Hannay, 44, 176, 193.
[27] See SUD, 23.

of the conformity of an individual's existence to ethical-religious ideality. That is, we saw in the discussion of subjective truth that such conformity appeared necessary, according to Kierkegaard, for a person to exist in a genuine sense.

Every human being, according to Kierkegaard, has an "eternally established essence" (CUP, 490).[28] According to Kierkegaard's interpretation of Christianity, however, no one actually exists according to this essence. Everyone is a sinner, but sin was not part of this essence.[29] "To exist [*at existere*]," observes Climacus,

> ordinarily means simply that, through having come to be, the individual is there and is in [the process of] becoming [*i Vorden*].[30] Now it means that having come to, he has become a sinner. Usually, "existing" is not a more closely defining predicate but the form of all the more closely defining predicates; one does not become something by coming to be, but now, coming to be is becoming a sinner. . . . [That is], by coming to be, the individual becomes another, or the moment he is to come to be, he becomes another by coming to be. (CUP, 490)[31]

God, according to Kierkegaard, has a plan for each individual. The difficulty is that no one's life actually represents the actualization of this plan. Thus it is not *this* plan that comes to be in the concrete existence of the person.[32] "Every human being," argues Anti-Climacus, "is a psychical synthesis intended to be spirit" (SUD, 43). God's plan for people is that they should

---

[28] Hannay translates "*evigt anlagte Væsen*" as "the being who is planned for eternity." "Planned" is, however, a contentious translation of *at anlægge*. Ferrall and Repp., for example, define *at anlægge* as "to found, establish, construct," and these are, in fact, the preferred translations even today (see, e.g., Vinterberg and Bodelsen, s.v. *anlægge*). "Being" is an acceptable translation of *Væsen*, but "essence" not only was the preferred translation in the first half of the nineteenth century (see Ferrall and Repp., s.v. *Væsen*) but also remains so even today (see Vinterberg and Bodelsen, s.v. *væsen*). More importantly, however, it is in the sense of "essence" that Kierkegaard most often uses the expression.

[29] It is important to remember that Kierkegaard is not an apologist for Christianity. That is, he offers no justification for the claim that everyone is a sinner. He simply assumes that this is one of the basic tenets of Christianity and that as the overwhelming majority of his readers would have professed to have been Christians, it is unlikely that many would have found the claim contentious.

[30] I have again altered Hannay's translation slightly. "*Vorden*" is Danish for "becoming" not "being." The Danish term that is ordinarily translated as "being," *Væren*, does not occur in the passage in question.

[31] I have altered the translation slightly. Hannay has "come about" throughout where I have "come to be." Not only is the former a less literal translation of the Danish *bliv til*, but also it is confusing in that it is generally only events, not things, that are spoken of as "coming about."

[32] See C, 141.

be spirits. "But what is spirit? Spirit is the self" (SUD, 13). To fail to exist according to God's plan, which is to say, to fail to realize the synthesis of the temporal and eternal as that synthesis is expressed by bringing one's particular, finite, temporal existence into conformity with universal, infinite, eternal ethical-religious ideality, is, according to Kierkegaard, to fail to have a self, or to fail to exist in a genuine sense.[33] Such an individual fails, according to Kierkegaard, to become actual in the technical sense.[34]

Ethically speaking, actuality (*Virkeligheden*), according to Kierkegaard, is ideality.[35] It is the ideality of ethical-religious prescriptions as they are concretely expressed in a person's life. To fail to express this ideality in one's existence is to fail, in an essential sense, to achieve actuality. "I know of no one," observes Kierkegaard, "of whom it is in the strictest sense true that his life has achieved actuality. There is a deceptive appearance, but on closer inspection hundreds of illusions are discernable, with the result that he does not exist altogether personally, that actuality cannot get hold of him altogether personally" (JP, 3:3217).

Actuality, in this sense, is the "unity of possibility and necessity" (SUD, 36). The self cannot become anything whatever but is limited by God's plan for it. Actuality, according to Kierkegaard, or actually to become a self, is to become what, according to the divine plan, it is *necessary* for one to become if one is to become anything at all. "To become oneself," according to Kierkegaard, is a movement within necessity.[36] It is the free appropriation of that self that it has been eternally determined one *ought* to become, or the actualization of that self that it is necessary to actualize in order actually to exist.[37]

To exist as a human being, argues Johannes Climacus, is not to be [*være*] in "the same sense in which a potato is. . . . Human existence," he continues, "has idea [or ideality] in it" (CUP, 277). To fail to instantiate ethical-religious ideality in one's existence is thus to fail to have authentic human existence.[38] But it is precisely such authentic human existence that is constitutive of the self.

The justification of objective knowledge in the strict sense, I argued, was equivalent to the knower's insight into the necessity of the correspondence

---

[33] See chapter 2 and, e.g., CUP, 290.

[34] See, e.g., JP, 3:3217.

[35] See, e.g., CUP, 272.

[36] See, e.g., SUD, 36.

[37] Compare this to Hügli's contention that "I can will, freely will what I must do [*was ich notwendigerweise tunß*]. My freedom, according to Kierkegaard, consists in this and only in this" (Hügli, 175).

[38] See, e.g., CUP, 290.

of a particular thought to being. The justification of subjective knowledge proper is just the reverse. It is the knower's insight into the necessity of the correspondence of being (i.e., the actuality of his existence) to thought (i.e., to abstract ethical or religious prescriptions). Now, however, the necessity is subjective rather than objective. Such correspondence is not objectively necessary but subjectively necessary in the sense that it is necessary for the knower to achieve authentic existence.

The knower's insight into this necessity is, however, just as was the insight that justified objective knowledge, possible only to the extent that he is immediately related to the object of knowledge. The object of subjective knowledge is, of course, subjective truth, which is again a conformity of the knower's existence to ethical-religious ideality. As this conformity is some-thing to which he is immediately related, its necessity becomes apparent to him with the conformity itself.[39] That is, the knower becomes aware, to the extent that his existence expresses truth in the subjective sense, that such an expression is necessary if he is to exist as an authentic human being. And, indeed, people sometimes say things such as that they become convinced, when they are living rightly (e.g., as a vegetarian, animal-rights activist, or public servant, or just ethically in a more general sense), that this is how they "must" live.

Ethical-religious prescriptions express a necessity—you shall![40] That is, as a human being, a person does not, according to Kierkegaard, have the option of existing in the same sense that a potato exists. The express sub-jective truth is to become convinced of this, or to attain an insight into the necessity of the correspondence of one's existence to ethical-religious ideality. Thus Anti-Climacus argues that "knowing [at vide] the truth fol-lows of itself from being the truth" (PC, 205),[41] and that "nobody knows [veed] more of the truth than what he is of the truth" (PC, 205–6).[42] Insight into the necessity of expressing ethical-religious ideality in one's existence is a product of that expression, or of the immediate relation to this truth

---

[39] The inseparability of religious knowledge and experience is a recurrent theme of Kierkegaard's unpublished *Book on Adler* about a Danish pastor who purported to have had a revelation, where he argues, for example, that "it is easy to show that he does not even hold firmly to the Christian concept of revelation—*ergo*, we conclude that he has had no revela-tion" (BA, 121).

[40] See the varying emphases put on this phrase in Kierkegaard's *Works of Love*.

[41] I have altered the translation here slightly. The Hongs have "entirely of itself accom-panies," where I have "follows of itself." The latter is a less literal translation but, I believe, significantly more readable (see also Hügli, 228).

[42] See Hügli's claim that, according to Kierkegaard, "[s]ubjective truth does not exist because I know it; I know this truth because it is me" (Hügli, 228).

that it established in the expression of it. This is the "concrete intuition" (JP, 3:2324) referred to earlier.[43] It is this intuition that justifies the mental representation with which it is connected.[44] Thus a person's bringing his existence into conformity with ethical-religious ideality generates "a self-certainty which, instead of depending upon some conclusive evidence or argument . . . is immediately available in a self-guaranteeing form: that of a performative product of the agent's own independent decision" (Hannay, 46). That is, the insight concerning the necessity of bringing one's existence into conformity with one's mental representation of ethical religious ideality is equivalent to certainty concerning the correspondence of this representation to reality. The contact with the reality of ethical, or religious, ideality established as a result of the knower's having brought his existence into conformity with this ideality is the cause of his certainty concerning this correspondence. It is thus a person's experience of such contact with reality that causes his mental representation of it to be justified. "Such experience has cogency, of course," observes Slotty, "only for the individual whose experience it is . . . and even for this individual, the resultant certainty remains a certainty of belief" (Slotty, 64).[45]

We saw above, however, that subjective truth, according to Kierkegaard, is something a person approaches, but not something he ever completely expresses. There is thus, for Kierkegaard, a sense in which the certainty associated with subjective knowledge is problematic. That is, it is contingent on a person's being in a particular state. One can be certain of the substance of ethical religious ideality only to the extent that one's existence expresses this ideality. There is thus a sense in which the certainty of subjective knowledge "has in it, at every moment, the infinite dialectic of uncertainty" (CUP, 48). If a person fails to express ethical-religious ideality for even a moment, his insight into the essence of this ideality vanishes.

A representation of ethical-religious ideality in thought cannot be justified in itself but can be justified only to the extent that it is connected with the prescribed way of life. The task of bringing his existence into conformity with this prescribed way of life persists as a task as long as a person

---

[43] See chapter 3, "Objective Justification."

[44] See Jeremy Walker's discussion of what he refers to as "pragmatic proofs" (Walker, 302–4).

[45] Compare this to Hannay's suggestion that "Kierkegaard considered some states of mind, for example, those fortified by a life view, . . . to be self-confirming in the sense of providing their own form of justification, and not only not in need of further justification, but as belonging to a 'proof game' for which any other kind of confirmation, e.g., empirical proof, or disproof, is irrelevant" (Hannay, 139).

lives. Thus Slotty argues that, according to Kierkegaard, "only in eternity can there be eternal [i.e., absolute] certainty. Existence must be content with a militant certainty" (Slotty, 56).

I asserted above that there are two sorts of subjective knowledge according to Kierkegaard: subjective knowledge proper and pseudo-knowledge. There are thus two senses in which subjective knowledge may be said to be "justified." Subjective knowledge is, again, essentially prescriptive. Pseudo-knowledge, is thus objective "knowledge" of something essentially related to the existence of the individual "knower" in the sense that it prescribes how he should exist. That is, pseudo-knowledge is a mental representation of a prescription the substance of which is not actualized in the existence of the "knower." This, according to Kierkegaard, is what is often referred to in discussions of "Christian knowledge."[46]

We saw, in the case of objective knowledge, that if formal certainty concerning the correspondence of a particular mental representation to reality were not possible, then there might be another way such a mental representation could be justified. That is, objective knowledge of actuality was justified to the extent that the knower was said to appreciate that the correspondence of a particular mental representation to reality was probable as well as that new evidence could come to light that would be inconsistent with it and that could tip the scales of probability in favor of a competing interpretation. It is something like such an impression of probability, I will argue, that serves to "justify" pseudo-knowledge according to Kierkegaard.

Pseudo-knowledge may take two forms. That is, the object of pseudo-knowledge may be the correspondence of the existence of the "knower" to ethical or religious ideality, or it may be the correspondence of a mental representation of this ideality to reality. What distinguishes pseudo-knowledge from subjective knowledge proper is that pseudo-knowledge lacks the agreement between thought and being that must now be established not in thought but in the existence of the would-be knower. A person who fails to establish such agreement cannot even be said to know that he has failed to establish it. That is, there is an important sense, for Kierkegaard, in which a person could be said to know the status of his relation to ethical-religious ideality only if he is properly related to it—that is, only if his existence is an expression of this ideality.[47] To fail to actualize ethical or religious ideality is to fail to agree with that with which it is necessary to agree in order

---

[46] See, e.g., CUP, 180–81; PC, 206; and JP, 2:2303.

[47] See Kierkegaard's claim that "the truth is *index sui et falsi* [a mark of itself and of the false]" (C, 122). See also JP, 2:1340; and C, 118–20.

to achieve authentic existence. Since, as we saw, no one can fail, according to Kierkegaard, to be interested in attaining such existence, to fail to attain it, or, more properly, to fail to strive to attain it, must be because one is ignorant of the fact that one does not already have it. Thus neither the person who mistakenly believes that his existence corresponds to this ideality nor the person who would openly acknowledge that his existence fails to correspond to it can fully appreciate either the substance of this ideality or his status relative to it.[48]

The difference between subjective knowledge proper and pseudo-knowledge is that with the former, all the efforts of the knower are concentrated not on the object of knowledge but on the nature of his relation to this object, whereas with the latter, at least some of the "knower's" activity consists in a contemplation of the object of knowledge as such, or of his mental representation of this object and whether this representation corresponds to reality. "Let us," asserts Climacus, "take knowledge of God as an example. Objectively, reflection is on it being the true God, subjectively on the individual relating to something *in such a way* that his relation is truly a God-relationship" (CUP, 168).

Christianity, for reasons that need not be explored here, is the paradigm of subjective truth according to Kierkegaard, thus it is with respect to Christianity that Kierkegaard discusses the difficulty of endeavoring to justify subjective knowledge through reference to probability. There are two ways, according to Kierkegaard, one can objectively relate to the truth of Christianity. He refers to the first as "the historical view" (CUP, 21–43), and the second as "the speculative view" (CUP, 44–50). The objective of the speculative view, according to Kierkegaard, is to grasp Christianity as "the eternal thought" (CUP, 44). From a speculative point of view, a person endeavors to understand Christianity as ethical-religious ideality. He compares his mental representation of this ideality with his mental representation of Christianity to see if the one corresponds to the other. Part of the difficulty, according to Kierkegaard, concerns the fact that intrinsic to Christianity is the claim that any mental representation a person would have of ethical or religious ideality would, as a mental representation, fail to correspond to the reality of this ideality.

This is, however, not a difficulty that concerns us here. What is relevant to the present discussion is that from the speculative point of view, the "knower" compares one mental representation to another. This means

---

[48] Compare this to Hannay's claim that, according to Kierkegaard, "genuine identification of the moral (and the true) can occur only in a properly moral practice" (Hannay, 16).

the agreement between thought and being Kierkegaard describes as truth becomes, just as was the case with objective immanent metaphysical knowledge, the abstract self-identity of thought. From this perspective, there is no sense in which one could argue that the correspondence of the one representation to the other was probable.

This is, in fact, the situation of the "knower" relative to the issue of the correspondence of a mental representation of ethical ideality—to the extent that this can be distinguished from religious or Christian ideality—to the reality of this ideality. Any effort to establish the correspondence will always be an effort to establish the correspondence of one abstract, or ideal, object to another. Christianity, however, according to Kierkegaard, has a historical dimension that the moral law, as such, does not. Thus when Christianity is considered from this perspective—that is, when the "knower" attempts to establish the correspondence of a mental representation of Christianity to the reality of Christianity as a historical phenomenon—probability emerges as a candidate for the justification of religious knowledge. "If," argues Johannes Climacus,

> Christianity is looked on as a historical document, the important thing is to obtain completely reliable reports of what the Christian doctrine really is. Here, if the investigating subject were infinitely interested in his relation to this truth, he would despair straight away, because nothing is easier to see than that with regard to history the greatest certainty is after all only an *approximation*. (CUP, 21)

"In raising the historical question of the truth of Christianity," continues Climacus, "or of what is and what is not Christian truth, Holy Scripture immediately presents itself as a crucial document. The historical point of view therefore focuses first on the Bible" (CUP, 21). "If Scripture," he continues,

> is regarded as the secure resort for decisions about what is Christian and what is not, the important thing is to give Scripture a secure critical base historically.
> Here one deals with matters such as whether particular books belong in the canon, their authenticity and integrity, the author's trustworthiness, and a dogmatic guarantee is posited: inspiration. (CUP, 22)

The difficulty, of course, is that this guarantee cannot be absolute but rests on the probability of the authenticity of particular passages of Scripture. That is, certainty is not accessible with respect to the issue of the correspondence of a particular account of the past to the reality of the past. The closest a person can come to proving such correspondence is to establish its apparent probability.

We saw in chapters 3 and 4 that the appreciation of the apparent probability of the correspondence of a given mental representation to reality could serve, according to Kierkegaard, to justify knowledge in the loose sense—that is, scholarly and scientific knowledge—precisely because the correspondence of such representations to reality was inherently uncertain. This is not the case, according to Kierkegaard, however, with respect to subjective knowledge. Probability does not preclude the possibility that one could be mistaken as to the substance of the object with which it is connected. When, however, that object is essentially prescriptive and thus imposes a responsibility on the knower to conform his existence to the substance of the prescriptions, there cannot be any possibility that the knower is mistaken as to this substance. That is, such a possibility would negate the prescriptive nature of the object of knowledge in that a person could not be made responsible for doing something he did not fully appreciate he ought to have done.

To the extent that the "justification" of pseudo-knowledge is understood to be the impression of the "knower" that the correspondence of the mental representation in question to reality is probable, this "knowledge," according to Kierkegaard, is "justified" in the same pejorative sense in which it is said to be "knowledge"—that is, it is not really justified at all.[49]

---

[49] I have made no reference here to the arguments Kierkegaard actually uses in the *Postscript* against any significance that probability could have with respect to establishing the truth of Christianity. Kierkegaard argues that probability, or approximation, with respect to matters related to the truth of Christianity such as whether a particular part of the biblical canon was actually inspired or whether the church, as a spiritual entity, has actually existed since the time of Christ, is impossible to attain (see CUP, 21–43). My argument has been that even if it were possible to attain probability of this sort, the appreciation of it would fall short, for reasons given above, of justifying the mental representation with which it was associated.

CHAPTER SIX

SUBJECTIVE KNOWLEDGE

Subjective knowledge was Kierkegaard's primary epistemological interest. It is tempting to jump to the conclusion that subjective knowledge is something that is idiosyncratic to Kierkegaard. It should be clear, however, that while a fully developed theory of subjective knowledge such as is possible to extract from Kierkegaard's works may indeed be specific to Kierkegaard, it is not at all idiosyncratic. That is, there are some things that, because of their very nature, nearly everyone would agree, we cannot have purely objective knowledge of. Of course, Kierkegaard had very well-defined ontological (and hence also anthropological) ideas, so not everyone will agree with Kierkegaard's claims concerning what sorts of things can be known subjectively. Confirmed atheists, for example, would not accept that any sort of religious knowledge, even of the subjective sort, is possible. But then, atheists also have very different ontological views. Kierkegaard's views make a number of ontological assumptions, as all views about knowledge must. That many of these assumptions were religious was not at all controversial for Kierkegaard's audience, though many of their implications, as Kierkegaard develops them, were.

Not all subjective knowledge, as we will see, however, is religious or depends in any sense on religious assumptions. All subjective knowledge, as Kierkegaard understands it, however, does depend on an acceptance of the reality of ethical obligations, or what one might even call social obligations,

if the term "social" is understood in the anthropological sense. This will be
controversial only to people who are unfamiliar with recent work in anthro-
pology, zoology, and even neurology concerning how fundamental is our
sense of obligation to our fellow creatures.[1]

The reader might be inclined to think that, given the apparent symmetry
of the categories of objective and subjective knowledge, pseudo-knowledge
is analogous to objective knowledge in the loose sense and thus to expect
that a section of the present chapter will be devoted to pseudo-knowledge.
Pseudo-knowledge is not analogous to objective knowledge in the loose
sense, however. Objective knowledge in the loose sense is a legitimate form
of knowledge for Kierkegaard, whereas pseudo-knowledge is not. There
will thus be no section devoted to pseudo-knowledge. Pseudo-knowledge
is simply subjective knowledge that is not reflected in the existence of the
"knower."

Immanent Metaphysical Knowledge

We saw in chapters 2 and 3 that objective knowledge in the strict sense is
restricted to mathematics and what Kierkegaard calls ontology. They are part
of the realm of immanent metaphysical knowledge. According to Kierkegaard, immanent metaphysical knowledge is not restricted, however, to mathematics and ontology but includes such things as knowledge that there is a
God and that one has an immortal soul. The difficulty with these latter sorts
of knowledge, according to Kierkegaard, is that people are unwilling to let it
"get control of their minds" (JP, 3:3606). It is precisely the potential of this
knowledge to get control of the knower that distinguishes it from objective
immanent metaphysical knowledge, which is indifferent to the existence of
the individual knower as such.

Kierkegaard is widely believed to belong to a skeptical tradition that
would appear to preclude any claim to religious knowledge.[2] As early as
1835, however, there is a reference in his journals to the possibility of such
knowledge,[3] and in 1840 there is another reference, this one to his plans

---

[1] See, e.g., Leonard Katz, ed., *Evolutionary Origins of Morality* (Charlottesville, Va.:
Imprint Academic, 2000); and Joshua D. Greene, R. Brian Sommerville, Leigh E. Nystrom,
John M. Darley, and Jonathan D. Cohen, "An fMRI Investigation of Emotional Engagement
in Moral Judgment," *Science* 293, no. 5537 (2001): 2105–8.

[2] See, e.g., Popkin's "Kierkegaard and Skepticism" and Penelhum's "Skepticism and
Fideism."

[3] "I can indeed conceive of a philosophy after Christianity," writes Kierkegaard, "or
after one has become a Christian, but then it would be a Christian philosophy. Then the
relationship would not be one of philosophy to Christianity but of Christianity to Christian
knowledge [*christelige Erkjendelse*] or, if one insists, Christian philosophy" (JP, 3:3245).

for developing a "speculative Christian epistemology [*Erkjendelseslære*]" (JP, 2:2277).[4] The reader might be tempted to conclude that these remarks were written before Kierkegaard's thoughts were developed to the point where such knowledge would be precluded. We will see, however, concern with and references to religious knowledge continue throughout Kierkegaard's authorship. Christensen argues that Kierkegaard "emphasizes that God is present in human consciousness" (Christensen, 59), and Kierkegaard's pseudonym Johannes de Silentio does indeed refer to human beings as having an "eternal consciousness" that he associates with the love of God.[5]

It would appear Kierkegaard believes the idea that there is a God is built into human consciousness. Precisely *how* this is so is something he does not directly address. It seems safe to assume that it is simply part of the way that consciousness itself is constructed.[6] It might be associated with a person's appreciation that his is a finite, or limited, form of rationality. It might be roughly equivalent to a kind of Schleiermachean feeling of absolute dependence. There are a number of ways the idea that there is a God may be understood to be part of the contents of human consciousness. What is important, in this context, is not accounting for the presence of this idea in consciousness but providing an account of how the mere idea that there is a God is translated, according to Kierkegaard, into knowledge that there is a God.

"Eternally understood, one does not *believe* that there is a God," asserts Johannes Climacus, "even though one assumes that there is. This is a misuse of language. Socrates did not have faith that there was a God. What he knew about God he achieved through recollection" (C, 153). This reference to recollection recurs in Kierkegaard's journals where he observes that both proving that there is a God and being convinced of this by proofs are "equally fantastic,"

> for just as no one has ever proven it, so has there never been an atheist, even though there certainly have been many who have been unwilling to let what they knew get control of their minds. . . . With respect to the existence [*Tilværelsen*] of God, immortality, etc., in short with respect to all problems of immanence, recollection applies; it exists altogether in everyone only he does not know it. (JP, 3:3606)

The question is, how does recollection work according to Kierkegaard? The doctrine of recollection, according to Plato, is that all knowledge is implicitly

---

[4] "*Everything Is New In Christ.* This will be my position for a speculative Christian epistemology. (New not merely insofar as it is different but also as the relationship of the renewed, the rejuvenated, to the obsolescent, the obsolete)" (JP, 2:2277).

[5] FT, 48.

[6] See, e.g., SUD, 13; C, 153; and SV XII, 285.

part of the contents of a person's consciousness. People are understood to have had other lives during which they attained knowledge of all there was to know or to have had an eternal existence that preceded their temporal one in which they were in contact with eternal unchanging truth. This implicit knowledge may be made explicit, so the theory goes, through a process of recollection.[7] It is clear, however, that Kierkegaard is attributing neither multiple lives to people nor an eternal existence that precedes their temporal one; thus it is reasonable to ask in what sense he is using the expression "recollection."

Meno's slave is depicted in Plato's dialogue as coming to know something about geometry as a result of recollection, but he is also able (or at least potentially able) to demonstrate the truth of what he knows in a way one is not, according to Kierkegaard, able to demonstrate that there is a God. According to Kierkegaard, however, the fact that a person cannot demonstrate the truth of the claim that there is a God does not appear to deprive him of certainty concerning the correspondence of his idea that there is a God to reality.

Knowledge that there is a God is obtained, according to Kierkegaard, by a person's willing to be convinced of this. This is accomplished by allowing oneself to be immersed in the idea that there is a God.[8] Johannes Climacus argues, however, that this God, the idea of which is part of the contents of consciousness, "is not a name but a concept" (C, 114). The certainty of the knower that his belief that there is a God corresponds to reality is possible because the reality in question is conceptual reality. That is, the agreement here between thought and being that constitutes truth according to Kierkegaard is just as tautological as was the case with ontological and mathematical knowledge.

The reality in question is mere conceptual reality, which means that, objectively, all we can be said to know is that the idea of God has reality as *an idea*. When Kierkegaard argues, however, that one assumes there is a God, he means more than that one assumes the idea that there is a God has reality as an idea. Slotty claims, for example, that even though Kierkegaard acknowledges that "how one is oneself has an essential influence on one's mental representation of God . . . he felt he was presented with religious realities that existed independently of this subjective contribution" (Slotty, 63). This view is supported by Vigilius Haufniensis' assertion that "[e]very

---

[7] Both this articulation of Plato's theory of recollection and the question of whether it is actually appropriate to attribute the theory to Plato at all are problematic. These are not, however, issues with which the present work is concerned.

[8] See, e.g., JP, 3:3606.

human life is religiously designed [*lagt religieust an*]" and that "[t]o want to deny this confuses everything" (CA, 105).[9]

Kierkegaard does not believe that the idea of God is the product of human thought or that knowledge that there is a God is equivalent to the appreciation that the idea of God has reality as an idea. "The philosophers think," argues Kierkegaard,

> that all knowledge, yes, even the existence [*Tilværelsen*] of the deity, is something human beings produce themselves and that revelation can be referred to only in a figurative sense in somewhat the same sense as one may say that rain falls down from heaven, since rain is nothing but earth-produced mist; but they forget to keep the metaphor, that in the beginning God separated the waters of the heavens and of the earth and that there is something higher than the *atmosphere*. (JP, 2:2266)[10]

According to Kierkegaard, the idea that there is a God was placed among the contents of human consciousness by God himself. The difficulty is that the presence of the idea in a person's consciousness says nothing about how it came to be there.

What is important in this context is that, according to Kierkegaard, the idea that there is a God is not irrelevant to the existence of the person whose idea it is. That is, a person is not indifferent to this idea. It is at this point far from apparent, however, what sort of significance the idea has. That it is significant, however, is implied in Kierkegaard's observation that people are unwilling to let it "get control of their minds" (JP, 3:3606). It is in this reference to the potential that the idea that there is a God has to get control of the mind of the knower that we will find the key, I believe, to understanding how this idea is translated, according to Kierkegaard, into knowledge.

Subjective knowledge proper, like objective knowledge in the strict sense, is associated by Kierkegaard with psychological certainty. To the extent, however, that all subjective knowledge is prescriptive, the certainty of the knower that a given mental representation corresponds to reality will, as I explained above, be inexorably intertwined with his appreciation of the subjective necessity of the correspondence of, or conformity of, his existence to the substance of this representation.

"The thought of God's existence [*Tilværelsen*]," asserts Vigilius Haufniensis, "when it is posited as such for the individual's freedom, has an

---

[9] Compare this remark to, e.g., FT, 15.

[10] I have altered the translation slightly. The Hongs have "man" where I have "human beings." The Danish term in question is "*Menneskeheden*," which is properly translated as "humanity" or "human beings."

omnipresence . . . [and] [t]o live in beautiful intimate companionship with this conception [*Frestilling*] truly requires inwardness" (CA, 140). That is, the thought that there is a God, that is, an omnipotent, omniscient creator of the universe, brings with it an impression of obligation relative to this God. That the God in question is an idea (*Forestilling*) is unimportant to the extent that it engenders an impression of duty or obligation of which the knowing subject cannot rid himself. It is possible, that is, for a person to be uncertain as to whether there really is a God while at the same time having a relatively well-defined idea of what kind of behavior God, if he existed, would require of people and to feel such a strong obligation to conform his behavior to what he imagines would be these requirements that he would say something on the order of "there ought to be a God," even if it turned out there was not one. I know several people like this, and there are probably many more who hold such a view but who would be unable to articulate it in this way. In fact, many people who profess to believe in God are more properly described as holding such a view to the extent that they are aware that it is impossible to prove God's existence objectively and would not claim to have had a personal encounter with God.

The impression that one has a duty to God is equivalent to the impression of the necessity of bringing one's existence into conformity with what would appear to be the divine will. That is, to have the impression that one has a duty to God is to have an impression of the necessity of the correspondence of one's existence to one's mental representation of the substance of God's will.

A duty is essentially subjective in that it prescribes the character of the existence of the knower. This can be seen, according to Kierkegaard, even in the language we use to talk about duties. "I never say of a man," Kierkegaard's pseudonym Judge Wilhelm observes, "He is doing duty or duties; but I say: He is doing *his* duty; I say: I am doing my duty, do *your* duty" (EO II, 263; emphasis added). "Everyone has his duty," observes Hügli, "and no one can tell another person what his duty is. This is what makes each person an individual" (Hügli, 156). But to say that a duty is essentially subjective is to argue that it is necessarily related to the subject's appreciation of it as such. That is, for a person to fail, so to speak, to appreciate that he has a duty of a particular sort is not to have such a duty in that one can be made responsible only for fulfilling a duty one appreciated as such.[11] By the same logic,

[11] See, e.g., Hügli, 155. It is, of course, possible to make people legally responsible for things they may not have known they were responsible for on the grounds that they ought to have known. The issue in this context, however, is not the responsibility a person may have to make sure he is sufficiently informed concerning his obligations but the responsibility a

to have an impression of an obligation of a particular sort is equivalent to being obligated in this way. That is, to the extent a person cannot rid himself of this impression, he will experience a feeling of approval or disapproval, depending on whether he has succeeded, or failed, to realize the substance of what he believed to be his duty. To be unable to rid oneself of the impression of an obligation of a particular sort is thus to justify the feeling of approval or disapproval associated with the success or failure to fulfill this obligation. That is, to have realized the substance of what one believed to have been one's duty is to have done what one believed one ought to have done and thus to merit approval, whereas to fail to do what one believed one ought to have done is to merit disapproval.

We saw in chapters 3 and 4 that, according to Kierkegaard, there were two senses in which a mental representation of objective reality could be justified. When, as was the case with immanent metaphysical knowledge, the knower was understood to be immediately related to the reality to which his mental representation referred, the justification of it was equivalent to his appreciation of the objective necessity of its correspondence to reality. This necessity, as we saw, was associated with the inconceivability that the representation in question could fail to correspond to reality. The justification of a mental representation of actuality, on the other hand, was associated with an appreciation of the apparent probability of its correspondence to reality.

The question we must address now concerns the nature of the subjective conviction Kierkegaard argues people have that they have a duty to God. Is this feeling the result of an appreciation of the necessity of the correspondence of the mental representation in question to reality, or is it the result of the impression of the probability of such correspondence? Kierkegaard's answer must be the former. That is, to conceive of not having such a duty— that is, of there not being a God, for the idea of God implies the duty in question—would be equivalent to conceiving one's existence as devoid of this impression of duty, or actually to rid oneself of this impression in the activity of conceiving of one's existence without it, and this, on Kierkegaard's view, is impossible. That is, an individual always possesses an impression of this responsibility,[12] even if he is engaged in the activity of obscuring it from himself, or of calculating "exactly what he needs to keep safely in the state in which his consciousness does not disturbingly awaken" (JFY, 117).

To be unable to rid oneself of the impression that one has a duty to God thus means that, subjectively, one really does have such a duty and that the

---

person has, according to Kierkegaard, not to flee from his knowledge of these obligations or not to deceive himself concerning the substance of his duty to God and his fellow human beings.

[12] See, e.g., SE, 34; and JP, 1:230.

correspondence of the mental representation that one has such a duty to reality is subjectively necessary. The appreciation of this necessity is equivalent to psychological certainty in the same sense that the appreciation of the objective necessity of the correspondence of a given mental representation to reality was equivalent to such certainty. That the necessity in question is subjective is entirely in order, in that the knowledge with which it is associated is subjective knowledge.

To be certain, in this way, that one has a duty to God is to be certain that there is a God, or to be certain that this idea corresponds to reality in the sense that it is inconceivable that it does not so correspond. This is presumably what Kierkegaard means when he says, "I do not believe that there is a God, but I know it" (JP, 3:3085). That is, I know there is a God in that I am convinced I have a duty to this God, the idea of whom is part of the contents of my consciousness. We are certain that the mental representation that there is a God whom we have a duty to obey corresponds to reality because we are immediately related to the reality of this duty, and thus of God, through our impression of this responsibility.

Knowledge that there is a God would thus appear equivalent to the justified true mental representation that there is a God in the sense that the knower is certain he has an obligation relative to the idea of God that is part of the contents of his consciousness. This is to say that the mental representation that he has such a duty is justified by his appreciation of the truth of this representation in the sense of the necessity of its correspondence to reality.

The difficulty with this account of the knowledge that there is a God is that it would appear to make truth the property of the mental representation that there is a God, whereas I argued above that subjective truth cannot be the property of a mental representation as such but is the property of the existence of the knower. That is, the agreement in question between thought and being that constitutes truth must ultimately be established in being—that is, in the conformity of the existence of the knower to his mental representation that he has a duty to God. If the subject does not bring his existence into conformity with this mental representation, then he can be said to "disagree" with it.

It is because the knowledge that there is a God is inexorably intertwined with the subjective impression that one has a duty to God that it properly belongs to the realm of subjective knowledge on Kierkegaard's view. That is, knowledge that there is a God is indistinguishable from the knower's impression that there is something God wants from him and is thus essentially related to his existence as such. It might be argued that what God wants is not so clear. According to Kierkegaard, however, not only are we always aware, to some degree or other, that we have a religious duty, but also we are always aware, to some degree or other, of what this duty is. That is, the Socratic principle, asserts Anti-Climacus, that one does not knowingly do wrong is correct in that "sin has its roots in the will, not knowledge [*Erkjendelsen*], and this corruption of the will affects the individual's consciousness" (SUD, 95).[13] This corruption of the will affects a person's consciousness, according to Kierkegaard, in that it facilitates the dialectic of self-deception. Self-deception may, in turn, be carried out on such a scale that it becomes difficult to distinguish whether the person in question did, in fact, know what he ought to have done.[14]

"Every person," asserts Kierkegaard, "always knows the truth a good deal farther out than he expresses it existentially" (JP, 1:230). A person's failure to express in his existence what he "knows," on some level, he ought to express is not due to an inadequacy in his mental representation of the substance of this duty but to a weakness of the will.[15] Kierkegaard is compelled to assume a person knows his religious duty in the same sense that he has an adequate mental representation of this duty because this is the only way he can be held responsible for doing it.

But subjective truth cannot be a property of a mental representation. To the extent that the knowledge that there is a God is inexorably intertwined with the impression that one has a duty to God, this knowledge is prescriptive, and the truth to which it relates must be instantiated in the existence of the knower as a result of his having brought his existence into conformity with his mental representation of his duty. But if truth, in this context, is equivalent to the conformity of the knower to his mental representation of his duty to God, in what sense can he be said to know the truth farther out than he expresses it? That is, it appears we must retain a concept of truth that is the property of mental representations rather than of the existence of the knower, if Kierkegaard is not to contradict himself.

Again, truth is an agreement between thought and being, or between ideality and reality. There is a sense, however, in which one can speak of degrees of agreement. That is, the knower can be understood to establish an agreement between thought and being not merely in that he brings his existence into complete conformity with the mental representation in question but also in the sense that he can be said to approximate (*tilnærme*) such

---

[13] I have altered the translation slightly. The Hongs have "willing" and "knowing" where I have "the will" and "knowledge." The expressions are nouns in the original Danish.

[14] See, e.g., SUD, 88–89.

[15] See JP, 1:230.

conformity through the acceptance that he ought to feel guilty whenever he fails to establish complete conformity. The acceptance that he ought to feel guilty if he failed to establish such conformity is an act on the part of the knower. Such acceptance represents the canceled possibility of self-deception in the sense that while it is not possible, according to Kierkegaard, for a person to fail to appreciate that he becomes guilty to the extent that he fails to behave in the way he believes he ought to have behaved, it is possible to reject that one ought to feel guilty to the extent that he can endeavor to deceive himself with respect to his guilt.[16]

A person is said to be certain of the correspondence of his mental representation that there is a God to reality to the extent that he appreciates the subjective necessity of the correspondence of his existence to God's laws. This appreciation must, however, be the product of the latter correspondence.[17] A person cannot be said to appreciate the necessity of bringing his existence into conformity with God's law if he fails to do this. The acceptance, however, that one ought to feel guilty for failing to establish such conformity constitutes just such an agreement between reality and thought that was defined by Kierkegaard as truth. That is, to accept that one ought to feel guilty for failing to bring his existence into conformity with his religious duty is to agree with the reality of this duty and is thus the first step down the path of the fulfillment of this duty.

That the agreement between thought and being that constitutes subjective truth admits of degrees, in a sense in which the agreement between thought and being which constitutes objective truth does not, will turn out to be essential for understanding the nature of the former. That is, there is an important sense, as we will see, in which a person can never be entirely successful in bringing his existence into conformity with ethical-religious ideality. This does not mean, however, that the degree to which a person expresses truth is a matter of indifference. To come no closer to an expression of subjective truth than to accept that one ought to feel guilty for failing to conform one's existence to ethical-religious ideality is precisely to condemn oneself. According to Kierkegaard, "most terrible of all that one should have known everything, and not have begun to do the least" (CS, 18).[18] For "[t]he point," according to Kierkegaard, "is that where there is

[16] Compare this to Hannay's contention that the purpose of Kierkegaard's psychological works "is to offer an account of human life and its interests in which even the apparently most rational denials of a transcendent source of personal value are to be interpreted as an expression of a deep-seated dread, of fear of the very notion itself" (Hannay, 169).

[17] See, e.g., Hügli, 228.

[18] I have chosen the wording here of David Swenson's translation because I believe it is clearer than the Hongs'. The relevant passage in the Hongs' translation in on p. 22 of TDIO.

a deficiency in knowledge the truth does not, after all, become a charge against one's character, but where knowledge is present, then the truth becomes criminal" (JP, 4:4237).

I mentioned above that, according to Kierkegaard, not only are people assumed to know they have a duty to God, they are assumed to know in what precisely this duty consists. This duty will turn out to be indistinguishable from a person's ethical duty. Before proceeding, however, to an examination of the nature of a person's ethical-religious duty, we must look briefly at another type of immanent metaphysical knowledge, which, according to Kierkegaard, is essentially related to the existence of the knower.

Part of immanent metaphysical reality, according to Kierkegaard, concerns the nature of the knower himself. The self as an object of knowledge, however, is not entirely unproblematic. A human being has, again, what Johannes Climacus refers to as an "eternally established essence [*evigt anlagte Væsen*]" (CUP, 490), but his existence, as we saw earlier in this chapter, is not actually according to his essence. What characterizes his existence only accidentally rather than essentially would not appear, according to Kierkegaard, to be an object of knowledge for him. Sin, as we saw, is considered by Kierkegaard to be a contingent characteristic of human existence. That is, it does not belong to a person's eternally established essence but was something he appropriated through a free action. It is for this reason Anti-Climacus maintains that "a person [*Mennesket*] has to learn what sin is by a revelation from God" (SUD, 95).[19]

But if, according to Kierkegaard, a person cannot know he is a sinner, there are other things he can know about himself. Or, more precisely, there are things he is not merely able to know, but that, in a sense, he is assumed already to know. A person knows, for example, according to Kierkegaard, that he has a soul. It would appear that the idea that he has a soul, like the idea that there is a God, is part of the contents of the consciousness of the knower. Knowledge that one has a soul is somewhat different, however, from knowledge that there is a God. The soul, according to Kierkegaard, is one half of the synthesis that composes the knower. The Danish word for "soul," *Sjæl*, is similar in meaning to the English "intellect."[20] Knowledge that one has a soul is thus like knowledge that there is a God to the extent that the correspondence of the mental representation that one has a soul to reality is not established through objective demonstration but is the result of the subject's immersing himself in the contents of his consciousness. Certainty of this correspondence derives, again, from the tautological

---

[19] This, as we will see, is one of the differences between sin and guilt.
[20] See, e.g., Ferrall and Repp., Molbech, and Vinterberg and Bodelsen.

character of the representation. The tautology in question is of a different sort, however, than that associated with the belief that there is a God. That is, the correspondence of the idea that there is a God to reality was tautological because the reality in question was merely thought reality. The reality of the soul is also only thought reality, but in this instance it is not a particular thought reality; it is the subject's own reality as a thinking being. That the idea that he exists (*er til*) as a thinking being could fail to correspond to reality is inconceivable. Indeed, to try to conceive it, as Descartes famously pointed out, is to involve the subject in a self-contradiction. Such correspondence is thus necessary according to what one could call the rules of thought.

Self-knowledge in this context, however, is not restricted to knowledge that one exists as a thinking being. Knowledge of "immortality" also appears, according to Kierkegaard, to belong to the realm of immanent metaphysical knowledge.[21] The idea that the soul, or intellect, is immortal may be part of the contents of the consciousness of the subject to the extent that he is inclined to associate generation and destruction with physical, or tangible, being. The correspondence of the mental representation that the soul is immortal to reality is necessary in the sense that the individual cannot conceive of himself as not existing as a thinking being. Every such effort is doomed in the sense the he must use thought in order to conceive his own nonbeing, but to the extent that he uses thought, he is affirming his existence as a thinking being. The reality to which the mental representation that the soul is immortal corresponds is thought reality. The correspondence in question is thus nothing other than the self-identity of the individual's inability to conceive of himself as not existing as a thinking being.

Just as was the case, however, with the idea that there was a God, the idea that one has a soul is not obviously significant with respect to what it means to exist. That is, to the extent that this idea appears equivalent to the idea that the knower exists as a thinking being, it would not appear to impose any responsibilities on him—i.e., it would not appear prescriptive in the way I asserted earlier that all subjective knowledge was. Yet Vigilius Haufniensis asserts that the thought of the soul's immortality "possesses a weightiness in its consequences, a responsibility in the acceptance of it which perhaps will transform the whole of life in a way that is feared" (CA, 139).[22]

---

[21] See, e.g., Hannay's claim that "Kierkegaard's despairer proper is one who in some sense *knows* . . . that death is not the end" (Hannay, 33).

[22] I have altered the translation here slightly. The Hongs have "recreate" where I have "transform." The Danish expression in question is "*omskabe*," which Ferrall and Repp. translate as "remodel." "Remodel" is somewhat awkward, however, thus I have chosen "transform," which, I believe, preserves the sense of "remodel."

It would appear that it is only when the idea that there is a God is brought into relation to the idea that one has a soul that this latter knowledge has a prescriptive dimension.

The knowledge that there is a God is, again, inexorably intertwined with the impression that one has a duty to God. The full import of this becomes clear, however, only when it is brought into relation to the idea that one has a soul.[23] That is, the necessity of bringing one's existence into conformity with God's law is apparent in the formulation "you shall!" The failure to live up to this demand is, according to Kierkegaard, the failure to exist according to one's eternally established essence, which, as we saw in the preceding chapter, is in an important sense to fail to exist at all. This perspective is, however, as we will presently see, more ethical than it is religious, to the extent, that is, that the two can be distinguished for Kierkegaard. The idea that one has an immortal soul, which, when brought into relation to the knowledge that there is a God, means, in fact, more than that if one fails to bring his existence into conformity with God's law, then he will fail to exist in an authentic sense. It means that one will be subject to God's eternal disapprobation. That is, such failure will consign one to eternal damnation.[24]

Just as the certainty that one's mental representation that there was a God corresponded to reality was inexorably intertwined with an appreciation of the subjective necessity of the correspondence of the reality—that is, actuality—of one's existence to God's law, so is the certainty that the mental representation that one has an immortal soul corresponds to reality inexorably intertwined with an appreciation of the subjective necessity of the correspondence of the reality of one's existence to God's law. To the extent that this knowledge is essentially subjective, according to Kierkegaard, the truth with which it is associated is something that must be expressed in the existence of the knower. Just as was the case, however, with the knowledge that there was a God, the agreement here between reality and ideality, or between being and thought, that constitutes truth admits of degrees. That is, such agreement is not linked to the absolute conformity of the knower to his mental representation of the substance of God's law but may also be approached (*tilnærmet*) in the sense that he accepts that the failure to establish such conformity means he ought to be consigned to eternal damnation. To accept that one ought to be consigned to eternal damnation is to agree with the substance of God's law. Such acceptance is thus the first step down the path toward the actualization of this law.

[23] See CA, 138–39.
[24] See UDVS, 82–83; CD, 230, 292; and JP, 2:1638.

Kierkegaard rarely refers, however, to the necessity of obeying God's law in order to avoid eternal damnation. It is primarily the necessity of such obedience for the positive objective of attaining authentic human existence, or of becoming a self, that is his concern. Such an objective belongs to what Kierkegaard calls the ethical-religious sphere.

"Kierkegaard's psychology," observes Hannay, "flatly acknowledges the reality of ethics and attempts no scientific explanation of it" (Hannay, 160). Subjective immanent metaphysical knowledge thus encompasses not merely knowledge that there is a God and knowledge that one had a soul but also knowledge of eternally valid norms for human behavior.[25] To the extent that these norms are eternally valid, they are essentially the same, according to Kierkegaard, in both paganism and Christianity.[26] This is why Socrates is such an important figure for Kierkegaard. That is, Socrates is the paradigm of the ethical individual, according to Kierkegaard, in that although he "was surely a thinking person, . . . he placed all other knowledge in [the sphere of] indifference, infinitely accentuating ethical knowledge, which relates to the existing subject infinitely interested in existence" (CUP, 266).

According to Kierkegaard, however, there are two conceptions of ethics in that it is possible to consider ethical norms independently of the specific significance they receive when placed into relation to Christianity. Ethics considered in this way, Vigilius Haufniensis asserts, "points to ideality as a task and presumes that everyone possesses the requisite conditions (CA, 16).[27] This view of ethics founders, however, according to Kierkegaard, on the individual's sinfulness. That is, ethics, or what one could call the moral law, demands that a person be perfect, yet people cannot live up to this demand.[28] That is, while "speculative philosophy breaks down when it believes that, with the help of thought, it can deduce historical actuality from ideality, ethics breaks down when it believes it can actualize ideality through action" (Hügli, 222).[29] Dogmatics comes to the aid of ethics, however, with the concept of hereditary sin. Thus religious ethics, or "the new ethics[,] presupposes dogmatics and with it hereditary sin, . . . while at the same time it sets ideality as the task" (CA, 20).[30] It is in this way that ethical

[25] See, e.g., Malantschuk, *Nøglebegreber*, 44–45; and Hannay, 158.

[26] See CA, 20–21.

[27] See Hügli, 218.

[28] Compare this to Hannay's observation that Kierkegaard's "objection to traditional ethics [is] that it finds no real place for sin; that it assumes that persons are naturally capable of realizing whatever ideality reason dictates, and fails to appreciate that the significance of sin is its denial of this assumption" (Hannay, 170).

[29] See also FT 98–99; and Slotty, 69.

[30] I have altered the translation slightly. The Danish reads "*Den nye Ethik forudsætter*

duty becomes inseparable for Kierkegaard from religious duty. That is, ethical duty becomes religious duty.[31]

Ethically, asserts Johannes Climacus, "the individual has an infinite interest solely in his own actuality" (CUP, 271), and this actuality is, in turn, his infinite interest in existing according to ethical ideality.[32] To live ethically is thus to strive to bring one's existence into conformity with eternally valid ethical norms. Or, as Hügli expresses it, "The meaning of ethical action consists solely in my efforts to infuse my life with ideality" (Hügli, 229).[33] To instantiate these norms, according to Climacus, is to become actual, or to become "revealed before God" (CUP, 132), and to be revealed before God is equivalent to being "a whole human being" (CUP, 290).[34]

The ethical is not merely action, however; it is also a kind of knowledge that is related to action.[35] That is, in order to be able to do the good, a person must know what the good is.[36] The knower must thus be assumed to have an accurate mental representation of eternally valid ethical norms, just as he was assumed to have a mental representation that there was a God. "[T]here is no question," explains Hannay, "of 'teaching' the distinction between good and bad, for this comes of itself with the positing of spirit" (Hannay, 227). The consciousness of the knower must be assumed to be essentially characterized by an impression that he has a duty to God as well as by the impression of precisely in what this duty consists.[37]

Thus Kierkegaard argues that "the thing which a person [*et Menneske*] ought to do is always easy to understand . . . infinitely easy to understand" (JP, 3L:2874). That is, it is easy for a person to understand his ethical obligations—these obligations are equivalent to his subjective impression of what he ought to do. If this were not the case, then the ethical would be only

---

Dogmatik og med den Arvesynden." The Hongs have mistakenly attached "*og med den Arvesynden*" to the next clause of the sentence.

[31] See, e.g., CUP, 114, 257; and Hügli, 150.

[32] See CUP, 272.

[33] See also Hügli, 280.

[34] The ideas of God as well as a person's relationship to God are so bound up together, according to Kierkegaard, with what it means to be a human being that he argues that "to do away with God is to cease to be human" (CD, 38).

[35] See CUP, 134.

[36] See EUD, 361–62; and Hügli, 230. See also Hannay's observation that "it is assumed throughout ["Purity of Heart"] that the reader has a correct theoretical notion of what he aspires to" (Hannay, 228).

[37] Kierkegaard is careful to explain, however, that the fact that the individual has, so to speak, his teleology in himself in the sense that it is built into the contents of his consciousness does not mean that he "is sufficient unto himself [*er det centrale*]" (EO II, 274).

hypothetically valid. That is, *if* a person knew what he ought to do, *then* he would be responsible for doing it. Whereas *if* a person *did not know* what he ought to do, then he would not be responsible for doing it. But one is always responsible, according to Kierkegaard, for behaving ethically, because the ethical, as Climacus contends, is "the absolute" (CUP, 118). "The most limited poor creature," argues Kierkegaard, "cannot truly deny being able to understand this requirement" (FSE, 35).[38]

The correspondence of a person's mental representation of his ethical, or religious, duty to the reality of this duty is necessary in that it is impossible for there to be a discrepancy between his subjective impression of his duty and the reality of that duty. A person is responsible for doing only what he knows he ought to do.[39]

To argue, however, that the consciousness of the knower is essentially characterized by an impression of his ethical-religious duty is not equivalent to arguing that the substance of this duty can never become obscure. It is possible for a person to deceive himself with respect to his duty. To the extent that the consciousness of the knower is essentially characterized by an impression of his ethical-religious duty, self-deception cannot consist in willed ignorance of it but must consist in the efforts of this subject to deceive himself with respect to whether he has succeeded in fulfilling it.[40]

Just as was the case, however, with knowledge that there was a God, a mental representation of the substance of one's ethical-religious duty, viewed independently of its actualization, cannot be said to be true. That is, to the extent that this knowledge is essentially prescriptive, the agreement between the mental representation in question and reality that constitutes truth consists not in the correspondence of this representation to reality but in the knower's having brought his existence into conformity with the substance of the prescriptions. A person, explains Hügli, "is only in the truth to the extent that he has ideality in himself" (Hügli, 200).

Just as was the case, however, with knowledge that there was a God and knowledge that one had an immortal soul, it is possible to speak here of degrees of agreement. To agree that one is responsible for behaving in a certain way is not merely equivalent to behaving in this way. It is also equivalent to the acceptance that one ought to behave in this way in the sense that one accepts the guilt that is consequent upon one's failure to do this. That is, to accept guilt is to acknowledge that one failed to act as one ought to have acted. To accept one's guilt is thus to agree with the substance

[38] See JFY, 118.
[39] See JP, 4:4237.
[40] See JFY, 157–58.

of ethical-religious ideality in the sense that one brings one's existence into conformity with that ideality in this act of contrition.

It is only after the existence of a person can itself be identified with ethical-religious ideality that he can be said to have knowledge of this ideality. That is, his certainty that his mental representation of this ideality corresponds to reality is equivalent to his appreciation of the subjective necessity of the correspondence of his existence to the substance of this representation. This appreciation is a direct result, however, of his decision to accept that he is guilty when he fails to bring his existence into conformity with it.[41] Thus his certainty that his mental representation of ethical-religious ideality corresponds to reality is, once again, "a performative product of [his] . . . decision" (Hannay, 46) to accept his guilt.[42]

Living ethically-religiously requires more, however, than knowledge of ethical-religious ideality. That is, a person has, again, what Kierkegaard refers to as "a lower nature" (SUD, 94) that sees this knowledge as a threat and that is thus inclined in the direction away from recognizing it. To live ethically-religiously involves a self-control, or autonomy, that is essentially related to a different sort of self-knowledge than that which belongs under the heading of immanent metaphysical knowledge.

Subjective Knowledge of Actuality

Existence itself, according to Kierkegaard, like consciousness, is an *inter-esse* between ideality and actuality.[43] Objectively, this situation makes knowledge of actuality possible in only a loose sense. That is, knowledge, in the ordinary sense, is the result of the contemplation of reality, and contemplation is an activity of thought, the medium of which is ideality. This, as we saw, posed no problem for ontological and mathematical knowledge since the objects of such knowledge were themselves idealities—that is, abstractions. Actuality, on the other hand, is concrete. Thus when the object of contemplation was actuality, because our relation to actuality is mediated by thought, the categories of which are abstract, the closest we could come to an appreciation of actuality was to approximate it.

We cannot even know what Climacus refers to as our "historical externality" (CUP, 482), except in a loose sense. The only actuality to which

---

[41] This is the reason Hügli argues that "the ethical telos cannot be known objectively" (Hügli, 123).

[42] Thus Hügli argues that "the ethical is not an object of knowledge but of the will" (Hügli, 161).

[43] See chapter 2 above. See also CUP, 276; and Hügli, 57.

we can have an immediate relation, according to Kierkegaard, is our own individual ethical actuality.[44] But an immediate relation of this sort has a different kind of cognitive significance than that of the relations mediated by thought. The relation itself is not a cognitive one. It generates knowledge, but this knowledge is distinct from objective knowledge. That is, objective knowledge is obtained by abstracting from one's subjective experience or by directing one's attention not toward oneself but toward an object that has no essential relation to oneself, while subjective knowledge is the result of attention being directed toward one's subjective experience as such.

Subjective knowledge of actuality is problematic in a way that differs, however, from the way objective knowledge of actuality was problematic. An individual's knowledge of his own actuality appears to follow directly from experience; hence it appears easy to attain. The difficulty with this knowledge appears to relate to sustaining rather than attaining it.

Kierkegaard argues that "[i]nsofar as the ethical could be said to have knowledge in itself, it is 'self-knowledge'" (JP, 1:653). We saw above that self-knowledge consists in part in the knowledge that one has a soul. Kierkegaard argues, however, "[t]hat to know what a human soul is, . . . is still a long way from beginning to gain one's soul in patience" (EUD, 172) and that "if a person is to gain his soul, then he certainly must know [*kjende*] it before he begins," but that "this knowing [*Erkjenden*] would still be only . . . the condition for being able to gain his soul in patience" (EUD, 173). It is the latter, however, that constitutes a person's ethical development. That is, for a person to acquire his soul is synonymous with his bringing the actuality of his existence into conformity with ethical-religious ideality.

I asserted in the preceding section that in order for a person to be able to bring his existence into conformity with eternally valid ethical norms he had to have a great deal more self-knowledge than that which belongs to the realm of immanent metaphysical knowledge. That is, human beings, according to Kierkegaard, have a "lower nature" that is resistant to accepting these norms and that thus represents an obstacle to the objective of attaining such conformity. "It is very difficult to extricate oneself," argues Kierkegaard,

> from the lower conceptual sphere [*Forestillingskreds*], and the pact of earthly passions with the illusions. Just when one has understood the truth best, the old suddenly crops up again. The infinite, the eternal, hence the true, is so alien to the natural man that with him it is as with the dog, which can indeed learn to walk upright for a moment but yet continually wants to walk on all fours. (WOL, 244)

[44] See CUP, 482.

We saw in chapter 2 that all coming to be, according to Kierkegaard, is a suffering, and we now know that the becoming that primarily concerned him was that of the self. The self comes to be as a result of a person's efforts to bring his existence into conformity with eternally valid ethical norms. That is, to become a self is to actualize ethical ideality in one's existence. Kierkegaard argues, however, that only through suffering can the eternal come together with the temporal.[45] Part of this suffering concerns the fact that the purely animal aspect, or lower nature, of human beings is, in a sense, sacrificed to the higher nature in this synthesis. "To serve the idea," asserts Kierkegaard, "is to be tortured, to be martyred . . . —otherwise the idea cannot be brought out of the synthesis which a human being [*Mennesket*] is, since in one sense he is a human animal [*Dyre-Mennesket*]" (JP, 4:3834). That is, to accept eternally valid ethical norms as such is to subordinate one's will to these norms even when one's natural inclination is opposed to them. This is why Kierkegaard argues that "everyone is more or less afraid of the truth; and this is being human for the truth is related to being 'spirit'—and this is very hard for flesh and blood. . . . Between a human being and the truth lies dying to the world—this, you see, is why we are all more or less afraid" (Pap. XI³ A 614).

But if a person is assumed to know the truth, the question becomes, how does he avoid acting on this knowledge without becoming guilty in his own eyes? We've already seen the answer, but it will perhaps help to look at it again. When one understands something, observes Kierkegaard, "it takes ages before there is action" (SE, 120), and this is precisely the problem. It is this delay that provides the lower nature with an opportunity to keep the person from doing something his lower nature would rather avoid. "If a person," asserts Anti-Climacus,

[d]oes not do what is right at the very second he knows it—then first of all knowledge simmers down. Next comes the question of how the will appraises what is known. The will is dialectical and has under it the entire lower nature of man, if this does not agree with what is known, then it does not follow that the will goes out and does the opposite of what knowledge has understood (presumably such strong opposites are rare); rather the will allows some time to elapse, an interim called "we shall look at it tomorrow." During all this, knowledge becomes more and more obscure, and the lower nature gains the upper hand more and more. . . . And this is how perhaps the great majority of men live; they work gradually at eclipsing their ethical and ethical-religious knowledge which would lead them out into decisions and conclusions that their lower nature does not much care for. (SUD, 94)[46]

---

[45] See JP, 4:4712; and JP, 2:1447.

[46] There is, unfortunately, a mistake in the Hongs' translation. The translation reads, "Willing is dialectical and has under it the entire lower nature of man. If willing does not

A person must acquire knowledge of both his higher and his lower nature if there is to be any hope of his being able to bring his existence into conformity with ethical ideality. He must learn to use the former against the latter. This task is specific to each individual not merely because it is prerequisite to genuine ethical development but because people vary in respect of how these two aspects of human nature present themselves. Some people may find that their lower nature is inclined to present itself with particular force and frequency, whereas other people may find that it presents itself less frequently and with less force. That is, some people, observes Kierkegaard, may be "structured more eternally" (JP, 2:1123).[47]

What is important in this context, however, is not whether a person is structured more eternally but that everyone, according to Kierkegaard, is required to become a self, or to make his life an expression of ethical-religious ideality. To succeed in this task, a person must learn to know himself so that he will be able to develop a strategy for realizing his ethical-religious duty that will address the specific challenges presented by his unique personality. "Human frailty," explains Hannay, "does not vanish [even] at the touch of a positive decision; the kinds of pressure which postpone a decision usually also contrive once it is made, to delay its consumption" (Hannay, 206). It is for this reason Anti-Climacus argues that "[t]he law for the development of the self with respect to knowing, insofar as it is the case that the self becomes itself, is

---

agree with what is known it does not necessarily follow. . . ." It is the lower nature, however, rather than the will that is the subject of this second sentence. This distinction is important, because the dialectical character of the will, according to Kierkegaard, is precisely that it has under it not merely the entire lower nature of a person, but his higher nature as well. The will is not destined to serve the lower nature in the way it does above. If it were, people could not be held responsible for allowing their lower natures to do this. The point is that a person is supposed to use his will to bring his lower nature under the control of his higher nature.

The passage that is translated by the Hongs as, "Gradually willing's objection to this development lessens; it almost appears to be in collusion," appears in Danish as, "*Saa smaat har Villien ikke noget mod, at dette skeer, den seer næsten igennem Fingre dermed.*" This translates literally as "The will gradually comes to have nothing against that this happens, it almost looks through its fingers therewith." "To look through one's fingers" is an obvious reference to the practice of children who, by putting their hands in front of their faces, pretend they do not see what is in front of them, even though there is enough space between their fingers that they are quite able to see. To the extent that the will "looks through its fingers" at the lower nature's stretching things out, it is, in fact, aware of what is going on and is thus actually, and not merely apparently, in collusion with the lower nature.

[47] My own view here is that these differences will be a combination of nature and nurture. It is sad, but I think undeniable, that some people have genetic and environmental advantages over other people in terms of their ability to fulfill what one could call the moral law.

that the increase in knowledge corresponds to the increase in self-knowledge, that the more the self knows, the more it knows itself" (SUD, 31).

The reason, according to Kierkegaard, that the only actuality there is for an individual is his own ethical actuality is that this is the only actuality to which he is immediately related. That is, it is this relation that makes genuine self-knowledge possible. This means, however, that self-knowledge in the propositional sense begins with acquaintance knowledge. There is, of course, a sense in which all propositional knowledge may be said to begin with acquaintance knowledge. This becomes particularly significant, however, with respect to subjective knowledge. It is in this context that the English translations of the Danish expressions for acquaintance knowledge (i.e., *Kjendskab*) and for "know" in the sense of to be acquainted with (i.e., *kjende*) cause problems in relation to determining the substance of Kierkegaard's epistemology.

The anonymous author, B, of the second volume of Kierkegaard's *Either/ Or* claims, for example, that "ethical knowledge is not simply contemplation, . . . [i]t is a collecting oneself [*Besiddelse*] which is itself an action" (EO II, 258).[48] This may make it appear that he equates knowing with doing, and, indeed, he has been interpreted this way.[49] It is important to appreciate, however, that the "knowledge" in question is *Kjendskab* rather than *Erkjendelsen* or *Viden*. That is, truly knowing oneself in the sense of being acquainted with oneself cannot be separated, according to Kierkegaard, from a certain kind of activity, but this "knowledge" is distinct from propositional knowledge. What is important, in this context, is that a person appreciate that while self-knowledge of the acquaintance sort is prerequisite to self-knowledge of the propositional sort, Kierkegaard never conflates the two. Though, as we have seen, genuine subjective knowledge of the propositional sort can enjoy its status as such only when it is conjoined with a particular activity on the part of the knowing subject, it is still, as knowledge, a mental representation and is thus distinguished from that activity.

A mental representation that corresponds to the actuality of the knower is crucial, according to Kierkegaard, if that person is going to be able to become a self. That is, what Anti-Climacus calls the "law for the development of the self with respect to knowledge insofar as it is the case that the self becomes itself is that the increase in knowledge corresponds to an increase in self-knowledge" (SUD, 31). The same is true with respect to Kierkegaard's claim that "[t]here is only one kind of knowledge that brings a person completely to himself—self-knowledge; this is what it means to

---

[48] See also Hügli, 177.
[49] See, e.g., Emmanuel, 139.

be sober, sheer transparency" (JFY, 105). It is necessary for a person to have a correct mental representation of himself so that he may be prepared for situations that may represent a potential for conflict between his higher and his lower nature. He must know *that* in certain situations his lower nature is inclined to represent a threat to his goal of bringing his existence into conformity with ethical-religious ideality and he must know *that* it is inclined to represent a threat in X manner and *that* the best way to counter this threat is Y.[50]

"Let us imagine," for example, offers Kierkegaard,

> a pilot, and assume that he has passed with distinction all examinations with dis-
> tinction, but as yet has not been out to sea. Imagine him in a storm: he knows
> exactly what he has to do, but he is unacquainted with the terror that grips the
> sailor when the stars disappear into the pitch darkness of the night . . . he has not
> known [*vidste*] how the blood rushes to the head when in such a moment one must
> make calculations. (TDIO, 36)[51]

After this pilot has actually piloted a ship through a storm, his knowledge will have increased. It will no longer be purely theoretical but also practical. He will have a better mental representation of what is involved in piloting a ship in that he will know what to expect, not merely in terms of what is required of him technically but in terms of his subjective response to the storm and the obstacle that it may present to his fulfilling what is required of him technically. He will be able to factor in his fear as he does the height of the waves and the speed of the wind and, eventually, be able to develop a strategy for managing it. When he has learned to anticipate and control his fear, he will have acquired the skill of piloting a ship through a storm. He will then know how to pilot a ship through a storm in a way that can be learned only by experience. He will know how to "use his knowledge" (TDIO, 36).

This kind of knowledge is often called skill knowledge and distinguished from propositional knowledge. If, in a broad sense, one could speak of this pilot as having skill knowledge rather than propositional knowledge, this skill knowledge is clearly directly related to, or a direct consequence of, the fact that he has gained a mental representation of what is required to pilot a ship through a storm that can be gained only as a result of having

---

[50] Compare this to Hannay's observation that, according to Kierkegaard, "the (Christian) ethical way of life remains 'seriously deficient' without 'adequate knowledge of human
life, and sympathy for its interests'" (Hannay, 169).

[51] The wording here is a combination of the Hongs' translation and the Swenson translation (35–36). I have combined the two in order to eliminate several inconsistencies in the
former.

had that experience. He now knows not merely that one must do X or Y in order to pilot a ship through a storm; he knows that *he* must do X and Y and Z. That is, he has developed a mental representation of what to expect from himself in terms of his subjective response to danger and how to bring it under control.

The theoretical knowledge that was imparted to the pilot during his training is related to the actual experience of piloting a ship in a manner analogous to the relation between the drawing of a landscape and the actual landscape it depicts. "The drawing, of course, cannot be as large as the country," observes Kierkegaard, "but it also becomes all the easier for the viewer to survey the outlines of that country. And yet if the viewer were suddenly set down in the actuality of that country where the many, many miles have all their force, he very likely would not be able to recognize the country, . . . or as a traveler to get his bearings" (UDVS, 72).

Such an observer, like the pilot above, may learn, however, from the experience of having to find his way about in the country in question, so that his mental representation of the country receives a new dimension. He would still possess a mental representation of the country as it appeared in the drawing and hence be able to identify it from a distance, but he would also possess a mental representation of how the details of the drawing appear to a person who is right in the middle of the country depicted and hence, he would, in the future, be able to find his way about in it.

The "actual country" in which we are all suddenly set down is existence. The philosophers, according to Kierkegaard, sketch existence, or make outlines of it that simplify it. The philosophers' categories are abstract, or general, in nature. Existence, on the other hand, is full of unique situations, and it is these situations we, as individuals, are expected to navigate. We learn to do this, according to Kierkegaard, by coming to know ourselves.[52]

The question now is whether this increase in knowledge gained by experience is separable from the experience itself, or whether it is the case that wherever the subjective is of importance in knowledge, knowing and doing are equivalent. Or to put it another way, is it proper to say that the kind of knowledge we have been looking at—that is, piloting a ship or finding one's way about in a land—is equivalent to a skill in the sense of the mere ability to do something divorced from any kind of cognitive content?

It would appear that while experience of the sort described above results in an increase in the knowledge to which it is related, knowing and doing are still distinguished. "[T]he genius," asserts Vigilius Haufniensis,

---

[52] See, e.g., CUP, 259–60.

[d]iffers from everyone else only in that he consciously begins within his historical presuppositions just as primitively as Adam did. Every time a genius is born, existence is, as it were, put to a test, because he traverses and experiences all that is past, until he catches up with himself. Therefore, the knowledge the genius has of the past is entirely different from that offered in world-historical surveys. (CA, 104–5)

Kierkegaard does not mean here that the genius has actually experienced past events but that he has become acquainted with every passion and emotion in a manner equally intense to that of any historical personage and that, hence, his mental representations of historical figures are informed by his appreciation of the nature of the experiences of those individuals. In short, he can project himself imaginatively into the situation of Caesar, or Napoleon, or any other historical figure one might wish to name, and is thus able to form a better mental representation of these individuals, or of the past in general, than are ordinary people. It is for this reason that Kierkegaard argues that knowing is related to imagination.[53]

That the subjective is of importance with respect to the knowledge the genius has of the past does not mean that knowing, according to Kierkegaard, can be equated with doing. The difficulty with equating knowing and doing is that this would amount to a conflation of thought and being, and this, as we saw, is a move to which Kierkegaard has strong objections. The essence (*Væsen*) of human beings is, again, an *inter-esse*, or a being between these two realms. But if such a division between thought and being, or between thought and action, is essential to human beings, then knowledge, to the

---

[53] "When all is said and done, whatever feeling, knowing and willing a person has depends upon what imagination he has, upon how that person reflects himself" (SUD, 31). It is important to note here that Kierkegaard does not say that the knowledge the genius has of the past is better than that which is offered in world-historical surveys. In a sense, of course, it is better because the genius is concerned not merely with historical facts but with the nature of the experience of individuals in the past, and this is as important to understanding the past as such—i.e., to understanding past events as having come about through human agency—as is knowledge of the events themselves. The reader will remember that the historian, according to Kierkegaard, is concerned not merely with determining historical fact but also with understanding how historical events came about, which is to say, he is concerned to understand those events as the result of human decisions. The difficulty is that the genius can no more be certain that his imaginative reconstruction of the experience of Caesar precisely reduplicates the experience of Caesar himself than he can be certain that, for example, Caesar's decision to cross the Rubicon was made in freedom rather than simply determined by a myriad of factors acting upon him as causes. Thus when Kierkegaard says that the genius possesses a knowledge of the past that is quite different from that offered in world-historical surveys, this "knowledge" should be understood in the same loose sense in which, according to Kierkegaard, knowledge is claimed to be represented in world-historical surveys.

extent that it retains any cognitive significance, cannot ever be straightfor-
wardly equated with action.

"It is thought in our age," observes Johannes Climacus, "that knowledge
settles everything, and that one is helped if only one acquires knowledge of
the truth, the quicker and shorter the better. But existing is something quite
other than knowing" (CUP, 249). If we look again at the two references
with which we began this section, we will see that Kierkegaard did not use
them to support a theory concerning the nature of knowledge that would
represent an alternative to the theory described in the chapter on objective
knowledge but to emphasize the difference between knowing and existing or
between knowing and doing. "Alas," observes Kierkegaard,

> contemplation and the moment of contemplation . . . easily conceal an illusion,
> because its moment has something in common with the counterfeited eternity.
> There is a foreshortening that is necessary in order for the contemplation to come
> about; it must shorten time considerably—indeed, it actually has to call the mind
> and thought away from time in order to complete itself in a counterfeit eternal
> rounding off. In this it is something like the work of an artist in drawing a map of
> a country. The drawing, of course, cannot be as large as the country; it becomes
> infinitely smaller, but it also becomes all the easier for the viewer to survey the out-
> lines of that country. And yet if that viewer were suddenly set down in the actuality
> of that country, where the many, many miles have all their force, he very likely
> would not be able to recognize the country or . . . as a traveler to get his bearings in
> it. . . . His knowledge has certainly been an illusion. What was compacted airtight,
> as it were, in the completeness of the contemplation must now be stretched out to
> its full length. (UDVS, 72)

But the knowledge that is enriched by the knower's experience, though it
is fuller and more complete than it was when he started, is still the result,
according to Kierkegaard, of his reflection on that experience and its relation to the knowledge with which he started; hence it is distinguished from
experience.

If we look again at the example of the pilot who is navigating a ship
through a storm for the first time, we see that, again, Kierkegaard did not
use the example to develop or defend a theory of knowledge where knowing and doing are identified. The difficulty with the pilot, according to
Kierkegaard, is that he "had no *conception* [*Forestilling*] of the change that
takes place in the knower when he has to apply his knowledge" (CS, 36;
emphasis added).[54] The knowledge the pilot gains by actually navigating a

---

[54] I have chosen the wording of the older Swenson-Lowrie translation here (with the
exception of the substitution of the Hongs' "use" for the former's "apply," which I have kept
for the sake of consistency) because it is more accurate. The relevant passage in the Hongs'
translation is on p. 36 of UDVS.

ship through a storm enriches his original mental representation of how to pilot a ship through a storm in a tremendously important way. He becomes acquainted with himself in the sense that he experiences how he is inclined to react in such situations so his resultant mental representation is not of how *one* is to pilot a ship through a storm but of how *he* is to do it in the sense of how he is to control his fear and keep it from having a negative influence on his calculations. It is clear, however, that the self-knowledge he has gained from this experience does not eliminate the possibility that fear will again gain the upper hand, and the persistence of this possibility shows that knowing is always distinguished from doing.

The self-knowledge that relates to the skill of piloting a ship, or finding one's way around in a land, may not appear immediately to have ethical significance, but all self-knowledge, according to Kierkegaard, is ultimately ethical knowledge.[55] How well we know ourselves affects our relations to others. The pilot of a ship, for example, is responsible for the lives of the passengers and crew. If he does not take care to learn through experience how he is inclined to react to danger, he might find himself responsible for their injury or death.

The ethical significance of the latter example is even less obvious, yet it too, according to Kierkegaard, has ethical significance. Finding oneself in an unfamiliar landscape can be confusing and disorienting. If a person allowed such confusion to get the upper hand, he might never find his way about. If the country were large and he were not alone, he might also find himself responsible for the injury of others. This may seem unlikely. What is important, however, is that this possibility, no matter how apparently remote, points out the potential ethical significance of all self-knowledge. The less well a person knows himself, the less control he has over himself and thus the greater is the potential that he will act irresponsibly. The better a person knows himself, the more control he can have over himself and thus the greater is the potential that he will act responsibly. A person's animal nature might incline him to flee in the face of danger or to cling to others for support or protection, but if he knows himself to the extent that he can anticipate such a response to danger, then he can, so to speak, head it off, or at least bring it under control.

The real country, however, in which we are expected to find our way about, or the real storm we are asked to come through, is again that of existence itself. Existence is fraught with dangers and threats to our efforts to instantiate ethical ideality. We must learn this landscape, or learn specifically

[55] See Hügli's claim that "there is no analysis of the factual, in Kierkegaard, that is not also concerned with the ethical and the religious" (Hügli, 185).

where these dangers lie, if we are to be able to find our way about in existence, or to become ourselves. To come to know the landscape of existence, however, means nothing other than to come to know ourselves because this again is all we ever can know of existence, according to Kierkegaard, in a genuine sense.

The ethical significance of self-knowledge becomes clear if we turn to another sort of example. Say a person is asked to help someone in a crisis. The latter has been slandered and seeks support to help quell the damaging rumors that have begun to circulate about him. Assume the person whose help is sought knows the rumors to be untrue. He is unsure, however, of the extent to which the rumors have spread. Perhaps, he says to himself, they have spread so widely that I, if I speak out now in support of this person, will simply be tarred, so to speak, with the same brush so that all my help will be to no avail. He may well decide that it would be best to wait to find out the precise nature of the rumors and the precise extent to which they have spread before speaking out in support of the victim. It is best after all, he may tell himself, to be prepared in order to launch the most effective defense. He may say to himself, "I will look at this tomorrow, tomorrow I will give it my full attention." So he promises to help, and really intends to help (or so he tells himself), but precious time passes during which further and perhaps irreparable damage is done to the reputation of the poor victim.

To know oneself, Kierkegaard would argue, would be immediately to recognize that the original hesitation did not, in fact, stem from the desire to make the aid to the victim optimally effective but from a fear of making oneself vulnerable to injury. The desire to protect oneself is a natural, animal instinct and thus belongs to "the synthesis which a human being is, since in one sense he is a human-animal" (JP, 4:3834). The person who truly knows himself, however, will know this and will not be taken in by the efforts of his lower, that is, animal, nature to dress up this natural, but nonetheless thoroughly unethical, impulse in an ethical guise. He will dismiss the impulse as what it is, a diversion of his lower nature, and he will act. He will act because he knows that to come to the aid of someone in need, to respond immediately to a request for help, is what the moral law demands.

A person who knows himself knows his own animal nature and how it is inclined to present itself, knows when he has failed to act ethically, and knows when he has succeeded in acting ethically. Such knowledge is possible, again, because to the extent that all self-knowledge has ethical significance, it is always accompanied by an experience of self-approval or self-condemnation, or by a feeling of innocence or guilt. It is impossible, according to Kierkegaard, for a person not to appreciate that he becomes guilty when he fails to bring his existence into conformity with his mental representation of ethical-religious ideality. It is possible, however, for him to deceive himself with respect to his guilt. A person thus knows himself, knows his own animal nature and how it is inclined to represent a threat to his actualization of his ethical-religious duty, in that he knows the extent to which he has failed to act ethically to the extent that he accepts the guilt that is consequent upon this failure.

A person's acceptance, for example, of the guilt that is consequent upon his failure to come to the aid of someone who is being slandered does not merely give rise to knowledge of what he ought to do in such a situation; it gives rise to knowledge of what he ought to *have done*. To know, however, what one ought to have done is to know what one did in the sense that it is to know that one did not do what one ought to have done. A person who accepts that he is guilty for failing to act ethically thus forms a mental representation of how his higher nature is inclined to give in to his lower nature, and this representation is, in turn, justified by the insight he gains, through this acceptance, into the subjective necessity of the subordination of his lower to his higher nature.

To know oneself in the sense of knowing both one's higher nature and one's lower, or animal, nature and how these are inclined to relate to each other is to know that the latter is inclined to represent a threat to the objective of bringing one's existence into conformity with ethical-religious ideality.[56] To know how these two natures are inclined to relate to each other is to know that one has a certain tendency to self-deception. Self-deception, observes Walker however, "cannot be corrected by right information . . . it is the self-deceiver's will that requires purification. For he has a will to obscurity of vision, and hence to ignorance about himself" (Walker, 300). Thus for a person to know himself in the sense of knowing he has a certain tendency to self-deception is to know that no matter how successful, in one sense, he may have been in living up to eternally valid ethical norms, he has failed to realize ethical ideality in the sense that his will has not been pure. To equate self-knowledge with knowledge of oneself as guilty brings us back, however, to the realm of ethical-religious knowledge or, more specifically, to the realm of Christian knowledge.

It is tempting to give Christian knowledge a heading of its own. It is, after all, the locus of most of the epistemological confusion concerning Kierkegaard's thought. Any attempt to distinguish it, however, from

---

[56] Thus Kierkegaard refers to the individual as engaged in a "continual struggle" with himself (BA, 128).

subjective knowledge of actuality in a broader sense invites confusion. Christian knowledge has a profound effect, according to Kierkegaard, on the life of the knower. It is essentially the same, however, as subjective knowledge of actuality more generally in terms of how it is known.

Ethics, according to Vigilius Haufniensis, is an "ideal science [*ideel Videnskab*]" (CA, 16). It "points to ideality as a task and assumes that everyone possesses the conditions [i.e., the conditions requisite for achieving ideality]" (CA, 16).[57] Ethics, Haufniensis continues, "has nothing at all to do with the possibility of sin" (CA, 20).[58] That is, what was referred to above as the first ethics becomes "shipwrecked," according to Kierkegaard, "on the sinfulness of the . . . individual" (CA, 20). The first ethics need the help of dogmatics in order to give a satisfactory account of the individual's failure to live up to the moral law. The difference, however, between guilt consciousness and sin consciousness is decisive. "In the totality of guilt-consciousness," argues Johannes Climacus, "existence asserts itself as strongly as it can within immanence. But sin-consciousness is the break [i.e., with immanence]" (CUP, 490). "Guilt consciousness," continues Climacus,

> is a transformation of the subject within the subject. Sin-consciousness, however, is a transformation of the subject himself, which shows that outside the individual there must be the power that makes clear to him that he has become a person other than he was by coming to be, that he has become a sinner. This power is the god in time. (CUP, 491)[59]

To be sinful, according to Kierkegaard, is to be essentially outside the truth where ethical-religious truth is viewed as *the* truth rather than as simply one among many different truths. To be outside the truth in this way, argues Kierkegaard in the *Crumbs*, is to be unable to come to understand it, or to become properly related to it on one's own, because if this were possible, then in an important sense one could not be said to be essentially outside it. To be essentially outside the truth, according to Kierkegaard, is to need assistance in order to gain a proper understanding of it, or to be put into the proper relation to it. Such assistance, he argues, can come only from the truth itself.

[57] See FT, 98–99; Hügli, 222; and Slotty, 69.

[58] I have altered the Hongs' translation slightly for purposes of clarity.

[59] The wording here is actually from the Hongs' translation (584), which is, in this instance I believe, clearer than the Hannay translation. Hannay has "change of subject" where the Hongs have "transformation of the subject," which can make it appear that one person is being replaced by another when what is actually happening is that a single subject is being inwardly transformed. Also, Hannay has "coming about" where the Hongs have "coming to be." In American English, however, it is only events and not things (such as people) that are spoken of as "coming about."

That is, if a person cannot come to the truth himself, then the truth must come to him.[60]

This is the decisive difference between guilt consciousness and sin consciousness. A person's understanding of himself as sinful is inseparable from his understanding the truth as such, in that sin is what separates him from the truth. If a person is essentially ignorant of the truth, then the truth can be called "the unknown" (C, 111–18). Thus Climacus argues that

> the individual, if he is truly to come to know something about the unknown (God), must come to know that it is different from himself, absolutely different. The understanding cannot come to know this by itself (because, as we have seen, this is self-contradictory). If it is to come to know this, it must come to know this through God . . . One needs God simply in order to come to know God is different, and now comes to know that God is absolutely different from himself. But if God is absolutely different from human beings, this cannot have its basis in what human beings owe to God (for to this extent they are related), but in what they are themselves responsible for, or what they have themselves earned. What then is the difference? What else could it be but sin. . . . (C, 119)

"Christianity," asserts Anti-Climacus, "very consistently assumes that neither paganism, nor the natural man knows what sin is; in fact, it assumes that there has to be a revelation from God to show what sin is" (SUD, 89).

According to Kierkegaard, a person does not come to know in the sense of coming to have a correct mental representation that sin is the difference between himself and God, or himself and the truth, as a result of his own efforts to understand this difference. He comes to know this as a result of having been transformed in a manner that makes such a mental representation possible.[61] This transformation can be brought about only by God himself. Thus Kierkegaard asserts that "truth is a snare: you cannot get it without being caught yourself; you cannot get the truth by catching it yourself but only by its catching you" (JP, 4:4886).

A person cannot come to know this on his own because this would amount to his being essentially in possession of this knowledge. The truth must come to him. That is, the eternal ethical-religious truth must, of itself, come together with the temporal—must come to be in time. Kierkegaard refers to such an intersection of the temporal and the eternal as a paradox.[62] It is not primarily the synthesis of the opposing elements of temporality and eternality in the person of the god in time that presents an obstacle to the

---

[60] See, e.g., C, 92–93.

[61] See EUD, 303; CUP, 325, 355; and JP, 3:3109.

[62] See JP, 3:3085. The references to paradox in the pseudonymous works are too numerous to list. Most occur, however, in the *Crumbs* and the *Postscript* to the *Crumbs*.

understanding according to Kierkegaard, however. The subject himself, as we saw in chapter 2, is defined by Kierkegaard as such a synthesis. It is rather that a person's own eternal consciousness, or understanding of the truth, is supposed to come to be through his relation to this paradox. The resistance of the individual to such a proposition is made clearer when it is remembered that the knowledge in question—that is, knowledge of eternal ethical-religious truth—is essentially prescriptive. What a person comes to know is not that he must conform the actuality of his existence to ethical religious ideality. This is something that he is presumed to know already. What he is supposed to come to know, as a result of his encounter with the god in time, is that he is incapable of doing what he is eternally responsible for doing in order to exist in a genuine sense. "The task of ethics," explains Hügli,

> cannot be completed even if it is conceived as an eternal striving. It is a task at which the individual inevitably fails because, if subjectivity is only truth so long as it expresses the eternal in actuality, then this would appear to mean that as long as it has this goal, it is untruth. (Hügli, 218)[63]

Such a proposition is offensive, and the individual quite naturally rebels against it. It is self-contradictory to propose that a person could be eternally responsible for doing something he is incapable of doing. To the extent that this is the message of the god in time, a person will be unable to get this message into his head, so to speak.[64] But if what Kierkegaard calls the paradox of Christianity cannot be grasped intellectually,

> [h]ow does the learner come to an understanding with this paradox. . . . It happens when the understanding and the paradox meet happily in the moment, when the understanding sets itself aside and the paradox gives itself; and this third thing, in which this happens (because it happens neither through the understanding, which is excused, nor through the paradox which offers itself—but *in* something), is the happy passion we will now give a name. . . . We will call it: *faith*. (C, 128–29)

To learn the truth, argues Johannes Climacus, is thus to become a believer. A person becomes a believer when, after having surrendered his reason to the paradox, he receives the condition for understanding the truth.[65] "This condition," continues Climacus, "what does it determine—his understanding of the eternal" (C, 133).[66]

---

[63] Compare this with Slotty's claim that "sin becomes apparent in [one's] striving to actualize the ethical" (Slotty, 70).

[64] See C, 124.

[65] Thus Wisdo argues that "Kierkegaard's analysis of faith appeals to *non-epistemic* factors, namely Grace and will" (Wisdo, 100).

[66] See also Hannay, 128.

One might legitimately wonder, however, why the belief that he was a sinner would be referred to by Kierkegaard as a "happy passion." The answer is that sin is only half of that in which a person is expected to believe as a Christian. Grace is the other half, and Grace marks a person's deliverance from the impression of guilt, which, according to Kierkegaard, is omnipresent in human consciousness. It is for this reason that Kierkegaard argues that "the hope of the life-giving Spirit is against the hope of the understanding" (SE, 82–83). A person can understand guilt. What he cannot understand is that, in the eyes of the eternal, he is forgiven.[67]

The only sense in which eternity is present in a person's consciousness, in this context, is in the form of the moral law and its demand as absolute. The forgiveness of sins is thus "the absurd" (JP, 2:1215).[68] "The absurd," explains Slotty, however, "is not synonymous with nonsense" (Slotty, 57). The forgiveness of sins is absurd in the sense that, from the perspective of the sinner—that is, from the human perspective—it seems impossible.[69] "[W]hen the believer has faith," asserts Kierkegaard, "the absurd is not the absurd—faith transforms it. . . . The passion of faith is the only thing capable of mastering the absurd rightly understood" (JP, 1:10). The passion of faith can transform the absurd because this passion is precisely a person's encounter with the infinite. A person understands the forgiveness of sins to the extent that he encounters God's love in the passion of faith. And "love," asserts Kierkegaard, "hides a multitude of sins" (EUD, 78).

A person who has encountered—that is, become acquainted with—God's love is thus able to form a mental representation of himself as a sinner and of his sins as forgiven. Not only is he able to form such a mental representation; he is able to achieve certainty, in the psychological sense, of its correspondence to reality.[70] Such an individual is understood, by Kierkegaard, to be immediately related to the reality of God's love in this encounter.[71]

[67] See CUP, 189.

[68] See also CUP, 188.

[69] There is nothing inherently irrational in this, however. Julia Watkin asserts, for example, in the introduction to *Nutidens Religieuse Forvirring* (Contemporary Religious Confusion) that "Climacus made it clear in the *Postscript* that to 'believe against the understanding,' far from encouraging an irrational faith, was a defence against it. [That is], the individual must first, with the help of the understanding, distinguish between 'nonsense' and 'the incomprehensible' [*det Uuforstaaelig*], 'the absurd'" (Watkin, 19). See also JP, 3:3076; and Malantschuk, "*Das Verhältnis*," 55.

[70] I am thus taking exception to Daise's claim that "truth, in the context of the *Crumbs*, does not have any epistemological significance" (Daise, 2).

[71] See Slotty's observation that, according to Kierkegaard, "Christ is the only past actuality that can continue to be present to anyone whatever" (Slotty, 70) and Hügli's observation

Since the reality of God's love is presumably that his sins are forgiven, he is understood to appreciate this through an insight into the essence of this love made possible by his immediate relation to it. This forgiveness is essentially subjective in that it is equivalent to the subject's own appreciation that his sins are forgiven, which appreciation he gains through his encounter with God's infinite love. That is, the forgiveness of sins, according to Kierkegaard, is not something that awaits one in eternity. "The forgiveness of sins," he argues, "means to be helped temporally" (JP, 2:1123). For one's sins to be forgiven means precisely to escape the feeling of guilt that is omnipresent in human consciousness according to Kierkegaard.[72]

I argued, however, that since all subjective knowledge was essentially prescriptive, certainty that a given mental representation corresponded to reality was equivalent to an appreciation of the subjective necessity of the correspondence of one's existence to the substance of this representation. The certainty that his sins are forgiven that is a product of the knower's immediate relation to the reality of God's love in the passion of faith must be equivalent to the knower's appreciation of the subjective necessity of conforming his existence to the substance of his mental representation that his sins are forgiven through faith in this forgiveness.[73] To the extent, however, that the knowledge in question is essentially subjective, the truth to which it is related cannot be a property of a mental representation but must be instantiated in the existence of the knower. This truth is the knower's acceptance that his sins are forgiven. Such acceptance, to the extent that it represents the cancelled possibility of despair of the forgiveness of sins, is an act of the knower that thus represents his having brought his existence into conformity with ethical-religious ideality.[74]

A person's knowledge that his sins are forgiven is contingent on his being in the passion of faith. As soon as "the enthusiasm of faith" (CA, 27) disappears, argues Vigilius Haufniensis, the lower nature, or "cunning prudence," will assert itself by endeavoring to engage the knower in the dialectic of self-deception in order to "escape the knowledge of sin" (CA, 27). That is, a person can know his sins are forgiven in the sense that he has a mental representation

---

that "[i]n belief in Christ, the individual has the eternal in time, present in every moment" (Hügli, 223).

[72] See JP, 2:2249. Thus Hannay argues that, according to Kierkegaard, the truth of Christianity is "appropriated in feeling" rather than in thought (Hannay, 173).

[73] Thus Slotty argues that "[u]nder the stress of responsibility to God—i.e., through God—a conviction comes into being" (Slotty, 70).

[74] Thus Hügli argues, "I could no more receive certainty concerning my [true] determination without the free act of belief, than I could receive certainty that I could swim without risking going into the water" (Hügli, 132).

of such forgiveness of whose correspondence to reality he is certain, only while he is in the passion of faith, which is to say, only while he is in contact with God's infinite love. "Just as understanding," explains Slotty, "is acquired only through belief, so is deeper understanding reserved for the knowledge of faith" (Slotty, 59). The passion of faith cannot be sustained indefinitely, however, but is something at which a person can only repeatedly arrive.[75]

Faith is what Kierkegaard, through the mouth of Johannes Climacus, calls "the risky venture." Before a person has made this venture, he continues, "he can understand it only as madness . . . and when he has taken the risk he is no longer the same [person]" (CUP, 355). It is through this risky venture that a person is "infinitized" (CUP, 355). That is, one first comes into contact with God's infinite love, or first comes to feel "in kinship with God" (SUD, 120n) in faith.

"*Everything Is New In Christ*," observes Kierkegaard, "this will be my position for a speculative Christian epistemology" (JP, 2:2277). Climacus refers to what he calls "the certainty of faith" (CUP, 48). But if faith is a risky venture, it would appear problematic to argue that a person could attain certainty as a result of having faith. That is, as Climacus argues, "[r]isking is the correlative of uncertainty, once certainty is there, risking stops" (CUP, 356). It is clear, however, from the following remark that the certainty that threatens faith is an objective, rather than a subjective, or psychological, phenomenon. If the knowing subject "acquires certainty and definiteness . . . he cannot possibly come to risk everything; for in that case, even if he gives everything up he risks nothing" (CUP, 356). The certainty of faith is accessible, however, only in the moment of faith and thus cannot represent a threat to faith itself. The instant a person ceases to believe in the sense that he ceases to be in the passion of faith, the certainty vanishes, and to renew faith involves risk in the same sense it did the first time. Thus the certainty of faith, according to Kierkegaard, "has in it, at every moment, the infinite dialectic of uncertainty" (CUP, 48), not merely in the sense that the object of faith appears objectively uncertain but also in the sense that faith itself is difficult to sustain.

The certainty of faith is, however, in no sense arbitrary. It is a necessary consequence of the believer's contact with God's infinite love in the moment of faith. Every moment of faith is characterized by certainty. Indeed, this certainty is, in a sense, indistinguishable from faith.[76] The difficulty is that every moment of a believer's existence is not characterized by faith. We

[75] See, e.g., CUP, 48, 68–69.

[76] See Slotty's observation that Kierkegaard "strongly emphasized the certainty [*Selbstgewißheit*] of belief" (Slotty, 70).

saw above that a person attains knowledge of the forgiveness of sins in the moment of faith. What we need to look at now is the issue of whether there is any other sort of knowledge associated by Kierkegaard with faith.

Immanent religious knowledge is not the only sort of religious knowledge according to Kierkegaard; there is also transcendent religious knowledge. All specifically Christian knowledge is of the latter sort. This knowledge is the product of revelation, and the specific revelation with which Kierkegaard is concerned can be expressed as an encounter with Christ, or as contemporaneity with Christ, as Climacus expresses it in the *Crumbs*.[77] "Christ is the truth" (PC, 205), according to Kierkegaard, hence to know Christ is to know the truth.

It appears, however, that in every instance where Kierkegaard refers to "knowledge" of Christ, the Danish expression is either *Kjendskab*, or some form of the verb *kjende*, rather than *Erkjendelsen* or *Viden* or their associated verbs.[78] There is even at least one place where Kierkegaard alters the then-current Danish translation of the New Testament by replacing the expression "know" (*kiende*), in connection with the truth of Christianity, with "experience" (*erfarer*). The reference is from his papers where he quotes John 7:17 as, "If anyone's will is to do my father's will, he shall experience whether the teaching is from God or on my own authority" (JP, 2:1881).[79] This substitution is important and provides us with a key to understanding an early journal entry where Kierkegaard asserts that "[t]he historical anticipation of and also the position in human consciousness[80] corresponding to the Christian *'Credo ut intelligam'* [I believe in order that I might understand] is the ancient *Nihil est in intellectus quod non antea fuerit in sensu* [There is nothing in the intellect that has not previously been in the senses]" (JP, 2:1098). A person meets Christ in the moment of faith. This meeting is what is meant by "knowledge" of Christ, hence acquaintance knowledge of Christ precedes genuine Christian knowledge in the propositional sense. To become acquainted with Christ is an experience that is related to the

---

[77] See C, 138–39, 167–68.

[78] See, e.g., EUD, 325–26; and C, 136–37.

[79] I have altered the translation here slightly because the Hongs do not take account of the substitution of "*erfarer*" for "*kiende*." The Greek term in question is *gnosetai*, which is related to the noun *gnosis*. In another reference from Kierkegaard's journals and papers he translates the expression for "know" in the inscription over the oracle at Delphi, *gnothi seauton*, as "*kjende*," which supports the view that Kierkegaard considered *gnosis* to be knowledge of the substantive, or acquaintance, sort. See chapter 7.

[80] I have altered the Hongs' translation of "*Bevidsthed*" from "knowledge" to "consciousness" because the former is not an acceptable translation of *Bevidsthed* (see Ferrall and Repp., Molbech, and Vinterberg and Bodelsen, s.v. *Bevisdthed*).

intellect in the same way sense experience is related to the intellect. Experience, according to Kierkegaard, belongs to the realm of existence, or actuality; hence it cannot, in itself, be equivalent to knowledge (which is why, according to Kierkegaard, it cannot be deceptive)[81] but becomes knowledge, or a candidate for knowledge, only when it is brought into relation to ideality in the intellect. Hence Christian knowledge, in the propositional sense, is a consequence of, rather than equivalent to, Christian experience.[82] "Knowing the truth," argues Anti-Climacus, "*follows* of itself from being the truth" (PC, 205; emphasis added). It is not actually equivalent to being the truth.

If knowledge of the truth *follows* from being the truth, this knowledge must be distinguished from the truth itself, or from this way of being. To argue, however, that knowledge is distinguishable from the activity that makes it possible does not mean that it may be separated from this activity. Specifically Christian knowledge, like all subjective knowledge, is essentially prescriptive. It is impossible to separate it from a certain way of life. "The being of [this] truth," asserts Anti-Climacus, "is not the direct redoubling of being in relation to thinking, which gives only thought-being. . . . [I]t is the redoubling of truth within yourself, within me, within him, so that your life, my life, his life . . . is approximately [*Tilnærmelsesvis*] the being of truth in the striving for it" (PC, 205).

Kierkegaard's assertion that specifically Christian knowledge, or knowledge of the truth of Christianity, cannot be separated from a certain way of life may lead one to believe Christian knowledge and action are equivalent, but this is not the case. "That essential knowing is essentially related to existence," argues Climacus,

> does not, however, signify that abstract identity mentioned above between thought and being; nor objectively does it mean that knowledge corresponds to something that is there as its object. It means that knowledge relates to the knower, who is essentially someone existing, and that for this reason all essential knowledge essentially relates to existence and to existing. (CUP, 166)

It is possible to argue that while Christian knowledge may initially be a result of Christian experience, once it has been attained, it determines, for the knower, appropriate Christian behavior such that, from that point on, Christian experience, in terms of right action, is either indistinguishable from Christian knowledge or follows immediately and unproblematically from that knowledge. If this were the case, then knowing the good would become indistinguishable from doing the good. To know the good, on

---

[81] See chapter 4.
[82] Contra Emmanuel, 139.

Kierkegaard's view, however, is not necessarily to do it, even when the good in question is of the specifically Christian sort, and this becomes apparent if we return to the two examples we considered earlier. Ordinary life, lived at the same pace as others, is analogous, according to Kierkegaard, to fair weather for a sailor, but the moment of decision

> the dangerous moment of collecting himself when he is to withdraw from the surroundings and become alone before God and become a sinner—this is a stillness that changes the ordinary just as the storm does. He knows [*veed*] it all, knows [*veed*] what is to happen to him, but he did not know [*vidste ikke*] the anxiety that grips him when he feels himself abandoned by the multiplicity in which he had his soul; he did not know [*vidste ikke*] how the heart pounds when the help of others and the diversions of others vanish in stillness; he did not know [*vidste ikke*] the shuddering when it is too late to call for human help, when no one can hear him— in short, he had no conception [*Forestilling*] of how the knower is changed when he is to appropriate his knowledge. (TDIO, 36–37)

The knowledge referred to in this passage is clearly not acquaintance knowledge—that is, *Kjendskab*. It is propositional knowledge, or a mental representation of reality. This is apparent from both the Danish expressions used and the reference to "idea," or "mental representation" (which is arguably a better translation of *Forestilling* than is "idea") in the last sentence. The ideality of even specifically Christian knowledge is clearly distinguished from the actuality of Christian existence. The relation of Christian knowledge to right action is expressed even more clearly, however, in the other passage. "Perhaps," begins Kierkegaard, "the double-minded person did have a *knowledge of the good. . . . Alas*," he continues,

> contemplation [*Betragtning*] and the moment of contemplation, despite all its clarity, easily conceal an illusion, because its moment has something in common with the counterfeited eternity. There is a foreshortening that is necessary in order for the contemplation to come about; it must shorten time considerably—indeed, it actually has to call the mind and thought away from time in order to complete itself in a counterfeited eternal rounding off. In this it is something like the work of an artist in drawing a map of a country. The drawing . . . cannot be as large as the country . . . but it also becomes all the easier for the viewer to survey the outlines of that country. And yet if that viewer were suddenly set down in the actuality of that country, where the many, many miles have all their force, he very likely would not be able to recognize the country . . . or as a traveler to get his bearings in it. The same thing will also happen to the double-minded person. His knowledge has certainly been an illusion. What was compacted airtight, as it were, in the completeness of contemplation must now be stretched out to its full length. (UDVS, 72)

There are two things it is important to appreciate about the above quotations. The individual described in the first one "had a knowledge of the good." The problem was not an inadequacy in his mental representation of the good but an inadequacy in his character. Such an inadequacy in character, or double-mindedness, is not restricted, according to Kierkegaard, to certain sorts of people; it is an expression of sin, which is universal. We are all double-minded, on his view, and living as a Christian means striving to purge ourselves of this double-mindedness, or to purify our wills.[83]

It is for this reason Kierkegaard asserts that the life of a Christian only approaches (*tilnærmer*) the truth. Only in Christ, according to Kierkegaard, are truth and existence combined in such a way that they are indistinguishable from each other. "The being of truth," argues Kierkegaard,

> is the redoubling of truth within yourself, within me, within him, [so] that your life, my life, his life *approaches* truth in the striving for it, that your life, my life, his life *approaches* the being of the truth in the striving for it, just as the truth was in Christ, a *life*,[84] for he was the truth. (PC, 205; emphasis added)[85]

Knowledge of the truth of Christianity appears equivalent to knowledge that Christianity "is not a doctrine" but "a believing and a very particular kind of existing [*Existeren*] corresponding to it" (JP, 2:1880).[86] Or as Daise explains, "To give assent to the god's having come into existence, . . . is to accept that way of life as a model for one's own and to see this model as authoritative" (Daise, 9). But while there is clearly such a thing as Christian knowledge in this sense, according to Kierkegaard,[87] he argues that Christian truth, or the truth of Christianity, when viewed *merely* as knowledge—that is, as a mental representation abstracted from any existential situation—is untruth.[88] One can see, argues Anti-Climacus,

> what a monstrous mistake it is, almost the greatest possible, to didacticize Christianity, and how altered Christianity has become through this continual didacticizing is seen in this, that now all expressions are formed according to the view that truth is cognition [*Erkjendelsen*], knowledge [*Viden*] (now one speaks continually of comprehending, speculating, observing, etc.), whereas in original Christianity all the expressions were formed according to the view that truth is a [way of] being. (PC, 206)

[83] This is the theme of Kierkegaard's discourse titled "Purity of Heart" (UDVS, 5–155).

[84] See Daise, 6.

[85] I have altered the Hongs' translation slightly by replacing their "approximates" with "approaches" because this is a better translation of "*Tilnæremer*" than is "approximate." See chapter 5, p. 103.

[86] See Wisdo, 97.

[87] See JP, 1:653; and Hügli, 169.

[88] See PC, 206.

Christian knowledge is possible as something that follows from Christian experience, and it is reasonable to assume it was this knowledge to which Kierkegaard referred when he said he could conceive of a specifically Christian epistemology, the development of which, he asserted, could be undertaken only after a person had become a Christian.[89]

We have already seen that Christian knowledge, according to Kierkegaard, may be understood to include the appreciation of the believer that his sins are forgiven. To the extent that this knowledge is indistinguishable from the appreciation that God is love, the latter too may be understood to be known by the believer in the moment of faith. To these two sorts of Christian knowledge we may now add the knowledge that Christianity itself is neither the doctrine that one's sins are forgiven nor the doctrine that God is love, but that it is a way of life. That is, Christianity is the process of a person's striving to bring his existence into conformity with ethical-religious ideality, which is characterized by his belief that the activity itself is pleasing to God and that God does not hold his failure to establish such conformity in an absolute sense against him.

The knower's certainty that his mental representation of Christian truth corresponds to reality is equivalent to his appreciation of the subjective necessity of the correspondence of his existence to this mental representation. Such an appreciation, and the certainty to which it gives rise, is made possible through belief in Christ. Belief in Christ transforms guilt consciousness into sin consciousness; this transformation is equivalent to the revelation of the subjective necessity of making one's life an expression of Christian truth in order to obtain authentic human existence.

The truth in question, however, like all subjective truth, is not a property of a mental representation that Christianity is a way of life but a property of the existence of the knower to the extent that this existence is an actualization of the particular way of being as it is represented in thought.

There may be a great deal more that could be placed under the heading of Christian knowledge according to Kierkegaard. Whatever Christian knowledge comprises, however, it cannot include a knowledge that God came into being in the person of Christ, because all knowledge, according to Kierkegaard, is, again, either of the eternal, which excludes the temporal, or of the historical. No knowledge can have for its object that the eternal came into existence.[90] There is no evidence that Kierkegaard ever abandons the Leibnizian distinction between truths of reason and truths of fact.

[89] JP, 2:2277.
[90] C, 131.

It is possible, of course, to speak of the "truths" of Christianity in the sense in which "truths" were distinguished from "truth" in chapter 3. Even Kierkegaard refers to the "truths of Christianity" (CUP, 188). Knowledge of Christian truths, on his view, may be characterized as a mental representation that God is love or that it is God's will that people relate lovingly to their neighbors. A person cannot know, however, even when meeting Christ, *how* Christ came to be there. Just as a person must believe in the historicity of the people and events around him, so must he believe in the historicity of Christ, or in the historicity of God in Christ.

There is a reference to knowledge (*Viden*) of Christ in *The Sickness Unto Death*,[91] but the context of the reference makes it clear that it is not a reference to knowledge that Christ was God. That is, this knowledge is later referred to as a representation (*Forestilling*) that exists in the knowing subject to a greater of lesser degree. "[T]he greater the conception [*Forestilling*] of Christ," argues Anti-Climacus, "the more self" (SUD, 113). That is, the more complete the mental representation one has of this individual one believes to be God (i.e., the more complete a mental representation one has of what ethical-religious ideality would look like if it were expressed in the life of a particular person),[92] the more self one has.

Specifically Christian knowledge, according to Kierkegaard, is either knowledge of eternal truth or historical knowledge. It does not include knowledge that the eternal became historical. The knowledge, for example, that one is a sinner and that one's sins are forgiven is historical knowledge. Sin is not a part of a person's eternally established essence, according to Kierkegaard, but was freely appropriated at some point by the sinner.[93] To the extent that a believer was not always a sinner, his sins cannot for all eternity have been forgiven. Both a person's mental representation of himself as a sinner and his representation of his sins as forgiven relate to what was referred to above as truths of fact. Knowledge that there is a God, on the other hand, is knowledge of eternal truth. There may be more, as I observed already, to specifically Christian knowledge than I have so far detailed. The point of this book is not to present an exhaustive list of exactly what falls under the headings of each of the various types of knowledge Kierkegaard

[91] SUD, 113.

[92] That is, Christ's life, according to Kierkegaard, is essentially eternal truth that has come to be in time. It is because Christ's life is essentially eternal truth, however, that everyone can be contemporary with it, according to Kierkegaard (see PC, 64).

[93] With the exception, of course, of hereditary sin, which is something of a mystery for Kierkegaard (see CA), but also, one could argue, far less of a problem for the sinner in that he is not tortured by the consciousness that he is a sinner in a hereditary sense so much as he is tortured by the consciousness that he is a sinner in the actual sense.

appears to believe there are but to show the type of thing that would fall under each heading, as well as to show that it is impossible, according to Kierkegaard, to know that God became man.[94]

Kierkegaard does refer to "knowledge of the paradox" in his journals, where he argues in a draft of the *Postscript* that "Christian knowledge is not knowledge of the paradox, but knowledge of it in passion and the knowledge of the wise that it can be known only in passion."[95] If what Kierkegaard is referring to here by "paradox" is that one's sins are forgiven, then the meaning of the claim is clear. If, on the other hand, he is using "paradox" to refer to the claim that God became man in the person of Christ, then it would appear that what he means is that "objectively there is no truth, for an objective knowledge of the truth, or truths, of Christianity is precisely untruth. To know a declaration of faith by rote is paganism, because Christianity is inwardness" (CUP, 188).

Christian knowledge proper is not "knowledge," in the approximate sense, of what has historically been referred to as Christian doctrine, or, more specifically, "knowledge" in an approximate sense, that the proposition that God became man in Christ is part of this doctrine. Christian knowledge proper is the mental representation of this doctrine in the sense of "*the objective uncertainty maintained through appropriation in the most passionate inwardness*" (CUP, 171) as well as the wise person's insight that the only way one can properly relate to this "knowledge" is subjectively, in the passion of faith.

This account of the passage we looked at from Kierkegaard's draft of the *Postscript* may seem contrived. What makes it compelling, however, is that it is consistent with all other references to knowledge that appear in the *Postscript* as well as Kierkegaard's authorship more generally, while there is nothing in that authorship that would support an interpretation of this passage as a reference to knowledge that God became man in Christ.[96]

Kierkegaard never explicitly develops a Christian epistemology because, although knowledge figures prominently in his works, it is not knowledge, even of the Christian sort, that was his primary interest. He argues, for example, that even "the knowledge that contemplation and reflection are the

---

[94] See Kierkegaard's claim in his unpublished *Book on Adler* that "[e]ven if thought considered itself capable of assimilating the doctrine; it cannot assimilate the way in which the doctrine came into the world" (BA, 176).

[95] The wording here is from volume 2, page 50 of the Hongs' translation of the *Postscript*.

[96] It is likely the ambiguity of the reference to knowledge of the paradox that caused Kierkegaard to omit it from the final version of the *Postscript*.

distance of eternity away from time and actuality . . . because, [as knowledge] it exists in a spurious eternity before the imagination, develops double-mindedness, if it is not slowly and honestly earned by the will's purity" (POH, 116–17).[97] Christianity, according to Kierkegaard, is essentially oriented toward the will rather than toward knowledge.[98] It is thus the will, or human psychology, that primarily interests him. Willing, according to Kierkegaard, is a more basic activity than knowing, and this is part of the reason it is so significant with respect to issues in epistemology.[99]

Kierkegaard is concerned with the difficulties involved in being a Christian, or in trying to live a Christian life. He observes, as we saw earlier, that

> [j]ust when one has understood the truth best, the old suddenly crops up again. The infinite, the eternal, hence the true, is so alien to the natural man that with him it is as with the dog, which can indeed learn to walk upright for a moment but yet continually wants to walk on all fours. (WOL, 244)

There is indeed Christian knowledge according to Kierkegaard, in the sense that there are mental representations of the "truths" of Christianity, but possession of this "knowledge" is not sufficient to make a person a Christian. "If the rights of knowledge are to be given their fair due," he argues, "we must venture out into life, out upon the ocean, and scream in the hope that God will hear . . . only then does knowledge acquire its *official* registration" (JP, 2:2279). "Here in the world of knowledge," he observes, "there rests upon the human being a curse (blessing) which bids him eat his bread in the sweat of his brow" (JP, 2:2274).[100]

A "completely human life," according to Kierkegaard, is not merely one of knowledge,[101] because the medium of knowledge is thought, or

---

[97] The wording here is from the Steere translation. I have chosen it because it is both clearer and more idiomatic than the wording of the Hongs' translation. The relevant passage can be found on page 79 of the Hongs' UDVS.

[98] See JP, 2:1202, 4:4953, 6:6966; SUD, 90; and Hügli, 161, 210.

[99] Knowledge is always the result of willing. A person has to will to know even what he is inherently capable of knowing without assistance. This is true not merely with respect to scholarly and scientific knowledge but also with respect to knowledge of immanent metaphysical truths, although it is less apparent with respect to the latter.

[100] Compare this to the assertion of Kierkegaard's pseudonym Johannes de Silentio in *Fear and Trembling* that "[t]here is a knowledge that presumptuously wants to introduce into the world of spirit the same law of indifference under which the external world sighs. It believes that it is enough to know what is great—no other work is needed. But for this reason it does not get nourishment [*Brød*]; it perishes of hunger while everything changes to Gold" (FT, 27–28).

[101] See JP, 5:5100.

ideality, whereas a human being is an *interesse* between thought and being, or between ideality and reality. A completely human life consists of action as well as thought, and to be really complete, the action in question should represent the efforts of the individual to bring the actuality of his existence into conformity with ethical ideality.

The activity of knowledge is to bring being into relation to thought such that thought is made to conform to being, that is, to accurately reproduce or represent it. This is true even with respect to specifically Christian knowledge. That is, Christian knowledge is the result of an effort to bring the actuality of Christian experience into relation to thought, or to represent that experience in the categories of thought. But the medium of thought is ideality; hence the categories of thought are ideal categories, which means Christian knowledge is an idealized representation of Christian experience. This representation is important, however, because once possessed, the efforts of the knower must be directed to a reduplication of that ideality in actuality.[102] Ethical-religious activity involves bringing thought in the sense of a person's conception of ethical-religious ideality into relation to reality, or, more specifically, actuality, such that actuality is made to conform to it.[103] Hence the activity of the Christian is directed toward a repetition of Christian experience.[104] This is what Kierkegaard means when he observes that "Christian experience rather than reason seeks its corroboration in other experience" (JP, 2:2251).

Only by successfully willing to do the good, that is, to bring the actuality of his existence into conformity with ethical-religious ideality, can a person overcome the contradiction inherent in human existence (i.e., that a human being is composed of the apparently incompatible elements of temporality and eternity, actuality and ideality, etc.).[105] Such success is, however, always only momentary because each new instant renews the demand that ideality be actualized in time. "Eternity," explains Hügli, "is the telos that should be present in existence, but because it can be present only in the moment [*momentweise*], it is never fully present, but belongs in part to the future" (Hügli, 213).[106] This is the reason the self, according to

---

[102] "I certainly do not deny," observes Kierkegaard, "that I still accept an *imperative of knowledge* [*Erkjendelsens Imperativ*] and that through it people may be influenced, but *then it must come alive in me*, and this is what I now recognize as the most important of all" (JP, 5:5100).

[103] See Hannay, 67; and Hügli, 111, 203.

[104] See CA, 18n.

[105] See Hügli, 133, 200.

[106] See BA, 129–32.

Kierkegaard, "does not actually exist [*er ikke virkelig til*] [but] is simply that which ought to come to be" (SUD, 30). That is, the distinction, according to Kierkegaard, between "truth and truths . . . is recognizable in the distinction made between *way* and final decision, which is reached at the end, *the result*" (PC, 206). Certainly in one sense the Christian has a goal toward which he strives—to actualize the ideal of Christian existence. "That the existing subjective thinker is constantly striving does not, however, mean that he has a goal in a finite sense, towards which he strives and reaching which would mean he was finished. No, he strives infinitely, is constantly coming to be" (CUP, 77).

Only Christ's life, according to Kierkegaard, was an expression of the truth in an absolute sense.[107] That is, the self that each of us is to become, the self that is an expression of our eternally established essence, is morally perfect. Christ, argues Anti-Climacus, "himself had to express the truth with his own life, himself had to portray what it is to be the truth, and as truly human he had consequently this something else as his task—to accomplish this himself absolutely" (PC, 181–82).[108] That is, a fully human life, according to Kierkegaard, is an expression of moral perfection.[109] This objective cannot be separated from being a person, or a self, properly speaking.[110] It is precisely this demand, however, for moral perfection, or the equation of a genuine synthesis of the opposing elements that compose the self with such moral perfection, that makes Christian knowledge problematic.

To meet Christ, according to Kierkegaard, in the passion of faith, is to come to know that God is love, that love is a living, dynamic force, not a mere fact, and that Christian truth is a way of living rather than a set of propositions. To meet Christ in the moment of faith is to come into contact with the reality of God's love. The knower is said to be certain that the resultant mental representation that God is love corresponds to reality because he has "the certainty, which can be had only in infinitude" (CUP, 68),

---

[107] See WA, 181; and BA, 91.

[108] I have altered the Hongs' translation slightly. The Hongs have "to accomplish this himself." That is, they omit the qualification "absolutely." The Danish is "*selv saaledes at fulkomme det*," which translates literally as "himself thus to perfect it" (see Ferrall and Repp., and Vinterberg and Bodelsen, s.v. "*fulkomme*"). The Hongs' translation includes no reference to Christ's obligation to make his life a perfect, or absolute, expression of the truth. This qualification is important, however, in that it is in this respect that only Christ is the truth. That is, only Christ's life comes closer than an approximate (*tilnæremelsesvis*) expression of the truth.

[109] See CUP, 290.

[110] See Daise, 5.

that is, "the certainty of faith" (CUP, 48).[111] The difficulty, however, is that faith is not something a person can attain once and for all. The infinite passion of faith, of the contact established through faith with God's infinite love, cannot be indefinitely sustained. This infinitude, according to Kierkegaard, is something in which a person cannot, so long as he exists, rest, but to which he can only repeatedly arrive.[112]

All specifically Christian knowledge has its foundation, according to Kierkegaard, in the knower's belief in Christ. The certainty of faith, as we saw, is no more arbitrary, according to Kierkegaard, than the certainty associated with objective knowledge. The former certainty, like the latter, is the result of the contact of the knower with the substance of the reality in question. It is just that the contact in the former instance is problematic in a sense in which the contact in the latter is not. The knower is by definition immediately related to the reality of his ideas as such, whereas he is, to the extent that he is defined as a sinner, essentially separated from ethical-religious reality. Contact with this reality must be established through the joint efforts of God, in the person of Christ, and the individual himself.[113]

Part of the individual is strongly resistant to establishing contact with ethical-religious reality, however, because it appears that the truth, according to Kierkegaard, is that "to become a Christian is to become, humanly speaking, unhappy for this life" (TM, 212). Everyone has an interest in authentic human existence according to Kierkegaard.[114] The difficulty is that to the extent that such existence is equivalent to the actualization of ethical-religious ideality, to become Christian means to sacrifice one's animal, or lower, nature with all its drives and desires to the interests of one's higher nature.[115] But the lower nature is strongly opposed to being sacrificed in this way and thus always represents a threat to the maintenance of Christian faith. Even the believer, according to Kierkegaard, eventually "relapses to the low level of the worldly, to his customary speech and way of thinking" (EUD, 300)[116]

---

[111] See WOL, 379; and Slotty, 60.

[112] See CUP, 68.

[113] That is, Christ supplies the condition for understanding the truth, and the believer accepts this condition through the surrender of his worldly understanding (see C, 125, 133; Thulstrup, *Kommentar*, 181; and Wisdo, 100).

[114] See Slotty, 40; and Hannay, 335.

[115] See JP, 4:4872, 4:4885.

[116] I have altered the translation slightly. The Hongs have "ordinary conversation" where I have chosen to stick with Swenson's "customary speech." The Danish is "*sædvanlig Tale*," which translates literally as "customary speech" (see Ferrall and Repp., and Vinterberg and Bodelsen, s.v. *sædvanlig* and *Tale*).

and must thus continually renew his faith. Hence Kierkegaard argues that "[f]aith certainly requires an expression of will, and yet in another sense than when, for example, I must say that all cognition [*Erkjendelsen*] requires an expression of will" (JP, 2:1094).

Though Christian knowledge is possible as a result of the contact of the knower with God's infinite love as that contact is established through his belief in Christ, "[o]nly in his strongest moment,"

> can a person understand that something that is present weakly enough at his strongest moment [i.e., Christian truth] was present far more strongly and yet equally at every moment [of Christ's life], but the next moment he cannot understand this, and therefore he must believe and hold to the belief, so that his life will not become confused by understanding at one moment and not understanding at many other moments. (WOL, 101)[117]

[117] It is important to note that there is an ambiguity in a portion of this passage that I have not quoted. The passage refers to the idea that Christ was the fulfillment of the law. It begins as follows: "Every Christian believes this and appropriates it in faith, but no one has known it except for the Law and him who was the fulfilling of the Law" (WOL, 101). The Danish expression the Hongs translate as "except for" is "*uden*," which was properly translated as "without" in the mid-nineteenth century (see Ferrall and Repp., s.v. *uden*), and this is still the preferred translation (see Vinterberg and Bodelsen, s.v. *uden*). The Danish word that is normally translated as "except" is *undtagen*.

CHAPTER SEVEN

Conclusion
The Implications of Kierkegaard's Epistemology

Kierkegaard clearly believes that his account of subjective knowledge reflects what one could call a real category of knowledge, or a genuine sense in which the expression "knowledge" is used in common parlance. This use is enormously significant with respect to the issue of ethical, or religious, truth. There are some difficulties with the concept of subjective knowledge, however, that remain to be addressed. I would like to return now to the questions I put forward at the beginning of the last chapter. The first of these concerned whether it was possible for the objects of subjective knowledge to be objects of objective knowledge as well. The answer is both yes and no. Objective "knowledge" of things essentially related to subjective experience is what I identified as pseudo-knowledge. It bears only the faintest resemblance to subjective knowledge proper in that it is neither justified nor true. The certainty of the knower that a given mental representation corresponds to reality is a consequence of his contact with the object of this representation that is a result of his having brought his existence into conformity with it. Pseudo-knowledge, or objective "knowledge" of things that can properly be known only subjectively, is precisely a mental representation viewed in abstraction from any relation it might have to the existence of the individual whose representation it is. That is, it is a mental representation considered independently of the contact, or lack thereof, of the "knower" with the reality to which it is related. Since the intuition, or insight, into the essence of the object of a mental representation that serves to justify it is possible only to the extent that the knower is in contact with that object, a mental representation viewed independently of such contact cannot be said to be justified.

According to Kierkegaard, subjective truth, as we saw, is not the property of a mental representation but a property of the existence of the knower. Pseudo-knowledge is precisely a mental representation viewed in abstraction from any relation it might have to the existence of the "knower." To the extent, however, that subjective truth consists in a particular kind of relation between such a mental representation and the existence of the individual whose representation it is, pseudo-knowledge cannot be said to be true. Subjective knowledge proper cannot be separated from the efforts of the knower to bring the actuality of his existence into conformity with the mental representation in question. Thus Climacus contends, "objective knowledge of the truth, or truths, of Christianity is precisely untruth" (CUP, 188).

The relation of subjective to objective knowledge should now be clear. Both concern aspects of reality with which the individual knower is faced. It is neither desirable, nor even possible, according to Kierkegaard, for a person to live a life informed exclusively by knowledge of one or the other sort. Objective reality can be the object only of objective knowledge. That is, there cannot be any discrepancy between objective reality and the knower's existence; thus there can be no question of the knower bringing his existence into conformity with this reality. Neither ontological knowledge, mathematical knowledge, nor any other knowledge that belongs to what we have called immanent metaphysical knowledge is essentially related to the existence of the knower, and the same thing is true with respect to scientific and scholarly knowledge. Objective knowledge of these sorts is appropriate and indeed is the only sort of knowledge possible with respect to certain kinds of objects because these objects are what they are independently of the experience of any particular individual. This is not true, however, as we have seen, with respect to knowledge that is essentially related to such experience.

The final question concerns whether one ought to subsume subjective knowledge under the general heading of Kierkegaard's epistemology. This is not an easy question to answer because of the differences, already detailed, between objective and subjective knowledge. There are also many similarities, however. Both types of knowledge are interested, although they are distinguished according to the nature of the object of interest. Insofar as objective knowledge is associated with interest, the object of interest is not the knower himself but something that is assumed to have an independent existence. The interest that is associated with subjective knowledge, on the other hand, is precisely the interest of the knower in himself. That is, this interest is his interest in attaining authentic human existence in the sense of becoming a self. Subjective knowledge proper, like objective knowledge in the strict sense, is a mental representation whose correspondence to reality is understood by the knower to be certain, and it is also, like the latter, concerned with truth, even if it cannot, in itself, be said to be true.

I argued in the introduction that Kierkegaard's epistemology was both procedural and substantive and that it involved both internalist and externalist accounts of justification. Subjective knowledge proper is substantive. That is, ethical-religious knowledge proper is the result of the contact of the knower with ethical-religious reality to the extent that that reality is built into the contents of his consciousness in the form of a mental representation and to the extent that he has brought the reality—that is, actuality—of his existence into conformity with this mental representation. Subjective knowledge proper is also justified internally in that its justification is precisely the psychological certainty that is a product of the knower's contact with the reality in question.

According to Kierkegaard, to instantiate ethical-religious reality in this way is to be in two places at once. That is, to instantiate ethical-religious ideality is to be at once both actual and ideal. It is to be an identity of subject and object—that is, an identity of the knowing subject and the ethical-religious ideality that is the object of his mental representation.[1] According to Kierkegaard, however, no one is ever entirely successful in actualizing ethical-religious ideality or in being in two places in this way. When a person is "closest to being in two places at once he is in passion; but passion is only momentary" (CUP, 168). This passion, as we saw, is the knower's personal interest in his own ethical actuality,[2] and it is this passion, or interest, that is the means through which contact with ethical-religious reality is established.[3]

Pseudo-knowledge, in contrast to subjective knowledge proper, is procedural just as objective knowledge in the loose sense is procedural. A person may have a correct mental representation of ethical-religious reality yet not have knowledge to the extent that his existence does not constitute a reduplication of the substance of this representation.[4] We saw above that such a reduplication admits of degree and that even the acceptance of guilt for failing to actualize ethical-religious ideality amounts to an actualization

---

[1] See Hügli, 200.
[2] See CUP, 271.
[3] See Hügli, 200.
[4] See EUD, 173; and JP, 1:656.

of that ideality to the extent that it represents the annihilation of the possibility of self-deception concerning one's guilt. To the extent, however, that
a person does deceive himself in this respect, his "knowledge," instead of
involving contact with ethical-religious reality as did subjective knowledge
proper, involves, or is associated with, the process of self-deception and may
thus be described as procedural "knowledge."[5]

There is another respect, however, in which a mental representation of
something essentially prescriptive may be considered independently of the
existence of the individual "knower." One may be objectively preoccupied
with determining the essence of ethical-religious ideality as such. That is, a
person may endeavor to determine the precise nature of norms that would
be eternally valid for human behavior by attempting to read the essence
of these norms from human history, which, of course, Kierkegaard repeatedly argues is impossible.[6] Pseudo-knowledge of this sort relates to what
is referred to in Danish as *Sædelighed*. That is, this "knowledge" refers to a
mental representation of culturally and historically established (rather than
eternally valid) norms that is attained through the same sort of procedure
as that which is used to attain scholarly and scientific knowledge—that is,
through the collection of data pertaining to such norms and the calculation
of the apparent probability of the correspondence of a particular mental
representation of these norms to reality. Such a justification is also externalist in that what is most important in determining whether the person in
question can be said to have knowledge is not how rigorously he followed
the requisite procedure but whether the results of his efforts are in line with
the prevailing views on the matter.

Pseudo-knowledge fails to be substantive, or to consist in contact with
the reality in question, precisely because the "knower," in this instance, lacks
infinite, personal, passionate interest in this reality. Pseudo-knowledge is
distinguished from knowledge in the loose sense, however, in that while a
"disinterested" perspective relative to the latter is quite proper, according
to Kierkegaard, such a relation to the objects of subjective knowledge is
improper.[7] "The assumption," argues Hannay, "is that individual human

---

[5] It is important to point out, however, that Kierkegaard did not believe in the possibility of complete self-deception. He asserts, for example, in his unpublished *Book on Adler* that
"cowardly and soft religious people are basically aware that their religiousness is a hypocritical
made-up thing" (BA, 108). I have chosen Lowrie's "made-up [as in cosmetics] thing" over the
Hongs' "prinked-up thing" because the former is more idiomatic.

[6] See CUP, 127.

[7] See Hannay's claim that Climacus assumes there is an "objective basis" for an individual's interest in an eternal happiness (Hannay, 193).

beings do indeed have this interest, and furthermore . . . that it is fitting that they should have it even if there are those, even a majority, who claim they do not" (Hannay, 44). The knower is defined by Kierkegaard as interest in the sense of both the interest he *has* and the interest he *takes* in attaining authentic existence in the sense in which this existence is equivalent to an instantiation of ethical-religious ideality. To fail to be interested in such existence is thus, according to Kierkegaard, to fail to be both what one essentially *is* and what one essentially *ought to be*.

I argued in the introduction that, according to Kierkegaard, knowledge was a justified, true mental representation and that subjective knowledge proper was thus problematic in that it could not in itself—that is, as a mental representation—be true. There is another respect, however, in which subjective knowledge is problematic. Truth, according to Kierkegaard, is an agreement between thought and being. The difficulty is that the agreement between the individual knower and ethical-religious reality that constitutes subjective truth admits of degrees and indeed must admit of degrees if Kierkegaard is not to contradict himself. That is, Kierkegaard argues that living ethically/religiously means endeavoring to bring one's existence into conformity with eternally valid ethical-religious norms, yet he argues that no one except Christ is ever entirely successful in this endeavor. But to express truth is to be in contact with it, and if this contact is necessary to secure knowledge of these truths, in what sense can a person be understood to be in contact with a truth the expression of which he only approaches (*tilnærmer*), and in what sense can such contact be said to yield knowledge?

In what sense can a person be only partly in contact with something? It might appear immediately that contact is something that one either obtains or fails to obtain. There is a sense, however, in which a person can be said to be partly in contact with something. To correspond with someone, for example, is to be in contact with that person, although such contact is of a lesser sort than that which characterizes face-to-face contact.[8] Kierkegaard argues, however, that to express ethical-religious truth only partly is to "approach" (*tilnæreme*) it; hence the analogy that will be most helpful is one that incorporates this aspect of subjective truth. This, I believe, can be found in the experience of approaching the ocean. As one approaches the ocean one becomes gradually surrounded by the sight, the smell, the sound, and even the feel of it. At the edge of the ocean, where the waves meet the shore, there is a fine mist thrown off by the waves. To approach the ocean is to feel this mist on one's face and to feel it thus, cool and wet like the ocean itself,

---

[8] Hence the resistance of many university faculty to teaching courses entirely online.

is to know something of that reality stretched out before one. To approach ethical-religious truth is to be in contact with it in this sense. But this too is a kind of contact that yields, in turn, a kind of knowledge, even if this knowledge is only "in part" (1 Cor 13:12).

I stated in the introduction that I was going to argue that Kierkegaard was an epistemological pluralist in that there were actually several kinds of knowledge described in his works. Knowledge, in general, I asserted in chapter 3, could be defined as a justified, true mental representation where the precise meaning of each of these terms is understood to be relative to the nature of the object of knowledge. Truth, as we saw, is defined by Kierkegaard as an agreement of thought with reality, or of reality with thought. We also saw, however, that it was possible to speak of truth and *truth*, or of truth in both a relative and an absolute sense.

Justification, in the strict sense, was identified as an insight into the essence of the object of knowledge that is made possible by the contact of the knower with that object. This insight gave rise to the knower's appreciation of the correspondence of the mental representation in question to reality. This appreciation, in turn, was said to be equivalent to psychological certainty concerning this correspondence. This was the case with both objective knowledge in the strict sense and subjective knowledge proper.

It was clear, however, that, according to Kierkegaard, such contact with the object of knowledge was not always possible. There was thus, as we saw, also a loose sense in which a mental representation could be said to be justified. Justification in this sense was equivalent to the impression of the knower that the correspondence of the mental representation in question to reality was probable.

Subjective knowledge proper was distinguished from objective knowledge in the strict sense in that it was essentially prescriptive rather than descriptive. The certainty of the knower that a given mental representation of reality corresponded to reality could not properly be separated from the correspondence of the reality in question—that is, the existence of the knower—to the mental representation. It was, in fact, this latter correspondence that constituted subjective truth. That is, subjective truth, as we saw, was not a property of a mental representation, as was objective truth, but was a property of the existence of the knower.

Objective knowledge was a justified, true mental representation, though the meaning of these terms depended on whether the object of knowledge was something abstract or something concrete. Objective knowledge of abstract objects was of the traditional, foundationalist sort in that it was substantive and involved an internalist account of justification, whereas objective knowledge of concrete objects was procedural and ultimately nonfoundationalist in that it involved an externalist account of justification. Subjective knowledge proper was also foundationalist in that it was anchored in the same kind of contact with reality as was objective knowledge in the strict sense. It turned out, however, that it was a justified mental representation that was neither true nor false. It was not false because it was associated with the way of life it prescribed and thus represented the agreement between thought and reality requisite to knowledge, but neither was it true in that the truth in question was precisely this way of life rather than a property of a mental representation as such. Subjective knowledge proper was substantive, just as was objective knowledge in the strict sense, and, like the latter, also involved an internalist account of justification.

Each of the above types of knowledge was related, as we saw, to specific sorts of objects and represented a legitimate way these objects could be known. Pseudo-knowledge, on the other hand, was not an expression of a legitimate way of knowing. Pseudo-knowledge, like objective knowledge in the loose sense, was associated with probability rather than with certainty. The appreciation of the probability of the correspondence of a given mental representation of reality to reality was acceptable, however, as a justification of objective knowledge in the loose sense precisely because the correspondence of such representations to reality was inherently uncertain. This was not the case, however, with subjective knowledge. That is, there is, for Kierkegaard, one determinate ethical-religious truth—Christianity—and this means that certainty, in the psychological sense, is accessible with respect to every object of subjective knowledge and that thus probability, or the impression that the correspondence of a given mental representation of ethical religious reality to that reality was probable, could not serve to justify this representation. The truth to which pseudo-knowledge related was a property of reality, or of the existence of the knower, rather than of the mental representation in question; thus, like subjective knowledge proper, it could not, as a mental representation, be said to be true. Pseudo-knowledge thus turned out to be a mental representation that was neither justified nor true.

I asserted in the introduction that the variety of uses Kierkegaard made of the expression "knowledge" did not represent an equivocation on his part as to its meaning, but that each of the senses in which he used the expression reflected a sense in which it is used in common parlance and that each sense served an important purpose within his authorship as a whole. Kierkegaard believed there was a "genius" to common parlance.[9] The various senses in which we use the expression "knowledge" reflect important differences in

[9] See P, 41.

the various objects of knowledge. Kierkegaard's objective, however, in detailing the various senses in which "knowledge" is used in everyday contexts was to show that there was no sense in which Christian knowledge could be understood to be superior to Christian faith.[10]

It might have been easier for scholars to determine the substance of Kierkegaard's thought if he had chosen a different term to designate each of the various types of knowledge referred to in his works. Technical terminology of this sort would, however, represent a substantial departure from ordinary language and would thus have made his work inaccessible to anyone who was not himself a scholar. It is, of course, not unusual for philosophers to eschew a popular readership. Nothing could have been further, however, from Kierkegaard's own authorial intentions. His epistemology is, as should be clear now, quite sophisticated, but his message was essentially a religious rather than a scholarly one and was thus aimed, despite his occasional references to "my reader" in the singular, at a broader audience.

Each type of knowledge referred to in Kierkegaard's works represents the clarification of a way the expression is used in everyday contexts. When we say, for example, that we know the sum of the interior angles of a triangle is 180°, what we mean by "know" differs somewhat from what we mean by this same expression when we say we know what causes mononucleosis; and surely neither of these senses of "know" gives a satisfactory account of what it meant by this expression when we say we know we have failed to behave as we ought to have done. Nor, finally, will the last sense give an adequate account of what is meant by statements such as, "I know I ought to have done X, but I don't care."

I asserted in the introduction that Kierkegaard's interest in epistemology was very likely a result of what he believed was an essential confusion concerning the nature of, and relation between, knowledge and belief in the thought of the then-prominent Danish theologian Hans Lassen Martensen. That is, much of Kierkegaard's authorship appears to be directed at Martensen in an effort to bring this issue to his attention.[11] Kierkegaard's primary objection, however, to the philosophy of both Hegel and Martensen related, as we saw, to their contention concerning the possibility of absolute knowledge.

I asserted in the introduction that Kierkegaard rejected the Hegelian doctrine of the identity of thought and being. It would appear that this rejection stemmed from his preoccupation with ethics and his appreciation that an identification of thought with being would create a monistic system, or view of reality, that would do away with ethics. Ethics, for Kierkegaard,

---

[10] See Slotty, 43.
[11] See JP, 1:707; Barfod, 419; Slotty, 41; and Horn, 261–68.

is one of the most important "problems" of philosophy.[12] "There can be no ethics," explains Hügli however, "in a monistic system [*Identitäts System*]. All ethical thought leads necessarily to dualism" (Hügli, 114). "The metaphysical decision between monism and dualism," Hügli argues, "is fundamentally an ethical decision. If the meaning of life consists in action, then there can be no monism" (Hügli, 113).

Kierkegaard's dualism meant that there could be no such thing as absolute knowledge in the sense of knowledge that has no presuppositions.[13] All knowledge, according to Kierkegaard, was ultimately based on the assumption that reality lies within the grasp of the understanding. This does not mean, however, that Kierkegaard was guilty of the same conflation of knowledge and belief that characterizes Martensen's thought when he claims that the foundation of dogmatics is both Christian faith and immediate religious knowledge.[14] There is a difference, according to Kierkegaard, between knowledge and the belief, or faith, on which it is based. Belief in the power of reason to attain knowledge of the external world is more fundamental, according to Kierkegaard, than is skepticism concerning the possibility of such knowledge. That is, this belief characterizes human beings immediately, and it is upon this belief that the edifice of human knowledge is constructed. Knowledge itself is distinguished, however, from the belief on which it is based in that while the latter is immediate, the former is not. That is, knowledge, according to Kierkegaard, is a representation of reality in thought and is thus a mediation of reality, or of the experience of the individual whose knowledge it is.

Kierkegaard's criticisms of the substance of Martensen's thought are not restricted, however, to Martensen's contention that there is such a thing as immediate knowledge. Kierkegaard also persistently emphasized that even the faith that Martensen alternatively argues is the foundation of Christian dogmatics cannot be immediate. Christian faith represents an immediate relation to ethical-religious truth in the sense that it represents the contact of the knower with this truth, but it is a contact that does not characterize the individual immediately, but only to the extent that he has deliberately and with, as we saw, great struggle brought his existence into conformity with this truth.

[12] See Malantschuk, "*Das Verhältnis*," 55.
[13] Slotty argues that Kierkegaard's reason for denying the possibility of presupposition-less knowledge is that Christianity precludes the possibility of such knowledge by the simple fact that "it claims the divine *revealed* itself in the world in the person of Christ [*in ihm*]" (Slotty, 49; emphasis added).
[14] See Martensen, *Dogmatik*, 6 and 12–13, respectively.

There is a difference, as we saw, according to Kierkegaard, between belief in the power of the understanding to grasp objective reality and belief in the truth of Christianity. That is, there is a difference between belief in general and faith, or belief in the "absolutely eminent sense" (C, 152).[15] That is, while the former can be said to characterize a person immediately, the latter is possible only as the result of an experience of personal transformation. "Kierkegaard," explains Hügli, "made the claim of Empedocles, that like was understood only by like, the fundamental principle of his epistemology" (Hügli, 233).[16] "According to Kierkegaard," explains Slotty,

> conviction concerning the truth of Christianity comes from God—i.e., one learns this truth from God himself. With this the circle is closed. Presuppositionless knowledge is also impossible from the side of the knowing subject in that the subject must be in the same condition as the object of knowledge. (Slotty, 71)

Christ gives a person the condition for understanding ethical-religious truth, and that person receives this condition to the extent that he endeavors to accept this truth. This task, as we saw, can never be completed. So long as a person lives, he will have this task as his goal. So long as he lives, his contact with the reality of God's love will be threatened by the resistance of his lower nature to the burden of responsibility that such contact imposes. "Even rebirth," explains Slotty, "does not elevate one above the human condition" (Slotty, 59).[17]

According to Kierkegaard, Christian knowledge cannot be viewed independently of the faith on which it is based. Christian faith is what one could call the wellspring of Christian knowledge and thus occupies a more fundamental position in the schema of Christian existence. Mental representations of ethical-religious reality cannot, as we saw, be said to be justified when separated from the contact of the individual whose representations they are with the reality to which they refer. Not only, however, is the justification of such representations dependent upon the contact of the individual with the reality of God's love that is established through faith in this love, but also truth in this context is indistinguishable from such contact. It is only the believer as such—that is, his faith—which can be said to be true. The efforts of the believer must thus be directed toward the maintenance of belief in God's infinite love rather than toward the contemplation of the mental representation of this love. The latter, according to Kierkegaard, represents "the beginning of the dissolution of Christian belief" (Slotty, 43).

[15] See Thulstrup, "Inledning," xxx, and *Kommentar*, 200.
[16] See also EO I, 236; CUP, 46; and WOL, 16.
[17] See also Hannay, 206.

We are now in a position to resolve the dispute to which I referred in the introduction between Steven Emmanuel and Louis Pojman concerning whether it is possible, according to Kierkegaard, to have propositional knowledge that God became man as well as to answer the related question of whether Christian knowledge, according to Kierkegaard, is equivalent to skill knowledge in the sense that it means nothing other than the ability to lead a certain kind of life. We are also finally in a position to be able to answer the more general charge, made by Pojman, that Kierkegaard's position on this issue is inherently irrational.

Let us begin with the issue of whether it is possible to have propositional knowledge that God became man. Pojman argues that, according to Kierkegaard, it is possible to have propositional knowledge that God became man. Emmanuel argues, on the other hand, that such a claim is inconsistent with both Kierkegaard's secular epistemology and his "epistemology based entirely on Christian terms" (Emmanuel, 79).[18] We can see now that Emmanuel is correct in his claim that Kierkegaard's epistemology precludes the possibility of knowledge that God became man and that Pojman is correct in his claim that there is such a thing as Christian knowledge—that is, propositional knowledge—that follows from Christian experience. It is also clear, however, that Emmanuel is not correct to the extent that he claims Christian knowledge is equivalent to a certain kind of action and that Pojman is not correct in his claim that the knowledge to which Christian experience gives rise is equivalent to, or indeed even includes, propositional knowledge that God became man.

Knowledge (i.e., *Erkjendelsen*), according to Kierkegaard, is, as we saw, a result of reality being brought into relation to ideality or of being having been brought into relation to thought. Truth, on the other hand, is an *agreement* between thought and being. Hence truth can be defined as either an agreement between some abstract, or ideal, object and thought or as an agreement between some concrete or actual object and thought. According to Kierkegaard, all thought consists, in some sense, of language. Hence when the agreement between thought and being is established in thought, truth becomes a property of sentences or propositions. The activity of knowledge, as we saw, is precisely the bringing of reality, whether the reality is ideal or actual, into relation to thought; thus all knowledge, according to Kierkegaard, would appear to be propositional. This is the case whether truth is construed as an agreement between ideality and thought, as is the case in mathematics, or whether it is construed as an agreement between actuality

---

[18] See JP, 3:3245.

and thought, as is the case with respect to historical scholarship. Truth is not what is the case about the world but an agreement between a particular expression, or proposition, about the world and what is the case. The truth of whether Caesar crossed the Rubicon, for example, is the property of a proposition relating to this event, not of Caesar or of the past.

The traditional interpretation of Kierkegaard is that it is not possible to know that God became man because this claim represents a combination of the mutually exclusive categories of eternal and historical truth. This is, as is well known, Kierkegaard's position in *Philosophical Crumbs*, where he argues that "all knowledge is either knowledge of the eternal that excludes the temporal and the historical as unimportant, or it is purely historical knowledge. . . . No knowledge can have as its object the absurdity that the eternal [i.e., God] is the historical" (C, 131). This is one aspect of what Kierkegaard refers to as the "paradox of Christianity." Christianity is not alone, however, according to Kierkegaard, in exhibiting this paradoxical character. "[T]he paradox always arises," he asserts, "by the joining of existing and eternal truths" (JP, 3:3085). "I do not believe," he continues, "that God exists [*er til*] (the eternal), but I know it; whereas I believe that God has existed [*har været til*] (the historical). . . . [E]ven from the Greek point of view," he argues, "the eternal truth, by being for an existing person, becomes an object of faith and a paradox" (JP, 3:3085).

Pojman appears correct when he argues that Kierkegaard believes "he is serving a doctrine that is objectively true but can only be appropriated subjectively with the help of God" (Pojman, "Kierkegaard's Epistemology," 151). The question is whether he is correct in his claim that it is Kierkegaard's view that this doctrine can be known to be true. Pojman argues that, according to Kierkegaard, "[d]ivine law and order prevails in the world of spirit, so that seekers after truth and righteousness gradually approach their object" and that "[i]f this is true, it would appear that not only can we be assured of finding immanent truth, we should also be granted revelatory truth" (Pojman, "Kierkegaard's Epistemology," 149). Such a seeker after truth, continues Pojman, "should finally have the truth manifested to him, and—presuming Christianity is true—should come to see that the doctrine of the absolute paradox is the truth" (Pojman, "Kierkegaard's Epistemology," 149). There is also no question that Kierkegaard claims that "knowing the truth follows of itself from being the truth" (PC, 205) and, furthermore, that since the knowledge in question is distinguished from a way of being it is a representation of that way of being in thought and is thus knowledge of the propositional sort. The question is, what is the proposition? "Christianity," argues Kierkegaard, "is not a doctrine" (JP, 2:1880); it is a way of life, a way of being or existing.[19]

The truth that, according to Kierkegaard, is the property of sentences is the expression of reality in thought, and this, again, is the activity of knowledge [*Erkjendelse*]. This is entirely in order because knowledge, according to Kierkegaard, is essentially descriptive. Ethics and religion, on the other hand, are essentially prescriptive. This means that while ethical or religious "knowledge" may be possible in the sense that an abstract representation of the prescriptions, or the prescribed way of life, is possible, "[a]ll Christian knowing," according to Kierkegaard, "is not what it is when it is separated from its situation. A situation," he continues, "(namely actuality, or to express that which is known in actuality) is the *conditio sine qua non* for ethical knowing" (JP, 1:978).

Kierkegaard argues that "[i]f a person does not become what he understands, then he does not understand it" (JP, 4:4540). The claim, explains Hügli,

> that he does not understand it does not mean that he understands it in the general, intellectual sense, but not in the genuine, existential sense. It refers rather to understanding in the general sense because the failure to appropriate what one understands . . . affects not merely the form of understanding, but the content as well. One has the word instead of the thing, the abstract instead of the concrete;[20] one knows [*kennt*] the explanation without, however, having understood what it is that is being explained. (Hügli, 242)[21]

Ethical or religious truth is not the property of abstract representations of what is the case ethically or religiously; it is the reduplication of what is "known" in the existence of the knower. It is the agreement between the ideality of ethical or religious prescriptions and the actuality of the knower's existence.[22] According to Kierkegaard, the truth of Christianity is not a property of the proposition that God became man; it is a way of being that was the very life of Christ. "Thus Christ is the truth," argues Kierkegaard, "in the sense that to *be* the truth is the only true explanation of what the truth is" (PC, 205).

The knowledge that follows as a matter of course from being the truth is the abstract representation of that way of being in thought. Thus Christian

---

[19] See JP, 2:1880; PC, 204ff.; and CUP, 338–39.
[20] See JP, 3:3224.
[21] See CA, 40; and SUD, 90.
[22] See R, 18–19; and Hügli, 203.

knowledge is still knowledge of ideality rather than actuality. The knower can propose that truth is a way of being, but the statement itself is neither true nor false. It is not false because it was uttered by a knower (i.e., someone whose existence has the prescribed character), and it is not true because the truth in question cannot be the property of a statement. This truth cannot be found abstractly, but only concretely in the life of the individual. Thus Kierkegaard argues that "Christian experience, rather than reason, seeks its corroboration in other experience" (JP, 2:2251).

Kierkegaard does occasionally refer to knowledge of Christ, as in *Crumbs*, where the believer is said to know Christ "as he was known" (C, 136). This would appear to support Pojman's claim that knowledge of the truth of the proposition that this particular individual is God is possible. If we turn to the original text, however, it becomes clear that this is not what Kierkegaard meant. The expression here is "*kjende*," not *erkjende* or *vide*, as one would expect if the knowledge in question were of the propositional sort. To know something, or someone, in the sense of *kjende* is to be acquainted with it.

Pojman rightly points out that there is a strong relation between acquaintance knowledge and propositional knowledge. That is, he argues that "[i]f I claim to know Professor Emmanuel, I must be able to give some description of him" (Pojman, "Kierkegaard's Epistemology," 150). Such acquaintance is clearly not equivalent, however, to propositional knowledge of that person or thing. If I am acquainted with Professor Emmanuel, for example, I will undoubtedly be able to give a description of him. I may claim, for example, that he is soft-spoken and kind. I may be mistaken, however, in my assessment of his character. He may appear this way to me because I have seen him only a few times, when he was relaxed and in a particularly good mood. My acquaintance knowledge can, of course, be translated into propositions about Professor Emmanuel. This does not mean, however, that acquaintance knowledge and propositional knowledge are coextensive or that I have exhaustive propositional knowledge of Professor Emmanuel because I am acquainted with him.

The same thing is clearly true, according to Kierkegaard, of Christ. If we were acquainted with the historical individual, then there would be much we could say about him. We could *say* that this man we had met was God. The question is, could we know whether this statement were true? It would appear that, according to Kierkegaard, we could not. That is, knowledge of Christ, to the extent that he is a particular person, is historical knowledge, whereas knowledge of God is eternal knowledge.

One could legitimately argue, however, that when Kierkegaard refers to the believer "knowing" Christ as he was known, the acquaintance in

question is not with the historical person of Jesus but with the eternal ethical-religious truth that this person was purported to embody. This latter
sort of acquaintance is, in fact, clearly what Kierkegaard had in mind in
Crumbs when he argued that a person who is genuinely contemporary with
"the god in time" "is not that by virtue of an immediate contemporaneous-
ness" (C, 135–36). To be contemporary with Christ in the genuine sense is
not to meet him in the street but to meet him in faith. The believer believes
that the eternal ethical-religious truth was once exemplified in the life of a
particular individual, and this belief, argues Kierkegaard, affects his understanding of the eternal in the sense that it reveals to him the necessity of his
bringing his life into conformity with it.[23] The knowledge that is consequent
upon acquaintance with Christ is thus knowledge of eternal ethical-religious
truth, not knowledge that this truth had a historical point of departure.
What is problematic about Christian knowledge, according to Kierkegaard,
is not that its object is at once temporal and eternal but that its object is
eternal, but can properly be understood—that is, known—only as a consequence of the belief that it was once historical.

Emmanuel argues that the claim that propositional knowledge of Christ's
divinity is possible goes against not only Kierkegaard's secular epistemology
but also traditional Christian doctrine that this must be an object of faith
and thus that it is an unlikely view for Kierkegaard to have held. Pojman
counters, however, that on the contrary, nothing "could be more Christian
than to hold that the believer knows that God became man in Jesus Christ.
The Gospel of John," he continues, "certainly holds this position" (Pojman,
"Kierkegaard's Epistemology," 149). Pojman then cites passages from John
that he believes substantiate this view.

It is not my intention to argue that the position Pojman claims can be
found in the Gospel of John cannot, in fact, be found there but to argue that
there is good reason to believe Kierkegaard did not interpret John in this
way. Pojman cites John 7:17 as a reference to the possibility of propositional
knowledge of Christ's divinity. "Anyone who resolves to do the will of God
will know whether the teaching is from God or whether I am speaking on my
own."[24] When Kierkegaard quotes this passage, however, he translates it as, "If
any man's will is to do the will of God he shall experience [*erfarer*] whether the
teaching is from God or on my own authority" (JP, 2:1881). This reference
supports his observation, cited earlier, that "Christian experience [*Erfaring*]

---

[23] See C, 133.
[24] This wording, which differs slightly from the wording of Pojman's reference, is that of
the New Revised Standard Version.

rather than reason seeks its corroboration in other experience" (JP, 2:2251).
It would appear that Kierkegaard considers *erfare* and *kjende*, or "experience"
and "know," in the sense of "to be acquainted with," to be roughly equivalent, since the authorized translation of the New Testament of his day used
kjende rather than *erfarer*,[25] and Kierkegaard does not acknowledge, when
quoting this passage, either that he has altered the existing translation or
that there is anything problematic with this translation.

It appears Kierkegaard considers that both *kjende* and *erfarer* are acceptable translations of *ginosko* the verb form of the Greek *gnosis*. That is, the
Greek expression that is translated as "know" at John 7:17 is *"gnosetai"* (will
know), and Kierkegaard also translates the inscription over the oracle at
Delphi, *"gnothi seauton,"* as "know [*kjende*] yourself" (JP, 5:5100). But if
Kierkegaard considers both *erfarer* and *kjende* to be appropriate translations
of *ginosko*, then the passages from the New Testament that Pojman cites cannot serve to discredit Emmanuel's argument that propositional knowledge
of Christ's divinity would be inconsistent, in Kierkegaard's mind, with the
Christianity of the New Testament because in every instance where Pojman
cites a reference to knowledge of Christ's divinity in John, the Greek expression in question is related to *ginosko*.[26]

Kierkegaard does indeed, as Pojman observes, "hold to propositional
knowledge of [at least some] metaphysical truths" (Pojman, "Kierkegaard's
Epistemology," 151), but these propositions do not appear to include the
proposition that God became man. One who believes in the divinity of this
individual Christ (for this, again, is not something that can be known) and
thus endeavors to bring his life into line with Christ's teachings can come
to represent the kind of life Christ prescribes in thought, and, to the extent
that his life actualizes these prescriptions, the knowledge in question may be
said to be *of* the truth, although it cannot in itself be true.

I argued in the introduction that, according to Kierkegaard, all knowledge was ultimately based on belief. That is, all knowledge, as we saw, was
based either on the knower's belief that his relation to objective reality was
such that that reality could come to be known by him or on his belief in
Christ. Such a view does not, however, make him an enemy either of rationality or of speculative thought.[27] Kierkegaard's position would indeed be

---

[25] See *Vor Herres og Frelsers Jesu Christi Nye Testament, ved Kong Frederik den Siettes
christelig Omsorg* [Our Lord and Savior Jesus Christ's New Testament, with King Frederik the
Sixth's Christian care] (Copenhagen: det Kongelig Vaisenshuses Forlag. 1833).

[26] There are, in fact, forty-nine occurrences of *ginosko* in John, more than any other of
the various Greek expressions for "knowledge."

[27] See FT, 33–34; Slotty, 38; and Hügli, 143.

irrational if he set up our situation as knowers such that Christ's divinity did not belong to the class of possible objects of knowledge and then claimed we could know it despite this, but this is not what he does.[28]

Kierkegaard's position on the issue of his purported antipathy for systematic, or speculative, thought is best summed up by himself in a remark from the *Postscript*:

> Just a word here, however, in order to make it clear, should anyone misunderstand many of these remarks of mine, that it is they who wish to misunderstand me and not I who am at fault. All honor to speculative philosophy, praise be to everyone who genuinely devotes himself to it. To deny the value of speculation . . . would to my mind be to prostitute oneself, and particularly foolish in one whose life has in its little way been consecrated to its service, especially foolish in one who admires the Greeks. For he must know that in discussing the nature of happiness Aristotle places the highest happiness in thinking, reminding us that thinking was the blessed pastime of the eternal gods. And furthermore he must have some conception of and respect for the fearless enthusiasm of the scholar, his perseverance in the service of the idea. (CUP, 49)[29]

The task of the speculative philosopher, or indeed of any scholar or scientist, according to Kierkegaard, is to become objective, to get "more and more away from himself" (CUP, 49), to "vanish" from himself, as Kierkegaard expresses it.[30] The difficulty is that ethics and religion, when they are what is at issue, demand that a person be present to himself.

What Kierkegaard objects to is not speculative thought as such but the assumption that often characterizes speculative thinkers, that *all* truth can be known objectively and, in particular, that the truth of Christianity can be known objectively.[31] For Kierkegaard, there were many things that could not really be grasped intellectually, many things that could be understood only by being lived. For Kierkegaard, as devoted as he was to intellectual rigor, there was something higher than "speculative happiness" (CUP, 49)—eternal blessedness—and while its pursuit did not preclude the pursuit of speculative happiness, it was absolutely crucial that the two not be confused. The point was not to grasp Christianity intellectually. The point was to believe. And Kierkegaard's point as an author was to make clear, in as intellectually rigorous a manner as possible, what that meant.

---

[28] See Evans' defense of Kierkegaard against the charge that he was an irrationalist (Evans, 117–32).

[29] See Slotty, 40.

[30] See CUP, 49.

[31] See Slotty's claim that "what Kierkegaard protested with all his might was that one could become objectively, or speculatively, convinced of the truth of Christianity" (Slotty, 57).

WORKS CITED

General Reference Works

Bresemann, Friederich. *Hand-Wörterbuch der deutschen und dänischen Sprache* [Concise dictionary of the German and Danish languages]. Copenhagen: C. Steen & Sohn, 1855.

Ferrall, J. S., and Thorl. Gudm. Repp. *A Danish-English Dictionary*. Copenhagen: Gyldendal, 1845.

Lübcke, Poul. *Politikens Filosofi Leksikon* [Politiken's philosophical lexicon]. Copenhagen: Politikens Forlag, 1983.

Meyer, Ludvig. *Fremmedordbog* [Dictionary of foreign words]. Copenhagen: J. H. Schubothes Boghandling, 1863.

Molbech, Christian. *Dansk Ordbog* [Danish dictionary]. 2 vols. Copenhagen: den Gyldendalske Boghandling, 1859.

Müller, G. H. *Deutsch-Dänisches Wörterbuch, Revidirt von Profess. Fr. Høeg Guldberg* [German-Danish dictionary, revised by Prof. Fr. Høeg Guldberg]. Kiel, Germany: Akademischen Buchhandlung, 1807–1810.

Scholze-Stubenrecht, W., and J. B. Sykes. *The Oxford Duden German Dictionary*. Oxford: Clarendon, 1990.

Vinterberg, Herman, and C. A. Bodelsen. *Dansk-Engelsk Ordbog* [Danish-English dictionary]. 2 vols. 2nd rev. and expanded ed. Copenhagen: Gyldendal, 1966.

Vor Herres og Frelsers Jesu Christi Nye Testament, ved Kong Frederik den Siettes christelig Omsorg [Our Lord and Savior Jesus Christ's New Testament, with

King Frederik the Sixth's Christian care]. Copenhagen: det Kongelig Vaisens-
huses Forlag, 1833.
Watkin, Julia. *A Key to Kierkegaard's Abbreviations and Spelling/Nøgle til Kierkegaards
Forkortelser og Stavemåde*. Copenhagen: C. A. Reitzels Boghandel, 1981.

Works by Kierkegaard in Danish

Kierkegaard, Søren. *Nutidens Religieuse Forvirring: Bogen om Adler* [Contemporary
religious confusion: The book on Adler]. *Udgivet med indledning og noter af
Julia Watkin* [Edited with an introduction and notes by Julia Watkin]. Copenhagen: C. A. Reitzels Forlag, 1984.

————. *Philosophiske Smuler* [Philosophical crumbs]. *Udgivet med Inledning og
Kommentar af Niels Thulstrup* [Edited with an introduction and commentary
by Niels Thulstrup]. Copenhagen: C. A. Reitzel, 1977.

————. *Søren Kierkegaards Skrifter*. Edited by Niels Jørgen Cappelørn, Joakim
Garff, Johnny Kondrup, Tonny Aagaard Olesen, and Steen Tullberg. 55 vols.
Copenhagen: GAD, 1997–present.

————. *Søren Kierkegaards Papirer* [Søren Kierkegaard's papers]. Edited by P. A.
Heiberg, V. Kuhr, and E. Torsting. By N. Thulstrup. 2nd ed. 16 vols. Copenhagen: Gyldendal, 1968–1978.

————. *Søren Kierkegaards Samlede Værker* [Søren Kierkegaard's collected works].
Edited by A. B. Drachman, J. L. Heiberg, and H. O. Lange. 2nd ed. 15 vols.
Copenhagen: Gyldendal, 1920–1936.

Translations of Kierkegaard

Kierkegaard, Søren. *The Book on Adler*. Translated by Howard V. Hong and Edna
H. Hong. Princeton: Princeton University Press, 1998.

————. *Christian Discourses*. Translated by Howard V. Hong and Edna H. Hong.
Princeton: Princeton University Press, 1997.

————. *The Concept of Anxiety*. Translated by Reidar Thomte, in collaboration with
Albert B. Anderson. Princeton: Princeton University Press, 1980.

————. *The Concept of Irony*. Translated by Howard V. Hong and Edna H. Hong.
Princeton: Princeton University Press, 1989.

————. *Concluding Unscientific Postscript to the "Philosophical Crumbs."* Translated
by Alastair Hannay. Cambridge: Cambridge University Press, 2009.

————. *Concluding Unscientific Postscript to "Philosophical Fragments."* Translated
by Howard V. Hong and Edna H. Hong. 2 vols. Princeton: Princeton University Press, 1992.

————. *Concluding Unscientific Postscript to the "Philosophical Fragments."* Translated by David F. Swenson and Walter Lowrie. Princeton: Princeton University
Press, 1992.

————. *The Corsair Affair*. Translated by Howard V. Hong and Edna H. Hong.
Princeton: Princeton University Press, 1982.

―――. *Eighteen Upbuilding Discourses.* Translated by Howard V. Hong and Edna H. Hong. Princeton: Princeton University Press, 1990.

―――. *Either/Or.* Translated by Howard V. Hong and Edna H. Hong. 2 vols. Princeton: Princeton University Press, 1987.

―――. *"Fear and Trembling" and "Repetition."* Translated by Howard V. Hong and Edna H. Hong. Princeton: Princeton University Press, 1983.

―――. *"For Self-Examination" and "Judge for Yourself!"* Translated by Howard V. Hong and Edna H. Hong. Princeton: Princeton University Press, 1983.

―――. *Kierkegaard's Attack upon Christendom.* Translated by Walter Lowrie. Princeton: Princeton University Press, 1944.

―――. *Letters and Documents.* Translated by Henrik Rosenmeier. Princeton: Princeton University Press, 1978.

―――. *"The Moment" and Late Writings.* Translated by Howard V. Hong and Edna H. Hong. Princeton: Princeton University Press, 1998.

―――. *Philosophical Fragments; Johannes Climacus.* Translated by Howard V. Hong and Edna H. Hong. Princeton: Princeton University Press, 1985.

―――. *Philosophische Bissen.* Über. mit Einl. U. Kommentar von Hans Rochol [Philosophical bits. Translated with an introduction and commentary by Hans Rochol]. Hamburg: Felix Meiner Verlag, 1989.

―――. *Philosophische Brocken.* Übers. von Chr. Schremf [Philosophical crumbs. Translated by Chr. Schremf]. Jena, Germany: Eugen Diederichs, 1910.

―――. *Philosophische Brocken.* Übers. von Emanuel Hirsh [Philosophical crumbs. Translated by Emanuel Hirsh]. Dusseldorf: Eugen Diederichs, 1967.

―――. *The Point of View for My Work as an Author.* Translated by Howard V. Hong and Edna H. Hong. Princeton: Princeton University Press, 1998.

―――. *Practice in Christianity.* Translated by Howard V. Hong and Edna H. Hong. Princeton: Princeton University Press, 1991.

―――. *"Prefaces" and "Writing Sampler."* Edited and translated by Todd W. Nichol. Princeton: Princeton University Press, 1997.

―――. *Purity of Heart, Is to Will One Thing; Spiritual Preparation for the Office of Confession.* Translated by Douglas V. Steere. New York: Harper Torchbooks, 1964.

―――. *"Repetition" and "Philosophical Crumbs."* Translated by M. G. Piety. Oxford: Oxford University Press, 2009.

―――. *The Sickness Unto Death.* Translated by Howard V. Hong and Edna H. Hong. Princeton: Princeton University Press, 1980.

―――. *Søren Kierkegaard's Journals and Papers.* Edited and translated by Howard V. Hong and Edna H. Hong, assisted by Gregor Malantschuk. 7 vols. Bloomington: Indiana University Press, 1967–1978.

―――. *The Stages on Life's Way.* Translated by Howard V. Hong and Edna H. Hong. Princeton: Princeton University Press, 1988.

―――. *Thoughts on Crucial Situations in Human Life: Three Discourses on Imagined Occasions.* Edited by Lillian Marvin Swenson. Translated by David F. Swenson. Minneapolis: Augsburg, 1941.

————. *Three Discourses on Imagined Occasions*. Translated by Howard V. Hong and Edna H. Hong. Princeton: Princeton University Press, 1993.

————. *Two Ages: The Age of Revolution and the Present Age: A Literary Review*. Translated by Howard V. Hong and Edna H. Hong. Princeton: Princeton University Press, 1978.

————. *Upbuilding Discourses in Various Spirits*. Translated by Howard V. Hong and Edna H. Hong. Princeton: Princeton University Press, 1993.

————. *Without Authority*. Translated by Howard V. Hong and Edna H. Hong. Princeton: Princeton University Press, 1997.

————. *Works of Love*. Translated by Howard V. Hong and Edna H. Hong. Princeton: Princeton University Press, 1995.

Primary Works by Authors Other Than Kierkegaard

Aristotle. *Prior Analytics, The Complete Works of Aristotle, The Revised Oxford Translation*. Edited by Jonathan Barnes. 2 vols. Bollingen Series 81, no. 2. Princeton: Princeton University Press, 1984.

Empiricus, Sextus. *Outlines of Pyrrhonism*. Vol. 1. Cambridge, Mass.: Loeb Classical Library, Harvard University Press, 1933.

Greene, Joshua D., R. Brian Sommerville, Leigh E. Nystrom, John M. Darley, and Jonathan D. Cohen. "An fMRI Investigation of Emotional Engagement in Moral Judgment." *Science* 293, no. 5537 (2001): 2105–8.

Hegel, G. W. F. *Hegel's Science of Logic*. Translated by A. V. Miller. London: Allen & Unwin, 1969.

————. *The Phenomenology of Spirit*. Translated by A. V. Miller. Oxford: Clarendon, 1977.

Katz, Leonard, ed. *Evolutionary Origins of Morality*. Charlottesville, Va.: Imprint Academic, 2000.

Leibniz, G. W. *Philosophical Writings*. Edited by G. H. R. Parkinson. Translated by Mary Morris and G. H. R. Parkinson. London: J. M. Dent, 1973.

Lessing, G. E. *Über den Beweis des Geistes und der Kraft* [On the proof of spirit and its power]. In *Die Erziehung des Menschengeschlechts und andere Schriften* [The education of the human race and other writings]. Universal Bibliotek No. 8968. Stuttgart: Philipp Reclam Jun., 1976.

MacIntyre, Alasdair. *After Virtue*. Notre Dame: University of Notre Dame Press, 1984.

Martensen, Dr. H. *Den Christelige Dogmatik* [Christian dogmatics]. Copenhagen: C. A. Reitzels Forlag, 1849.

————. *Den menneskelige Selvbevidstheds Autonomie i vor Tids dogmatiske Teologie* [The autonomy of human self-consciousness in contemporary dogmatic theology]. Translated by L. V. Petersen. Copenhagen, 1841.

Møller, P. M. *Efterladte Skrifter* [Posthumously published writings]. Copenhagen: C. A. Reitzels Forlag, 1843.

Mynster, J. P. *Blandede Skrifter* [Miscellaneous writings]. 3 vols. Copenhagen: Gyldendalske Boghandlings Forlag, 1852.

Plato. *The Dialogues of Plato.* Translated by B. Jowett. 4 vols. Oxford: Clarendon, 1953.

Polanyi, Michael. *Personal Knowledge.* Chicago: University of Chicago Press, 1962.

Rorty, Richard. *Philosophy and the Mirror of Nature.* Princeton: Princeton University Press, 1979.

Weaver, George. "Reading Proofs with Understanding." *Theoria* 54 (1988): 31–47.

Secondary Works

Barfod, Frederik. *Fortællinger af Fæderlandets Historie* [A narrative history of the fatherland]. Copenhagen: Gyldendal, 1874.

Bejerholm, Lars. *"Meddelelsens Dialektik": Studier i Søren Kierkegaards teorier om språk, kommunikation och pseudonymitet* ["The dialectic of communication": Studies of Kierkegaard's theories of language, communication and pseudonymity]. Publications of the Søren Kierkegaard Society II. Copenhagen: Munksgaard, 1962.

Bertung, Brigit. *Om Kierkegaard, Kvinder og Kærlighed—en studie i Søren Kierkegaards Kvindesyn* [On Kierkegaard, women and love—A study of Kierkegaard's views on women]. Copenhagen: Reitzel, 1987.

Burnyeat, Myles F., ed. *The Skeptical Tradition.* Berkeley: University of California Press, 1983.

Cappelørn, Niels Jørgen, and Paul Müller, eds. *Frihed og Eksistens: Studier I Søren Kierkegaards Tænkning* [Freedom and existence: Studies in the thought of Søren Kierkegaard]. Copenhagen: C. A. Reitzels Forlag, 1980.

Christensen, Arild. *"Efterskriftens Opgør med Martensen"* [The confrontation with Martensen in the *Postscript*]. *Kierkegaardiana* 4 (1962): 45–62.

Daise, Benjamin. "The Will to Truth in Kierkegaard's *Philosophical Fragments.*" *Philosophy of Religion* 31 (1992): 1–12.

Deuser, Hermann. *"Kierkegaards Verteidigung der Kontingenz: «Daß etwas Inkommensurables in einem Menschenleben ist»"* [Kierkegaard's defense of contingency: "That there is something incommensurable in a human life"]. *Kierkegaardiana* 15 (1991): 104–16.

Disse, Jörg. *Kierkegaards Phänomenologie der Freiheitserfahrung* [Kierkegaard's phenomenology of the experience of freedom]. Symposion. *Philosophische Schriftenreihe.* Freiberg: Verlag Karl Alber, 1991.

Dunning, Stephen N. *Kierkegaard's Dialectic of Inwardness: A Structural Analysis of the Theory of Stages.* Princeton: Princeton University Press, 1985.

Emmanuel, Steven N. "Kierkegaard on Faith and Knowledge." *Kierkegaardiana* 15 (1991): 136–46.

Evans, C. Stephen. *Kierkegaard on Faith and the Self.* Waco, Tex.: Baylor University Press, 2006.

Hannay, Alastair. *Kierkegaard*. London: Routledge & Kegan Paul, 1982.

Henningfeld, Jochem. *"Denken der Existenz. Einubung in Kierkegaard"* [The thought of existence: Practice in Kierkegaard]. *Philosophische Rundschau* 40 (1993): 310–19.

Høffding, Harald. *Kierkegaard som Filosof* [Kierkegaard as philosopher]. Copenhagen: Gyldendal, 1919.

Holmer, Paul. "On Understanding Kierkegaard." In Johnson and Thulstrup, *A Kierkegaard Critique*, 40–53.

Horn, Robert L. "Positivity and Dialectic: A Study of the Theological Method of Hans Lassen Martensen." Ph.D. diss., Union Theological Seminary, 1969.

Hügli, Anton. *Die Erkenntnis der Subjektivität und die Objektivität des Erkennens bei Søren Kierkegaard* [Knowledge of subjectivity and the objectivity of knowing in Søren Kierkegaard]. Basel, Switzerland: Editio Academica, 1973.

Johnson, Howard A., and Niels Thulstrup, eds. *A Kierkegaard Critique: An International Selection of Essays Interpreting Kierkegaard*. New York: Harper, 1962.

Mackey, Louis. *Kierkegaard: A Kind of Poet*. Philadelphia: University of Pennsylvania Press, 1971.

———. "The Loss of the World in Kierkegaard's Ethics." In Thompson, *Kierkegaard*, 266–88.

Malantschuk, Gregor. *Fra Individ til den Enkelte* [From an individual to the single one]. Copenhagen: C. A. Reitzel, 1978.

———. *Nøglebegreber I Søren Kierkegaards Tænkning* [Key concepts in the thought of Søren Kierkegaard]. Edited by Grethe Kjær and Paul Müller. Copenhagen: C. A. Reitzels Forlag, 1993.

———. *"Søren Kierkegaard og Poul Martin Møller"* [Søren Kierkegaard and Poul Martin Møller]." In Cappelørn and Müller, *Frihed og Eksistens*, 101–13.

———. *Søren Kierkegaard's Thought*. Edited and translated by Howard V. Hong and Edna H. Hong. Princeton: Princeton University Press, 1971.

Mehl, Peter. *Thinking through Kierkegaard: Existential Identity in a Pluralistic World*. Urbana: University of Illinois Press, 2005.

Müller, Paul. *"Tvivlens former og deres rolle I erkendelsen af det historiske: En studie i Søren Kierkegaards erkendelsesteori"* [The forms of doubt and their role in knowledge of the historical: A study of Søren Kierkegaard's epistemology]. *Dansk Teologisk Tidsskrift* 37 (1977): 177–216.

Nielsen, R. *Mag. S. Kierkegaards "Johannes Climacus" og Dr. H. Martensens "Christelige Dogmatik": En undersøgende Anmeldelse af R. Nielsen, Professor i Philosophien* [Master S. Kierkegaard's "Johannes Climacus" and Dr. H. Martensen's "Christian Dogmatics": A critical review by R. Nielsen, professor of philosophy]. Copenhagen: C. A. Reitzels Forlag, 1849.

Pattison, George, and Stephen Shakespeare, eds. *Kierkegaard: The Self in Society*. London: Macmillan, 1998.

Penelhum, Terence. "Skepticism and Fideism." In Burnyeat, *The Skeptical Tradition*, 287–318.

Perkins, Robert L. "Kierkegaard, a Kind of Epistemologist." *History of European Ideas* 12, no. 1 (1990): 7–18.

———. "Kierkegaard's Epistemological Preferences." *International Journal for Philosophy of Religion* 4, no. 4 (1973): 197–217.

Piety, Marilyn Gaye. "The Dangers of Clarity." *Times Literary Supplement*, April 18, 1997: 8–10.

———."Kierkegaard on Rationality." *Faith and Philosophy* 10, no. 3 (1993): 365–79.

———. "Kierkegaard on Religious Knowledge." *History of European Ideas* 22 (1996): 105–12.

———. "The Place of the World in Kierkegaard's Ethics." In Pattison and Shakespeare, *Kierkegaard: The Self in Society*, 24–42.

Pojman, Louis P. "Kierkegaard on Faith and Freedom." *International Journal for Philosophy of Religion* 27 (1990): 41–46.

———. "Kierkegaard's Epistemology." *Kierkegaardiana* 15 (1991): 147–52.

Popkin, Richard. "Kierkegaard and Skepticism." In Thompson, *Kierkegaard*, 342–72.

Schmidinger, Heinrich M. *Das Problem des Interesses und die Philosophie Sören Kierkegaards* [The problem of interest and the philosophy of Søren Kierkegaard]. Symposion. *Philosophische Schriftenreihe*. Freiburg: Verlag Karl Alber, 1983.

Schmüeli, Adi. *Kierkegaard and Consciousness*. Translated by Naomi Handelman. Princeton: Princeton University Press, 1971.

Shakespeare, Steven. *Kirkegaard, Language and the Reality of God*. Aldershot: UK: Ashgate, 2001.

Sløk, Johannes. "*En Studie I Kierkegaards Erkendelsesteori*" [A study of Kierkegaard's epistemology]. *Dansk Teologisk Tidsskrift* 1 Hefte (1941).

Slotty, Martin. "*Die Erkenntnislehre S. A. Kierkegaards*" [The epistemology of S. A. Kierkegaard]. Diss., Friedrich-Alexanders-Universität, 1915.

Smith, Joseph H., ed. *Kierkegaard's Truth: The Disclosure of the Self. Psychiatry and the Humanities*. Vol. 5. New Haven: Yale University Press, 1981.

Stewart, Jon, ed. *Kierkegaard's Relations to Hegel Reconsidered. Modern European Philosophy*. General editor Robert B. Pippin. Cambridge: Cambridge University Press, 2003.

Swain, Marshall. "Knowledge, Causal Theory of." In *Routledge Encyclopedia of Philosophy*. Edited by E. Craig. London: Routledge, 1998. http://www.rep.routledge.com/article/P004SECT4.

Taylor, Mark C. *Journeys to Selfhood: Hegel and Kierkegaard*. Berkeley: University of California Press, 1980.

———. *Kierkegaard's Pseudonymous Authorship: A Study of Time and the Self*. Princeton: Princeton University Press, 1975.

Thomas, J. Heywood. "Logic and Existence in Kierkegaard." *Journal of the British Society for Phenomenology* 2, no. 3 (1971): 3–11.

Thompson, Josiah, ed. *Kierkegaard: A Collection of Critical Essays*. Garden City, N.Y.: Doubleday, 1972.

Thulstrup, Niels. *Kierkegaard's Relation to Hegel*. Translated by George L. Stengren. Princeton: Princeton University Press, 1980.

Walker, Jeremy. "Ethical Beliefs: A Theory of Truth without Truth Values." *Thought* 55, no. 218 (1980): 295–305.

Widenman, Robert. "Kierkegaard's Terminology and English." *Kierkegaardiana* 7 (1968): 113–30.

Willows, David. *Divine Knowledge: A Kierkegaardian Perspective on Christian Education*. Aldershot, UK: Ashgate, 2001.

Wisdo, David. "Kierkegaard on the Limits of Christian Epistemology." *International Journal for Philosophy of Religion* 29, no. 2 (1991): 97–112.

INDEX

good, the Good, 8, 29–30, 47, 62, 84, 87, 123, 129, 150–52, 157
Grace, 145n. 65, 146
guilt, -y, 23, 30–32, 36–37, 78, 124, 125n. 19, 130–31, 133, 141–43, 146–47, 163–64; consciousness, 28, 31–32, 36, 143–44, 153

Hannay, Alastair, 9–10, 17–18, 18n. 57, 28, 33n. 28, 35–36, 51n. 31, 55, 70n. 18, 72n. 20, 81, 88n. 54, 90, 98n. 10, 100n. 12, 105n. 26, 106n. 28, n. 30, 109, 109n. 45, 111n. 48, 124n. 16, 126n. 21, 128, 128n. 25, 129, 129n. 36, 131, 134, 136n. 50, 143n. 59, 145n. 66, 147n. 72, 157n. 103, 159n. 114, 164, 164n. 7, 165, 170n. 17
Hegel, -ian, 5–6, 6n. 11, 7, 7n. 15, n. 19, 8–11, 25n. 7, 26n. 13, 40n. 49, 54n. 39, 168
hidden, 32, 59
history, 9n. 25, 27, 44, 53, 55, 87–89, 91, 112, 164
Hügli, Anton, 1n. 1, 7n. 16, n. 17, 8, 8n. 21, n. 23, 9, 9n. 27, n. 28, 16, 19n. 60, 25n. 7, 26n. 9, 28n. 17, n. 18, n. 20, 29n. 21, 33, 34n. 31, 35, 35n. 33, n. 36, n 37, 36n. 38, 37n. 42, 39n. 46, n. 47, 43n. 5, 44n. 8, 46n. 14, n. 15, 47n. 16, 48n. 22, 49n. 23, 50n. 26, 51–52, 52n. 34, 53, 54n. 38, n. 39, 55, 56n. 45, 65, 66n. 11, 67, 68n. 13, 70n. 17, 74n. 25, 79, 80n. 40, 85, 86n. 51, 89, 94, 100, 101n. 14, n. 16, 102n 18, 107n. 37, 108n. 41, n. 42, 120, 120n. 11, 124n. 17, 128, 128n. 27, 129, 129n. 31, n. 33, n. 36, 130, 131n. 41, n. 42, n. 43, 135n. 48, 140n. 55, 143n. 57, 145, 146n. 71, 147n. 74, 152n. 87, 156n. 98, 157, 157n. 103, n. 105, 163n. 1, n. 3, 169–70, 173, 173n. 22, 176n. 27

human, -ity, 2, 7n. 16, 9–10, 27, 33, 46, 49n, 23, 50–51, 87, 89, 133–34, 146, 151, 158–59, 170; agency, 138n. 53; behavior, 44, 81–82, 87, 88, 94, 96, 128, 164; being, 8, 11, 23, 25, 29, 31, 33, 35, 39, 45, 54n. 38, 55, 62, 81, 87, 89–90, 94, 96, 96n. 6, 100, 101n. 16, 102, 106, 107–8, 117; consciousness, 45, 117, 119, 146–47, 149; decision, 138; existence, 24, 35, 107, 125, 128, 153, 157, 159, 163; experience, 2; history, 27, 164; life, 119, 124, 136n. 50, 156–58; nature, 43, 87, 134; psychology, 86, 156; soul, 132; thought, 119; understanding, 80

idea(s), 6–7, 9, 21, 25n. 7, 37, 37n. 41, 55–56, 58n. 48, 63–64, 66–70, 97, 107, 120, 125, 126–27, 129n. 34, 133, 151, 159, 160n. 117, 177; innate, 63; of God, 21n. 1, 66–67, 117–22, 126–27
ideal, -ity, 7, 9, 21–26, 28, 32–33, 33n. 28, 34, 36–39, 39n. 45, 40, 45n. 10, 46–48, 56n. 45, 63, 65, 67, 74, 97, 100, 100n. 12, 101–2, 104–12, 123–24, 127–28, 128n. 28, 129–34, 136, 140, 142–43, 145, 147, 150–51, 153–54, 157–59, 163–65, 171, 173–74
idealism, 6n. 11, 8n. 20, 53, 56, 72, 72n. 20
ignorance, 130, 142
illusion, 39, 75, 79, 107, 132, 139, 151
imaginary, imagination, 138, 138n. 53, 156
immanent, 28, 41, 61, 65, 69, 71, 97, 100, 112, 116, 121, 125–26, 128, 131–32, 149, 156n. 99, 162, 172
immediate, 22, 30, 35–37, 37n. 41, 68, 72, 75, 88–89, 109, 112, 140–41, 150, 165, 169–70; apprehension, 28; cognition, 72–73, 88;